THE
DEFINITIVE
BOOK
OF
CHINESE
ASTROLOGY

By Shelly Wu

New Page BOOKS

A division of The Career Press, Inc.
Franklin Lakes, NJ

THE DEFINITIVE BOOK OF CHINESE ASTROLOGY
EDITED BY KIRSTEN DALLEY
TYPESET BY DIANA GHAZZAWI
Cover design by Lucia Rossman/DigiDog Design
Printed in the U.S.A. by Courier

To order this title, please call toll-free 1-800-CAREER-1 (NJ and Canada: 201-848-0310) to order using VISA or MasterCard, or for further information on books from Career Press.

The Career Press, Inc., 3 Tice Road, PO Box 687,
Franklin Lakes, NJ 07417
www.careerpress.com
www.newpagebooks.com

Library of Congress Cataloging-in-Publication Data

Wu, Shelly, 1959–
    The definitive book of Chinese astrology / by Shelly Wu.
        p. cm.
    Includes index.
    ISBN 978-1-60163-078-0
        1. Astrology, Chinese. I. Title.
BF1714.C5W798 2010
133.5'9251--dc22

2009045346

To my children and their children. Human nature is complex and only those with great understanding can fathom its depths.

He who rules by mind is like the North Star, steady in his seat, whilst the stars all bend to him.

—Confucius

To keep old knowledge warm and make new makes the teacher.

—Confucius

Contents

Introduction   9

Part I: The Four Pillars of Destiny: Ba Zi

Chapter 1: What Are the Four Pillars?   13

Chapter 2: The Year Pillar   21

Chapter 3: The Month Pillar   45

Chapter 4: The Day Pillar   55

Chapter 5: The Hour Pillar   87

Chapter 6: Compatibilities Between
           Pillars   99

Chapter 7: Incompatibilities Between Pillars   107

Chapter 8: Lucky and Unlucky Elements   113

Part II: Zi Wei Dou Shu: The Emperor/King of Stars

Chapter 9: What Is Zi Wei Dou Shu?   123

Chapter 10: The Life Palaces   127

Chapter 11: The Stars   133

Chapter 12: The Catalysts   143

Chapter 13: The Self or Destiny Palace   149

Chapter 14: The Elders, Parents, and Authority Palace   157

Chapter 15: The Karmic Luck Palace   159

Chapter 16: The Property Palace   161

Chapter 17: The Career and Vocation Palace   163

Chapter 18: The Friends and Staff Palace   165

Chapter 19: The Travel and Sociability Palace   167

Chapter 20: The Health Palace   169

Chapter 21: The Wealth and Prosperity Palace   173

Chapter 22: The Children Palace   175

Chapter 23: The Relationship Palace   177

Chapter 24: The Siblings and Peers Palace   181

Chapter 25: Interpreting Your Zi Wei Dou Shu Chart   183

Part III: The Eastern Astrological Subspecialties

Chapter 26: The I-Ching   189

Chapter 27: Feng Shui   193

Chapter 28: Chinese Palmistry   197

Chapter 29: The Emperor's Destiny Chart   205

Chapter 30: 9 Star Ki   209

Index   217

About the Author   223

Introduction

Like a sea captain's compass or a pilot's navigation system, the Eastern astrological system contains some of the most profound personal guidance tools ever discovered. With their roots planted deeply in Taoist and Buddhist traditions, the variety of intriguing practices that make up the Eastern astrological system are unparalleled. Two of the most insightful are the Ba Zi (four pillars of destiny) and the Zi Wei Dou Shu. Akin to our own personal weather maps, these systems offer us the choice to sail around life's storms or fly directly through its tempests.

In *Chinese Astrology: Exploring the Eastern Zodiac*, I examined the 12 earthly branches (animal signs) and their respective archetypal characteristics. We also discovered the five essential elements, and the relevance of one's birth year. These branches and stems are the stepping stones we will use to move about through the deeper intricacies of Chinese astrology. Each month, each day, and each two-hour segment of the 24-hour day is assigned a combination of animal sign (earthly branch) and element (heavenly stem). Together, they complete what is called the four pillars of destiny, or the Ba Zi (eight words). This ancient system uses the five elements, with special emphasis placed on the "daymaster," or element and sign that rules the day you were born.

The Zi Wei Dou Shu chart is the grandfather of all Chinese astrological specialties. This life chart (plotted in the form of a rectangular rice paddy) takes us on a tour of our destiny using the 12 palaces, or houses. Decade by life-decade, major and minor star energies move in and out of each life palace in the birth chart. These stars revolve around the placement of the all-important

Zi Wei, or "emperor star." Together, they paint a rich personality portrait and can help you understand your destiny and assess your life options.

I hope you enjoy this new journey and find these ancient arts good for thinking upon.

Part 1

The Four Pillars of Destiny: Ba Zi

Chapter 1

What Are the Four Pillars?

The four pillars are the cornerstones of Chinese astrology. Each year, month, day, and 2-hour period of each day is assigned a combination of one of the 12 animal signs (branches) and one of the 5 elements (stems). Ba Zi means "eight words" or "eight characters," and denotes the one element and one animal sign in each of the four "pillars." Two characters (one of the five elements placed on top of one of the 12 animal signs) times four pillars or positions (one for your birth year, one for your birth month, one for your birth day, and one for your birth hour) equal the eight words. These eight words (four elements and four animal signs) comprise what is called the four pillars of destiny, or Ba Zi. Here's an example:

Hour	Day	Month	Year
Metal (1)	Wood (2)	Fire (3)	Earth (4)
Snake (5)	Dog (6)	Horse (7)	Pig (8)

Eight Characters, Four Pillars

Ba Zi is a system of astrology invented by Li Xu Zhong in the Tang Dynasty (618–907 AD). The system was later revised and updated by Xu Zi Ping of the Song Dynasty (960–1279 AD). The most authoritative work is the San Ming Tong Hui by Wan Yu Wu of the Ming Dynasty (1368–1644 AD). As with each of the many forms of Chinese divination, the four pillars began with a hypothesis, which was then supplemented by and confirmed through observations and experimentation until a formula was found that

13

returned reliable and consistent results. The ancient Chinese developed the art of four pillars of destiny as a method for understanding and enhancing our life experiences.

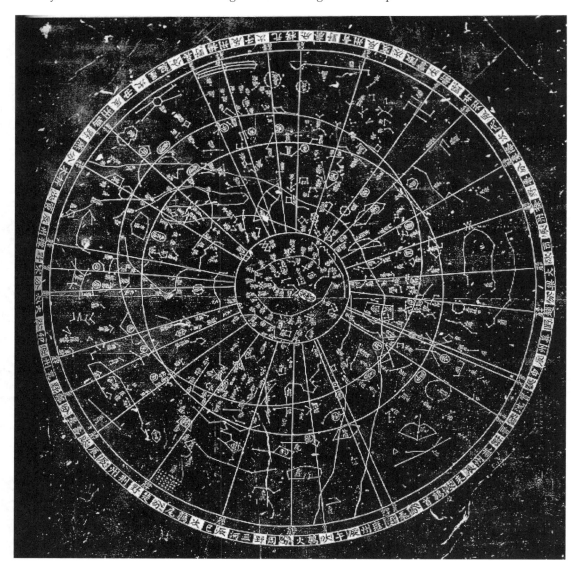

A Song Dynasty (960–1279 AD) star map of the heavens.

Each year, month, day, and hour has its own energy, or qi. The qi that surrounds you as you take your first breath is your destiny. These complex energy patterns, stacked on top of each other, are what form the four pillars. Each character (element and animal sign) placed in your birth chart carries with it a frequency, or unique energy pattern, and the combination of these frequencies forms a certain synergy, or influence. "Synergy" is the working together of separate entities (signs and elements, in this case), cooperating for an advantageous final outcome. This dynamic between the stems (elements) and the branches (animal signs) is what makes up the four pillars birth chart, and what forms the sum and substance of your astral signature, or horoscope.

Here is an example of a four pillars chart for a person born on September 5, 1959, at 10:34 a.m.:

Hour pillar	Day pillar	Month pillar	Year pillar
Yin Metal (Xin)	Yang Metal (Geng)	Yang Water (Ren)	Yin Earth (Ji)
Snake (Si)	Tiger (Yin)	Monkey (Shen)	Pig (Hai)

Each element (upper stem) and animal sign (lower branch) is strategically placed in one of eight locations to tell the story of your destiny. Using information gathered from the time and date of your birth, a Chinese astrologer is then able to draw up a blueprint or map of your karma and life, and advise you accordingly.

This earliest of Chinese divination systems uses the five element placements in an individual's birth chart, especially the element of the birth day, or daymaster, to examine and compare each pillar to the others. Forecasting is accomplished by comparing your birth chart to any given time, date, or person. The individual pillars are examined for harmony and conflict, balance and imbalance. Through these basic interactions and distinct patterns, each person can view his or her potential and determine his/her best days, months, years, and companions.

The five elements are Wood, Fire, Earth, Metal, and Water. These five types of qi (life force) also have their yin and yang attributes. Each element is expressed once in its negative, feminine yin form, and once in it's positive, masculine yang form. Yin is more subtle, and Yang is more active. Each element is produced and subsequently destroyed by another element in a delicate yet perfectly balanced cycle:

◈ The producing, enhancing cycle: Water → Wood → Fire → Earth → Metal

◈ The controlling cycle: Water → Fire → Metal → Wood → Earth

◈ The weakening cycle: Water → Metal → Earth → Fire → Wood

The five elements in their yin and yang expressions create 10 types of element qi, or the "10 heavenly stems." The 12 animal signs, alternating between yin and yang, are called the "12 earthly branches." Each energy interacts in a specific way with the others, just as we do with different people.

◈ Yang Wood Jia is like a tall tree, sturdy and growing upward.

◈ Yin Wood Yi is like a shrub, grass, or graceful plant.

◈ Yang Fire Bing is like a forest fire—hot, raging, and quick.

◈ Yin Fire Ding is like a candle flame, flickering and burning slowly.

◈ Yang Earth Wu is the tallest mountain, crusty soil, and parched desert.

◈ Yin Earth Ji is akin to garden soil, loamy and rich in nutrients.

◈ Yang Metal Geng is like a sharp sword, piercing and strong.

◈ Yin Metal Xin is like intricate jewelry that clasps and creates structure.

◈ Yang Water Ren is like the deep ocean with its tempests and waves.

◈ Yin Water Gui is like a lake or pool, calm on the surface.

We will discuss the various manifestations of each element and its effect on a chart further in Chapter 4.

Life qi also comes in combinations of the 12 earthly branches or animal signs. The 12 animal branches are: Rat (Zi), Ox (Chou), Tiger (Yin), Rabbit (Mao), Dragon (Chen), Snake (Si,) Horse (Wu), Goat (Wei), Monkey (Shen), Rooster (You), Dog (Xu), and Pig (Hai).

Once the chart is cast, the four pillars are examined for several salient features. Some of the questions an astrologer will ask are as follows: Are the pillar elements and signs within your chart harmonious with one another? Is there a certain element in the pillar that is supported or destroyed by any of the other elements? Are any of the five elements too "heavy" or too "light" in your chart? Is there an element that is absent? The CD-ROM included with this book will calculate your four pillars for you and make answering these questions easy.

The first and most important aspect of any chart is the balance of the elements contained within each pillar. The Chinese use various "cures" for elemental imbalances. If an element is light or weakened in a birth chart, that element becomes lucky when supplemented. If an element is heavy or overpowering the others in a birth chart, that element becomes unlucky and should be minimized. This is an important aspect of this art which, with practice, will become a revealing window into your destiny. The various remedies for each elemental imbalance will be addressed further in Chapter 8.

As mentioned previously, there are four pillars in the Ba Zi chart. Each pillar has an animal sign branch at the bottom and one of the five element stems (in either yin or yang expression) on the top. The first pillar is calculated on the year of birth, so it is called the year pillar. The second pillar is calculated on the month of birth, so it is called the month pillar. The third pillar is calculated on the day of birth, so it is called the day pillar (or "daymaster"). The fourth pillar is calculated on the hour of birth, so it is called the hour pillar. (It is important to adjust the time of birth to true local time—for example, if daylight saving time was in effect, this must be taken into account.) The year pillar is calculated using the Chinese solar year calendar (rather than the Chinese lunar calendar, which begins anywhere from mid-January to mid-February on a different date each year), which is based on the return of the sun and the subsequent cycles of the sun's orbit. The Chinese solar year begins on February 4 or 5, so if you were born in January in 1959, you would do your year pillar calculations based on 1958, an Earth Dog year. The four pillars can show family background; relationship with parents, grandparents, children; marriage and romances; and relationships with bosses, peers, partners, and subordinates. In each pillar, life qi combines, clashes, strengthens, weakens, assists, and controls in a complex tango of energies.

The most important pillar is the day pillar, or daymaster. The top element stem represents you—your spirit and your qi. The bottom animal sign branch is your marriage/partnership branch. It will tell you the quality of your intimate relationships. The month pillar, also called the parents pillar, reveals your early childhood and your relationship with your parents and children. The hour pillar, also called the children pillar, reveals your career, your relationships with your children, and old age. The year pillar reveals your karma, your family background, your ancestors, your grandparents, and the society in which you live. It also reveals your level of career achievement.

After evaluating the element harmonies and clashes in the pillars, the next important step is to look at the compatibility between the branches, or animal signs, in the chart. Are they compatible, in opposition, conflicted, or enhanced? Do the animal signs form any particular pattern? In Chapter 6 we will delve into these various patterns.

Depending on the month (season) in which someone is born, the daymaster element will be rated as strong or weak. This has nothing to do with the strength or weakness of character. In certain months (seasons), some elements will be strong and others weak. Elements that are weak become the lucky elements when supplemented. Usually what is weak in a chart is most desirable and what is strong (overpowering) is least desirable. In Chinese metaphysics, whether it is feng shui, traditional Chinese medicine, or the four pillars of destiny, when we talk about seasons and five elements we are talking about universal energy, both tangible and intangible. When we talk about strength and weakness of daymasters, therefore, we are not talking about local climate. When it is said that someone is born in the summer season, it means they were born in a month when the universal elemental energy of Fire and Earth was strong. It has nothing to do with the actual locale of the birth.

The elements go through 12 stages of life, so it is important to know at what stage the various elements were during birth, because this has an impact on one's life. If your daymaster element is Wood, it is strongest if you were born in the spring, and weakest in the fall. If your daymaster element is Fire, it is strongest if you were born in the summer, and weakest in the winter. If your daymaster element is Earth, it is strongest if you were born between seasons or during late summer, and weakest during the winter-spring transition. If your daymaster element is Metal, it is strongest if you were born in the fall, and weakest during the spring. If your daymaster element is Water, it is strongest if you were born in the winter, and weakest during the summer.

With the help of the four pillars chart, we can examine and analyze our inherent strengths and weaknesses, and set our life sails to catch the wind in just the right direction.

Pages 18–19: The binomial 60-year cycle. Chinese years are classified according to 10 heavenly stems and 12 earthly branches. The succession of stems and branches produces a 60-year calendar, or sexagenary cycle. Each year, each month, each day, and each 2-hour period of the day is assigned one stem and one branch, a paring that is called a ganzhi. *This sexagenary cycle has been used in some form for almost five millennia.*

No.	Stem	Pinyin	Element		No.	Stem	Pinyin	Element		No.	Stem	Pinyin	Element
1	甲	Jia	Yang Wood		11	甲	Jia	Yang Wood		21	甲	Jia	Yang Wood
2	乙	Yi	Yin Wood		12	乙	Yi	Yin Wood		22	乙	Yi	Yin Wood
3	丙	Bing	Yang Fire		13	丙	Bing	Yang Fire		23	丙	Bing	Yang Fire
4	丁	Ding	Yin Fire		14	丁	Ding	Yin Fire		24	丁	Ding	Yin Fire
5	戊	Wu	Yang Earth		15	戊	Wu	Yang Earth		25	戊	Wu	Yang Earth
6	己	Ji	Yin Earth		16	己	Ji	Yin Earth		26	己	Ji	Yin Earth
7	庚	Geng	Yang Metal		17	庚	Geng	Yang Metal		27	庚	Geng	Yang Metal
8	辛	Xin	Yin Metal		18	辛	Xin	Yin Metal		28	辛	Xin	Yin Metal
9	壬	Ren	Yang Water		19	壬	Ren	Yang Water		29	壬	Ren	Yang Water
10	癸	Gui	Yin Water		20	癸	Gui	Yin Water		30	癸	Gui	Yin Water

No.	Stem	Name / Element	No.	Stem	Name / Element	No.	Stem	Name / Element
31	甲	Jia — Yang Wood	41	甲	Jia — Yang Wood	51	甲	Jia — Yang Wood
32	乙	Yi — Yin Wood	42	乙	Yi — Yin Wood	52	乙	Yi — Yin Wood
33	丙	Bing — Yang Fire	43	丙	Bing — Yang Fire	53	丙	Bing — Yang Fire
34	丁	Ding — Yin Fire	44	丁	Ding — Yin Fire	54	丁	Ding — Yin Fire
35	戊	Wu — Yang Earth	45	戊	Wu — Yang Earth	55	戊	Wu — Yang Earth
36	己	Ji — Yin Earth	46	己	Ji — Yin Earth	56	己	Ji — Yin Earth
37	庚	Geng — Yang Metal	47	庚	Geng — Yang Metal	57	庚	Geng — Yang Metal
38	辛	Xin — Yin Metal	48	辛	Xin — Yin Metal	58	辛	Xin — Yin Metal
39	壬	Ren — Yang Water	49	壬	Ren — Yang Water	59	壬	Ren — Yang Water
40	癸	Gui — Yin Water	50	癸	Gui — Yin Water	60	癸	Gui — Yin Water

Chapter 2
The Year Pillar

The first pillar of destiny is the year pillar. Each year is composed of two Chinese characters that depict the cosmic qi that is distinct to the year in which you were born. Using the software included, find your year pillar (Chinese birth year St/Br) in the center of your Zi Wei Dou Shu chart.

Your year pillar is calculated using the Chinese solar calendar, rather than the familiar eastern lunar calendar which begins on a different date each year anywhere from mid-January to mid-February. Li Chun (the first day of spring, which falls on the 4th or 5th of February) begins the new earthly branch of each year for the Ba Zi. The year pillar changes at precisely this moment. The day pillar changes at midnight, local standard time, and is used for the hour pillar.

The Rat (Tze)

Feb 5, 1924 to Feb 4, 1925: Wood Rat on the rooftops

Feb 5, 1936 to Feb 4, 1937: Fire Rat of the fields

Feb 5, 1948 to Feb 4, 1949: Earth Rat of the granary

Feb 5, 1960 to Feb 4, 1961: Metal Rat on the crossbeams

Feb 5, 1972 to Feb 4, 1973: Water Rat on the hilltop

Feb 5, 1984 to Feb 4, 1985: Wood Rat of the mulberry tree

Feb 5, 1996 to Feb 4, 1997: Fire Rat of the grasslands

Feb 5 to Feb 4, 2009: Earth Rat of the granary

If your year pillar is ruled by Tze, the earthly branch of the Rat, you possess charisma, charm, intelligence, and the ability to express yourself both verbally and through the written word. Sociable and romantic, with complex emotions, you form deep emotional ties. Always thrifty, you count your pennies and know how to spot a bargain. Impatient with those of slower wit or action, you need an energetic (perhaps younger) partner with a good sense of humor. Talkative, creative, and a natural critic, you are curious, resourceful, and ever alert to your environment. Your tendency toward concealment makes you a natural for undercover work or any kind of profession that entails confidentiality or the need for secrecy. A strong survival instinct is inherent in this year pillar, as is great longevity. It is said that those born into this yearly branch will acquire the gift of prophecy in old age.

Wood Rat

The creative Wood element produces a Rat who is a lover of harmony, beauty, and elegance. Wood Rats are inclined to be carefree and blessed with a more relaxed style than other Rats, but they are still susceptible to worry. If you are a Wood Rat, you must allow your imagination a free rein via poetry, writing, and artistic endeavors of all types. Keep a close eye on your passions, impulses, and aggressive outbursts, as Wood is flammable and can stir anger and dangerous obsessions. The organ of Wood is the liver, so it is best to limit alcoholic beverages for optimum health.

Fire Rat

The impassioned Fire element makes for a lively, intense Rat who is a natural leader and transformer. If you are this sign, changes, makeovers, and animated conversions are your specialty. Lucid, clairvoyant and emotional, Fire Rats reject mediocrity, conformity, and bookish, conventional ways of expressing themselves. High-minded and with great moral thinking and principles, Fire Rats are nevertheless always susceptible to the Fire element's excesses. The organ of Fire is the heart and circulatory system, so keep an eye on blood pressure and arterial blockages.

Earth Rat

The practical Earth element yields a materialistic, prudent Rat who is concerned with the here-and-now. Shrewd, subtle, and contemplative, Earth Rats make knowledgeable businesspeople and entrepreneurs. If you are an Earth Rat, be careful of deliberating too long and thereby missing opportunities, as the Earth element makes you deeply contemplative and measured. Productive, cunning, and delightfully crafty, the Earth Rat must resist hiding away in subterranean passages of his or her own making. The organ of Earth is the spleen, so be moderate with sweets and watch a tendency toward diabetes and weight gain.

Metal Rat

The structured and defining Metal element brings forth an outspoken Rat who can be austere, scrupulous, and verbally astute to the point of hurling some profoundly stinging verbal barbs. These are merely truths to the Metal Rat, as they call 'em like they see 'em. Organizational geniuses and natural experts at putting plans into action, Metal Rats vacillate between beauty, creativity, and purity on one hand, and sadness, severity, and destruction on the other. The organ of Metal is the lungs, so be careful of breathing difficulties and take good care of your respiratory system.

Water Rat

The intuitive, deep, and placid Water element gives birth to a calmer Rat who knows how to listen. Water soothes the aggressive impulses of this earthly branch; this Rat knows how to control his or her passions. Skilled craftspeople, defenders of the peace, and determined humanists, Water Rats are humane and benevolent leaders who could easily rule the masses. Helpful, sympathetic, and tolerant, you can easily be encroached upon and taken advantage of if you are a Water Rat. Don't give more than you receive. The organ of Water is the kidneys, so be sparing with salty foods and take good care of your urinary system.

The Ox (Chou)

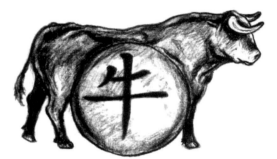

Feb 4, 1925 to Feb 5, 1926: Wood Ox of gold in the sea

Feb 4, 1937 to Feb 5, 1938: Fire Ox of the boiling stream (steam)

Feb 4, 1949 to Feb 5, 1950: Earth Ox of the shelter/roof

Feb 4, 1961 to Feb 5, 1962: Metal Ox of the main road

Feb 4, 1973 to Feb 5, 1974: Water Ox of the little stream

Feb 4, 1985 to Feb 5, 1986: Wood Ox of gold in the sea

Feb 4, 1997 to Feb 5, 1998: Fire Ox of the boiling stream (steam)

Feb 4, 2009 to Feb 5, 2010: Earth Ox of the shelter/roof

If your year pillar is ruled by Chou, the earthly branch of the Ox, you have been blessed with endurance, stamina, and the ability to efficiently run a home, a corporation, or even a country. Hardworking, serious, and opinionated, the Ox is a determined, strong, and conservative personality. The gift bequeathed from your ancestors is manual dexterity, nimbleness, and a proclivity for working with your hands. Family, country, and duty are of utmost importance to those born into this year pillar. They are powerful individuals with traditional, reliable, and sometimes stubborn personalities. This quiet and strong pillar reveals a homebody who possesses intense passion beneath a calm exterior. If you are an Ox, you will always need to be captain of your own ship. Your home will always be your castle—fill it with rosy-cheeked children, a healthy garden, and beloved pets.

Wood Ox

The creative Wood element produces an Ox who is a lover of harmony, beauty, and elegance. Wood Oxen are blessed with a more relaxed style than other Oxen, but they are still susceptible to being too serious or grim. Poets, musicians, and artists find themselves born into this astral pattern. You are full of ideas, yet you have your feet firmly on the ground. This is because you possess an affinity for the earth itself. A dignified attitude conceals your great sensitivity; others may be surprised at how tender your emotions are and how great your passion is. Strong of will, with an inborn sense of balance, you search for a quality life rather than allowing yourself to be driven by success as the world knows it. The organ of Wood is the liver, so be on guard against outbreaks of anger, social anxiety, and narrow-mindedness for optimum health.

Fire Ox

The Fire element emblazons this Ox's need for harmony and beauty. Fire Oxen are the dreamers and creatives of this world. Natural leaders with a mystical spark, Fire Oxen are drawn to politics, but always remain fiercely individualistic. Fond of combat and the spirit of the game, your tenacity will get the better of any resistance. Your extraordinary skills tend to move you at high speed. Take care not to run out of steam; slow down and don't overdo things. The sensual Fire Ox must be cautious, as Fire moves rapidly and can make you prone to excesses of all types, especially during middle age. Fire governs the heart and circulatory system, so relax and respect your body's limits and natural rhythms.

Earth Ox

The abundant Earth element brings into being a contemplative, hardworking Ox who is concerned with the here-and-now. Earth Oxen are blessed in any venture connected with the earth, soil, or food. Whether a winegrower, farmer, restaurant entrepreneur, or leader of a religious sect, the earth Ox is a hardworking, balanced, and patient individual. If this is your sign, be careful of being too leisurely or pondering too long and thereby missing opportunities. Thrifty, placid, and a lover of nature, the Earth Ox needs plenty of fresh air, freshly ploughed fields, serene ponds, and quiet spots unknown to others. The fertile earth is your preferred retreat and personal paradise. The organ of Earth is the spleen, so be moderate with rich foods and watch a tendency to put on weight.

Metal Ox

The structured and defining Metal element brings forth a serious and rigid Ox who can be austere, stern, and rigorously traditional. The element of Metal symbolizes clarity, purity, and precision, which makes Metal Oxen excellent administrators, organizers, and leaders. If you are a Metal Ox, you need the concrete, the real, and the workable. Achieving your goals is of the highest importance, and you believe wholeheartedly that the needs of the many outweigh the needs of a few. You are full of energy, constant, and true to your word; however, the Metal element can also cause you to be slightly cutting or take yourself too seriously—so relax! The organ of Metal is the lungs, so take good care of your respiratory system and refrain from smoking.

Water Ox

The sheltering, deep, and intuitive Water element gives birth to a sensitive and spiritually minded Ox who wears his/her heart on his/her sleeve. Water soothes the somber, serious side of this earthly branch, and enables this Ox to nurture and look after others. Defenders of peace and caretakers of the most vulnerable amongst us, Water Oxen make doting and attentive parents. Family life will make you happiest, and a cozy home filed with well-behaved children will be heaven on earth for you. Water Oxen have a fear of making scenes, which can make them appear timid or fearful; however, nothing could be further from the truth! When you decide to move out into the world, you could create a business, chair a political cause, or even found a new religion. The organ of Water is the kidneys, so be cautious regarding blockages, circulatory problems, edema, and emotional obstructions.

The Tiger (Yin)

1926 Feb 13 to Feb 1, 1927: Fire Tiger of the furnace

1938 Jan 31 to Feb 18, 1939: Earth Tiger climbing mountains

1950 Feb 17 to Feb 5, 1951: Metal Tiger of mountain pines

1962 Feb 5 to Jan 24, 1963: Water Tiger of the streams

1974 Jan 23 to Feb 10, 1975: Wood Tiger of the forest

1986 Feb 9 to Jan 28, 1987: Fire Tiger of the furnace

1998 Jan 28 to Feb 15, 1999: Earth Tiger climbing mountains

2010 Feb 14 to Feb 2, 2011: Metal Tiger of mountain pines

If your year pillar is ruled by Yin, the earthly branch of the Tiger, you are a restless, adventurous, risk-taker at heart. With your sense of empowerment and entitlement, noble and humanitarian causes appeal to you. Blessed with a tenderhearted and affectionate core, you are also self-reliant and fiercely independent. Graced with charm, bravery, and grand ideas, Tigers flash brilliantly through this life, sometimes without caution for their own safety and security. Courageous, enthusiastic, and optimistic, the passionate Tiger is an unconventional yet humanitarian soul who resists day-to-day routines in favor of a new adventure. Possessing a deep, almost old-fashioned sense of self-sacrifice, Tigers specialize in protecting those weaker than themselves. They make first-rate friends as well as the frankest of enemies.

Wood Tiger

The creative Wood element produces a Tiger who is a lover of harmony, beauty, and elegance. The Wood element brings gentleness to the Tiger, softening pride and giving full rein to a fertile imagination. Those born with the Wood Tiger as their year pillar seem at ease; however, this is an illusion and a mask, behind which they skillfully hide their anxious nature. Wood is a balancing element for Tigers, yet Wood is also flammable and the element of passion—even destruction. The Wood Tiger can therefore be confusing to others. If you are a Wood Tiger, beneath a peaceful exterior your spirit is stirred by excessive and explosive impulses. The organ of Wood is the liver, so it is best if Wood Tigers limit alcoholic beverages for optimum health. Passionate and engaging, Wood Tigers are lovers of liberty and personal freedom. The stage attracts you, the limelight awaits you, and the crowd's eyes are fixed upon you!

Fire Tiger

The impassioned Fire element makes for a Tiger who is, quite literally, born to be in charge. Fire is Yang, the positive, masculine day force which animates, transforms, and quickens. For Tigers, Fire is the flame of energy and dynamism, a creative and stimulating force. Ideas flash and fly as fast as lightning, and hunches will be right on target. This is a lucid and clairvoyant Tiger. However, Fire is often a symbol of war, passion, and violence. For the impetuous and ardent Fire Tiger, moderation is called for with this combination of element and sign. The Fire Tiger is high-minded, principled, and highly moral, yet will always be susceptible to the Fire element's excesses. If this is your sign, you are a loyal, royal, and highly virtuous individual. Fire governs the heart and circulatory system, so guard against stress.

Earth Tiger

The practical Earth element brings into being a worldly, wise, and sensible Tiger who has his or her feet planted firmly on the ground. Earth Tigers are concerned with the here-and-now and they obtain goals as a result of repeated and diligent efforts. Shrewd, assertive, and mature, Earth Tigers are knowledgeable businesspeople and entrepreneurs. If you are an Earth Tiger, you likely dream of a fortress with the security of impregnable castle walls; however, take a chance, go out of your comfort zone a bit, and expand your horizons. The Earth element makes you deeply thoughtful and measured, so be careful of deliberating too long and thereby missing opportunities. The organ of Earth is the spleen, so be moderate with sweets and watch a tendency toward weight gain. Also, beware of becoming mired, stuck, or trapped by the influence of the Earth element.

Metal Tiger

The structured and defining metal element brings forth a prepared Tiger who can be austere, scrupulous, and verbally astute to the point of handing down some shockingly candid assessments. These verbal barbs are merely observational truths to the Metal Tiger. Natural leaders and chiefs, Metal Tigers are experts when implementing plans of action and converting concepts and ideas into reality. "Do it my way and it will be fun" could be their motto. If you are a Metal Tiger, flexibility could benefit you, as could more tenderness, subtlety, and diplomacy. A lack of tact can seriously jeopardize delicate issues of negotiation; it is important to keep in mind that it easier to wound than to heal. The organ of Metal is the lungs, so get enough fresh air, be careful of breathing difficulties, and take good care of your respiratory system.

Water Tiger

The intuitive, deep, and placid Water element gives birth to a calmer and more spiritually perceptive Tiger. Water soothes the savage beast, so to speak, and dampens the inherent aggressive impulses of this earthly branch. Natural warriors of righteous causes and heroes in difficult dilemmas, Water Tigers can be found in foreign countries as missionaries and teachers, and are known to be great humanitarians of the highest order. Defenders of the peace and determined leaders, Water Tigers are humane and benevolent benefactors. If this is your sign, burnout and exhaustion can be your nemesis, so it is important to take time for rest and personal rejuvenation.

Don't give more than you receive, keep a healthy life balance, and, above all, avoid parasitic people who drain your vigor. The organ of Water is the kidneys, so go light on salty foods and take good care of your kidneys and urinary system.

The Rabbit (Mao)

Feb 5, 1927 to Feb 4, 1928: Fire Rabbit dreaming of the moon

Feb 5, 1939 to Feb 4, 1940: Earth Rabbit of mountain pines

Feb 5, 1951 to Feb 4, 1952: Metal Rabbit of the burrow

Feb 5, 1963 to Feb 4, 1964: Water Rabbit of the forest pond

Feb 5, 1975 to Feb 4, 1976: Wood Rabbit of enlightenment

Feb 5, 1987 to Feb 4, 1988: Fire Rabbit dreaming of the moon

Feb 5, 1999 to Feb 4, 2000: Earth Rabbit of mountain pines

Feb 5, 2011 to Feb 4, 2012: Metal Rabbit of the burrow

If your year pillar is ruled by Mao, the earthly branch of the Rabbit, you have been blessed with good manners, diplomacy, and, above all, virtue. One part of your being is easygoing, refined, and social; the other is detached and aloof, and will flee personal upheaval and disruption whenever possible. Those born with this year pillar are naturally talented and have been blessed with excellent taste. Most can excel in the fine arts, are highly creative, and are sensitive to beauty in all of its forms. Well-grounded and upright, you shun personal drama and emotional entanglements, choosing instead security and a peaceful existence. Rabbits are amazing business partners and supportive friends. Sensitive and easily hurt, these private souls keep their own council but are highly sought after for their advice. Nonviolent and relaxed strategists by nature, Rabbits possess a quiet sensuality and an aptitude for self-preservation.

Wood Rabbit

The creative Wood element produces a Rabbit who is a lover of harmony, beauty, and elegance. Wood Rabbits are the muses of the Rabbit family. Art, music, and literature are the gifts from your ancestors. The Wood element brings out a sense of adventure in the Rabbit, as well as a passion for travel and a love of nature. Socially, you are perceived as being calm and relaxed; however, the Wood element leaves you vulnerable to anxiety and excessive worry. The organ of Wood is the liver, so it is best to limit alcoholic beverages. Do not let yourself be drowned by your emotions for optimum health.

Fire Rabbit

The impassioned Fire element makes for a lively, intense Rabbit blessed with great fervor who is a natural leader and transformer. Lucid, clairvoyant, and emotional, Fire Rabbits reject mediocrity and conventional ways of expressing themselves. Virtuous, and with high-minded thinking and ethics, the naturally prudent and reserved Rabbit can also be bold and sometimes even rash. These two sides will continually fight for dominance, a process which can actually increase and strengthen this Rabbit's courage. If this is your sign, you will embrace your boldness, but always remember to remain faithful to your deepest nature. Reason should always be in control of your excesses. The organ of Fire is the heart and circulatory system, so keep an eye on your heart and watch a tendency toward aggressiveness.

Earth Rabbit

The no-nonsense Earth element brings into being a worldly yet sensible Rabbit who is concerned with practical pursuits. Shrewd, subtle, and thoughtful, Earth Rabbits are knowledgeable businesspeople and entrepreneurs. Your natural caution and insistence that time is always on your side may cause you to deliberate too long and miss opportunities. This is a stay-at-home, cozy Rabbit who prefers warm refuges over the challenges of the outside world. The Earth element is all about slow and profound transformations, and so is the Earth Rabbit. The Earth Rabbit must resist hiding away in a cushioned warren and risk the trials and tribulations of life outside. The organ of Earth is the spleen, so be moderate with sweets, get some exercise, and avoid weight gain.

Metal Rabbit

The structured and defining metal element brings forth a self-confident Rabbit who can be circumspect, severe, and even blunt. Metal Rabbits vacillate between beauty, creativity, purity on the one hand; and sadness, severity, and destruction on the other. The Metal element tends to be cutting, rigid, and even harsh at times. Remember not confuse strength of purpose with stiffness. The Metal Rabbit seeks solitude and is attracted to mystical pursuits, but may have difficulty harmonizing body and spirit. A stiff neck and a cold heart are not in your nature; forgiveness is always in your best interest no matter how grievous the perceived insult. The organ ruled by the element of Metal is the lungs, so be careful of breathing difficulties and take good care of your respiratory system.

Water Rabbit

The intuitive, deep, and placid Water element gives birth to a Rabbit who knows how to listen. If you are a Water Rabbit, you are calm and reflective, and generally refrain from excesses. A certain timidity holds you back at times—you may fear difficulties and be hesitant to rock the boat or complain. However, you are very much a pacifist and humanist, so you may find yourself embroiled in social problems and fighting against injustice, rather than pursuing introspective spiritual matters. A lack of self-confidence is your main weakness, so don't stay in the background—be less passive and take the plunge! You don't need to recoil from your passions, but merely control them. Helpful, sympathetic, and tolerant, you can be encroached upon if you are perceived as too passive, so don't give more than you receive. The organ of Water is the kidneys, so look after your spine and urinary tract.

The Dragon (Chen)

1928 Jan 23 to Feb 9, 1929: Earth Dragon of virtue

1940 Feb 8 to Jan 26, 1941: Metal Dragon of patience

1952 Jan 27 to Feb 13, 1953: Water Dragon of the rain

1964 Feb 13 to Feb 1, 1965: Wood Dragon of the whirlpool

1976 Jan 31 to Feb 17, 1977: Fire Dragon of the sky

1988 Feb 17 to Feb 5, 1989: Earth Dragon of virtue

2000 Feb 5 to Jan 23, 2001: Metal Dragon of patience

2012 Jan 23 to Feb 9, 2013: Water Dragon of the rain

If your year pillar is ruled by Chen, the earthly branch of the Dragon, you have been blessed with vital physical health, farsightedness, and the ability to envision the future. Outspoken, impatient, and self-assured, it is said that the lucky Dragon will have boundless energy and strength. You are the proudest of the 12 branches and do not like to be challenged. Your unpredictability assures that others are either your friends or your rivals. Fortunate, original, and enthusiastic, infatuate Dragons need a strong and intriguing partner, or else they may stray to greener pastures or live a solitary life. Egotistical and assertive attention-getters, those with the Dragon as their year pillar are boisterous, flamboyant, and showy. Successful and popular, this lucid sign produces individuals who are born to be in the public eye. If you are a Dragon, the stage attracts you, the limelight awaits you, and the crowd's eyes are fixed upon you!

Wood Dragon

The creative Wood element produces a Dragon who loves harmony, beauty, and elegance. The Wood element brings gentleness to the Dragon, softening pride and giving full rein to a fertile imagination. Those born with the Wood Dragon in their year pillar will always seem to be at ease; however, this is an illusion and a mask, behind which they skillfully hide an anxious and sometimes tormented personality. Beneath a peaceful exterior, your spirit is stirred by excessive and explosive impulses from the Wood element. Wood is the symbol for excessive passion or anger; the Wood Dragon should be careful of this tendency. The physical organ of Wood is the liver, so stand against anxiety and don't self-medicate with alcohol or excessive amounts of food for optimum health.

Fire Dragon

The impassioned Fire element makes for a Dragon who is born to be in the public eye in some way. Fire is yang, the positive, masculine day force that animates, burns, and transforms. Fire within the Dragon will strengthen your energy, making ideas flash and fly through your mind as fast as lightning. This is a lucid and clairvoyant Dragon; however, Fire is also a symbol of war, passion, and violence. Impetuous and ardent, the Fire Dragon will be in a permanent state of alertness, with a thirst for life and an inexhaustible wellspring of activity and imagination. Fire governs the heart and circulatory system, so control anger and aggressiveness before they get out of hand. Reserve your strength and do not burn your energy recklessly.

Earth Dragon

With its caverns and buried treasures, the practical Earth element is very beneficial for the Dragon. The Earth Dragon is more realistic than the other Dragons, and also more materialistic, cautious, and suspicious. Earth Dragons obtain goals as a result of their repeated and diligent efforts. If you are an Earth Dragon, you are a hard and conscientious worker, and you enjoy speculation and accumulating wealth. Although you dream of a refuge with the security of impregnable castle walls, there is a time for rest and a time for action and discoveries. Expand your horizons! Be careful of deliberating too long and thereby missing opportunities, as the Earth element makes you deeply prudent and guarded. The organ of Earth is the spleen, so be moderate with sweets and watch a tendency toward weight gain. Also, beware of becoming mired, stuck, or trapped in life. Quiver your scales and make the ground tremble, but do not close yourself up.

Metal Dragon

The structured and defining metal element brings forth a Dragon who is a gleaming sword. Outspoken, blunt, and future-oriented, Metal Dragons implement plans of action and convert visionary concepts into reality. If you are a Metal Dragon, you are an energetic and decisive person. You are also a natural-born leader—fair, just, and honest. However, your lack of tact can critically jeopardize fragile negotiations. A little more flexibility could benefit you, as could more tenderness, subtlety, and diplomacy. You can also be rather fanatical about work being done correctly and punctually, so relax, be more flexible, and take time to play a bit. The organ of Metal is the lungs, so be diligent to get enough fresh air, be vigilant concerning breathing difficulties, and take good care of your respiratory system.

Water Dragon

The intuitive, deep, and placid Water element should theoretically give birth to a calmer and more reflective person, but this is rarely the case with Water Dragons. They will be found involved in social problems as humanists and as advocates of justice. The Water element turns you toward the hearts of your fellow humans. Water Dragons are humane and benevolent benefactors given to charitable acts (the more public and well-connected, the better). This priest or priestess of the Dragons is naturally drawn to metaphysics as a visionary, a prophet, or a self-styled practitioner. The organ of Water is the kidneys, so be sparing with salty foods and take good care of your urinary system.

The Snake (Si)

Feb 4, 1929 to Feb 4, 1930: Earth Snake of the desert sands

Feb 4, 1941 to Feb 4, 1942: Metal Snake of molded bronze

Feb 4, 1953 to Feb 4, 1954: Water Snake of the wetlands

Feb 4, 1965 to Feb 4, 1966: Wood Snake of the forest trees

Feb 4, 1977 to Feb 4, 1978: Fire Snake of the lamps

Feb 4, 1989 to Feb 4, 1990: Earth Snake of the desert sands

Feb 4, 2001 to Feb 4, 2002: Metal Snake of molded bronze

Feb 4, 2013 to Feb 4, 2014: Water Snake of the wetlands

If your year pillar is ruled by Si, the earthly branch of the Snake, you are the wise philosopher and stealthy sage. Physically attractive, with flawless skin and flawless advice, the Snakes are the intellectuals, scholars, psychiatrists, and spiritual advisors of the world. Gradual, accumulated growth is your life pattern. Those born with the deep-thinking Snake as their year pillar lean toward aesthetic interests such as music, art, and interior design. Unusually gifted with deep intuition, Snakes are also uncommonly sexually attractive. Insight, compassion, subtlety, and discretion are their sum and substance. This highly sensual branch is possessive and needs an emotional partner who abandons him- or herself to passionate desire. The harmonious relationship between your well-kept, polished exterior and your reflective, lucid personality makes you irresistible!

Wood Snake

The creative Wood element produces a Snake who is a lover of the finer things in life. Wood Snakes love art, music, literature, and fine craftsmanship of any type. Inventive and creative, you have a gift for combining beauty and space. The Wood Snake has the soul of a connoisseur and artistic authority, and most are the personification of harmony, charm, and beauty. With intentional improvisation, Wood Snakes will disentangle themselves from even the most difficult situations with finesse and charisma. The organ of the body that corresponds to Wood is the liver, so it's best to limit alcoholic beverages and not let yourself be consumed by your powerful emotions. Wood Snakes sometimes suffer from psychosomatic illnesses.

Fire Snake

The fervent Fire element makes for a lively, intense Snake. Blessed with great feeling, this Snake is a natural power-behind-the-throne and influential personality. Lucid, level-headed, and intuitive, Fire Snakes reject ordinary or conventional ways of doing things. Individualists endowed with a power of rapid intellectual assimilation, Fire Snakes wish to constantly be learning something new. They make excellent teachers and philosophers. Fire Snakes enjoy giving advice and people naturally confide in them; they make excellent personal and financial advisors. The organ of Fire is the heart and circulatory system, so keep an eye on your heart and your blood pressure, and watch a tendency toward aggressiveness.

Earth Snake

The no-nonsense Earth element brings into being a worldly yet sensible Snake who is all about practicality. The protective and soothing Earth Snake has a slow and enticing personal style. This is a stay-at-home, cozy Snake who prefers warm refuges over the challenges and aggressions of the outside world. The Earth element is concerned with slow and profound transformations, and so is the Earth Snake. The downside of this is that it can incite idleness, passivity, and procrastination at times. If this is your sign, you must resist hiding away in a cushioned nest and risk moving out into the unsympathetic outside world. The organ of Earth is the spleen, so be moderate with sweets and watch a tendency toward becoming sedentary and weight gain.

Metal Snake

The structured and defining metal element brings forth a self-confident Snake who can be a bit severe. This Snake has no tolerance for fools. This is a no-nonsense individual who will vacillate between beauty, creativity, and purity on one hand; and sadness, severity, and destruction on the other. The Metal element tends to be cutting, rigid, and even harsh at times. The Metal Snake seeks solitude and is attracted to mystical pursuits. Despotic when angered or agitated, too much rigidity can engender sadness or remorse. If this is your sign, humor is your best friend and defense against drama and calamity. Surround yourself with positive, upbeat people; relax and stop chasing after inaccessible or "perfect" ideals. The organ ruled by the element of Metal is the lungs, so breathe deeply, seek the open air, and take good care of your respiratory system.

Water Snake

The intuitive, deep, and placid Water element gives birth to a Snake who is sensitive to the point of being psychic. Calm, reflective, and generally able to refrain from excesses, the Water Snake is a consummate sage, philosopher, and literary connoisseur. Those with the Water Snake in their year pillar will be led by their pacifist and humanistic leanings as they listen to the problems of their fellow man. This is a cool-headed leader as well as a warm, good-hearted character. Helpful, sympathetic, and tolerant, you could be taken advantage of if you are perceived as too passive, so don't give more than you receive. Your wisdom and moderation are based on deep inner reflection. The organ of Water is the kidneys, so look after your spine and urinary system. Dry warmth and sunshine are vital for your optimum health.

The Horse (Wu)

Feb 4, 1930 to Feb 4, 1931: Metal Horse of the palace gates

Feb 4, 1942 to Feb 4, 1943: Water Horse of the clouds

Feb 4, 1954 to Feb 4, 1955: Wood Horse of the stable

Feb 4, 1966 to Feb 4, 1967: Fire Horse of the celestial river (stars)

Feb 4, 1978 to Feb 4, 1979: Earth Horse of the battlefield

Feb 4, 1990 to Feb 4, 1991: Metal Horse of the palace gates

Feb 4, 2002 to Feb 4, 2003: Water Horse of the clouds

Feb 4, 2014 to Feb 4, 2015: Wood Horse of the stable

If your year pillar is ruled by Wu, the earthly branch of the Horse, you are a verbally astute, quick-witted sportsperson and competitor. Charming, independent, and decisive, the Horse prefers to be always on the move, with places to go and people to see. If you are a Horse, you are of the yang/masculine/day-force disposition, a natural leader who is both idealistic and humanitarian. You are also a gifted speaker and strong communicator. Elegant, witty, and talkative, you are difficult to defeat in a dispute and can always argue a persuasive case. You could be very successful in politics, public speaking, or sales. Those with an independent Horse year pillar need a partner who stimulates their mind and appreciates their wit. Loquacious and friendly, you will always need freedom to change your course at whim and maneuver unencumbered through life's pastures.

Wood Horse

The creative Wood element produces an ardent and elegant Horse who scorns routine and the banalities of life. You are a lover of harmony and beauty, and prefer anything creative and imaginative to reason and discipline. A natural sportsperson, the Wood Horse hates to lose and is extremely competitive. However, the Wood element brings a certain gentleness to this Horse, softening pride and giving full rein to a fertile imagination. Those born with the Wood Horse as their year pillar will give the outward appearance of being at ease; however, inner anxieties and a secret fear of failure can cause difficulties such as depression and obsessions. Active and engaging, Wood Horses need absolute liberty and personal freedom. The limelight calls to you, and the public's eyes are fixed upon you!

Fire Horse

The impassioned Fire element makes for a lucid and clairvoyant Horse who is destined for either fame or infamy. Fire is yang, the positive, masculine day-force that animates, transforms, and urges resolution. For Horses, Fire (the symbol of war, passion, and violence) intensifies an already formidable personality. Impetuous and ardent, moderation is called for with this combination of element and sign. The Fire Horse is fair-minded, with high moral principles, yet can be susceptible to the Fire element's excesses, as well. Artistically and aesthetically gifted, you reject outdated laws, traditional mores, and passé customs. Fire Horses rarely join the establishment. Remember that Fire governs the heart and circulatory system, so keep a tight rein over your passions and do not allow yourself to become overwhelmed. Spend your energy in small doses to avoid burnout.

Earth Horse

The practical Earth element brings into being a worldly, wise, yet sensible Horse who is more realistic than other Horses. Earth Horses are realists and materialists who advance prudently and skeptically through life. Lucky when it comes to financial speculation, you have the potential to amass a considerable fortune. Full of ardor and initiative when young, middle age can bring preoccupation with comfort and security. Later years are spent devoting yourself to the needs of your family and investments. The Earth Horse is first and foremost an elegant and seductive conqueror—always preserve those youthful and dynamic qualities! The organ of Earth is the spleen, so be moderate with sweets and watch a tendency toward weight gain.

Metal Horse

The structured and defining metal element brings forth an orderly and even rigid Horse who is austere, scrupulous, and verbally astute. Natural communicators and leaders, Metal Horses are experts at implementing plans of action and converting concept ideas into reality. If you are a Metal Horse, you are usually able to gain the upper hand in an argument or debate. You are also unhesitant when acting on a decision. However, your blunt observations and candid assessments can be shocking to some. Also, your lack of tact could jeopardize delicate negotiations. Some flexibility could benefit you, as could more subtlety and diplomacy. On the positive side, you have been bestowed a just and honest personality. An ardent idealist, you are also a conscientious worker and a stickler for principles. The organ of Metal is the lungs, so do be diligent to get enough fresh air, be careful of breathing difficulties, and take good care of your respiratory system.

Water Horse

The intuitive, deep, and placid Water element gives birth to a calmer and more spiritually perceptive Horse. Natural decision-makers and idealistic warriors of righteous causes, Water Horses are known to be humanitarians, defenders of the peace, and generous benefactors. Those born with the Water Horse as their year pillar can dominate their passions, impulses, and excesses in order to successfully channel their energies constructively. Great adventurers and masters in the art of governing and leadership, Water Horses are naturally confident and will always live according to the rhythms of their own heart. Like your Fire Horse brothers and sisters, you have been bequeathed rare powers of perception handed down from your ancestors. Bizarre occurrences seem to befall those surrounding you. The organ of Water is the kidneys, so be sparing with salty foods and take good care of your kidneys and urinary system.

The Goat (Wei)

Feb 4, 1931 to Feb 4, 1932: Metal Goat of the mines (fortune)

Feb 4, 1943 to Feb 4, 1944: Water Goat of the gathering storm

Feb 4, 1955 to Feb 4, 1956: Wood Goat of dedication

Feb 4, 1967 to Feb 4, 1968: Fire Goat of lost sheep (shepherd)

Feb 4, 1979 to Feb 4, 1980: Earth Goat of the pasture

Feb 4, 1991 to Feb 4, 1992: Metal Goat of the mines (fortune)

Feb 4, 2003 to Feb 4, 2004: Water Goat of the gathering storm

Feb 4, 2015 to Feb 4, 2016: Wood Goat of dedication

If your year pillar is ruled by Wei, the earthly branch of the Goat, you are an artist in spirit and likely in practice. Those born with a year pillar of the Goat are changeable free spirits who love social gatherings, stimulating conversation, and a beautiful environment. Polite, decent, and gentle, Goats desire a peaceful spot to exist undisturbed and unhurried. Creative, sensitive, and kind, those souls with Goat year pillars are also dependent, disorganized, and extremely vulnerable. They are capricious, work when least expected to, and are never reached by being pressured with a heavy hand. Sometimes insecure and generous to a fault, you are a good Samaritan who has a soft heart toward those less fortunate. Whether a homeless puppy or a needy friend, you will always try to help out if at all possible.

Wood Goat

The creative Wood element produces a Goat who is a lover of luxury, beauty, and style. Wood Goats are artistic muses; most have been blessed with many creative gifts from their ancestors. Art, music, and literature are their specialties. The Wood Goat's art can also be expressed through cooking, modeling, photography, and many other aesthetic pursuits. If you are a Wood Goat, you are usually perceived as being calm and relaxed; however, the flammable Wood element can also leave you vulnerable to internal jolts, anxieties, and excessive worry. The sensitive Wood Goat is sometimes referred to as "the mother of nature," as the natural world and environment holds a strong attraction for this element and branch combination. The organ of Wood is the liver, so it is best to limit alcoholic beverages and keep your emotions in perspective for optimum health.

Fire Goat

The impassioned Fire element makes for a lively, intense Goat who is blessed with great powers of persuasion. Lucid, clairvoyant and emotional, Fire Goats are natural survivors and manipulators of circumstances. They also tend to have strong personalities and high expectations of others. The Fire element puts an exclamation mark after this Goat's personality. If this is your sign, it will take all of your willpower to restrain the latent aggressiveness of the Fire element. The Fire element is also a catalyst for expressiveness, so be careful not to dissipate your energy and exhaust your talents by entertaining your associates. The organ of Fire is the heart and circulatory system, so keep an eye on these systems and watch for blockages of various kinds.

Earth Goat

The no-nonsense Earth element brings into being a worldly, more realistic Goat who is concerned with the here-and-now. Earth Goats are talented artisans, artistic entrepreneurs, and charming personalities in general. This is a stay-at-home, cozy Goat who prefers warm refuges over the aggressions of the outside world. If you are an Earth Goat, the Earth element endows you with a natural caution and reticence; however, your impulsive sense of humor and carefree, whimsical nature will always gain the upper hand. You may be financially fortunate, as many Earth Goats are left with an inheritance, trust fund, or other financial windfall. The organ of Earth is the spleen, so be moderate with sweets and watch a tendency toward becoming sedentary or putting on weight.

Metal Goat

The structured and defining Metal element brings forth a more confident Goat who never limits him- or herself with dogmas or rules. Metal Goats need to follow their own drummer in religion, philosophy, and ethics. These intuitive and empathic souls have the potential to be great healers, with sharp judgment and purpose. Metal Goats vacillate between beauty, creativity, and purity on one hand; and sadness, severity, and destruction on the other. They are attracted to mystical pursuits, but may have difficulty harmonizing body and spirit. If you are a Metal Goat, you are a curious mixture of fantasy and exactitude, tolerance and stubbornness. The Metal element tends to be cutting, rigid, and even harsh at times, which can conflict with your gentle yin nature. Remember not confuse strength of purpose with stiffness. The organ ruled by the element of Metal is the lungs, so be careful of breathing difficulties and blockages, and take good care of your respiratory system.

Water Goat

The intuitive, deep, and placid Water element gives birth to a highly emotional, yet calm and reflective Goat. Water Goats are temperate and reflective, with a capacity to listen to others; however, they also avoid difficulties and can be the first ones to despair or complain about a problem. If this is your sign, a certain timidity can hold you back at times. Don't recoil from your passions—merely control them. When you're not pursuing introspective spiritual matters, you may find yourself embroiled in a protest or fighting against injustice as a pacifist and a humanist. The organ of Water is the kidneys, so look after your and urinary tract system, remain active, and drink plenty of water to hydrate your body. The Water element is a symbol of fertility and a token of good health for all Goats throughout their lives.

The Monkey (Shen)

Feb 5, 1932 to Feb 4, 1933: Water Monkey of elegance

Feb 5, 1944 to Feb 4, 1945: Wood Monkey of the forest trees

Feb 5, 1956 to Feb 4, 1957: Fire Monkey of independence

Feb 5, 1968 to Feb 4, 1969: Earth Monkey of the foothills

Feb 5, 1980 to Feb 4, 1981: Metal Monkey eating pomegranate

Feb 5, 1992 to Feb 4, 1993: Water Monkey of elegance

Feb 5, 2004 to Feb 4, 2005: Wood Monkey of the forest trees

Feb 5, 2016 to Feb 4, 2017: Fire Monkey of independence

If your year pillar is ruled by Shen, the earthly branch of the Monkey, you are an eternally youthful, highly diverse, and clever individual. Monkeys are quick, restless, enterprising, and irrepressible. Mischievous and high-spirited, those with this year pillar are social, active, convincing, and blessed with an entertaining sense of humor. Imagination, ingenuity, and resourcefulness characterize those born with their year pillar in a year of the multifaceted Monkey. Versatile, curious, and easily bored, mischievous Monkeys are witty companions—indulgent, intelligent, and ready to play. Those with this earthly branch are difficult to define due to their complex and sometimes contradictory natures. If you are a Monkey, at times you may secretly suffer from feelings of exclusion, which can make you pessimistic, skeptical, and even bitter. In reality, you only wish to be admired, loved with indulgence, and understood. You must have movement, discussion, and an open exchange of ideas.

Wood Monkey

The creative Wood element produces a Monkey who is a lover of harmony, beauty, and elegance. Wood Monkeys are inclined to be carefree and blessed with a more relaxed style than other Monkeys. Understanding and tolerant, they are humanists of the first order. Temperate in nature and sensitive to nuances and tradition, you appreciate the art of living. When angered or impassioned, quietness in nature and solitude will appease your frustrations and obsessions. Wood is flammable and can stir anger and dangerous fascinations, so keep a close eye on your passions, impulses, and aggressive outbursts. The organ of Wood is the liver, so it is best to limit alcoholic beverages for optimum health. You may also battle depression and have to exercise control over your deepest impulses to overcome dark moods and stop worrying about details.

Fire Monkey

The aggressive Fire element makes for an impassioned, intense Monkey blessed with great fervor who is a natural leader and agent of change. Lucid, clairvoyant, and emotional, Fire Monkeys reject mediocrity, conformity, and conventional ways of expressing themselves. If you are a Fire Monkey, changes, makeovers, and conversions are your specialty. You are a person of action and leadership, which is always couched in terms of vehement anti-conformism. Fire Monkeys seesaw between the satisfaction of strong material needs and mystical aspirations, so your fervor and inner demands may press you toward the monkish solitude of a philosopher. Be careful to avoid fanaticism or a tendency to isolate yourself from your fellow man. The Fire element is subject to excesses, and the organ of Fire is the heart and circulatory system. Keep an eye on your heart, circulatory system, and blood pressure.

Earth Monkey

The levelheaded Earth element brings into being a reasonable, shrewd Monkey who is concerned with practical pursuits. Shrewd, subtle, and materialistic, Earth Monkeys are knowledgeable businesspeople, convincing salespeople, and successful entrepreneurs. Productive, cunning, and delightfully crafty, the Earth Monkey likes activities that bear fruit and will be attracted to speculation, banking, and real estate—anything of tangible value, really. If you are an Earth Monkey, many of your enterprises will be motivated by an overriding need for expansion and an ever-increasing desire for worldly possessions. You can often feel distrustful and suspicious of those near you, which can make you difficult to live with. This usually stems from your worries about your financial security and future. The organ of Earth is the spleen, so be moderate with sweets and watch a tendency toward overeating and weight gain.

Metal Monkey

The structured and defining Metal element brings forth an uncompromising, outspoken Monkey. The Metal Monkey can be austere, narrow-minded, scrupulous, and verbally astute to the point of hurling some profoundly stinging verbal barbs. However, these are merely truths to the Metal Monkey. Organizational geniuses and natural experts at putting plans into action, Metal Monkeys will aim for high positions and great responsibilities, but will need diversity and innovation in their work. Metal Monkeys always stand apart and have a desire to be different. If this is your sign, you cannot tolerate the tedious routine of the daily grind. You also dislike having to explain or justify yourself, which comes from a taste for solitude as well as your communication problems. The organ of Metal is the lungs, so be careful of breathing difficulties and take good care of your respiratory system.

Water Monkey

The intuitive, deep, and placid Water element gives birth to a clever and secretive Monkey who is an observant student of human nature. This trait can be used for better (encouragement and counseling) or worse (conning and tricking). The Water Monkey looks at life uncertainly, through foggy lenses and with slightly confused vision. Water Monkeys need action, change, movement, novelty, and new discoveries. If you are a Water Monkey, the boredom of routine is your greatest enemy; mental stagnation can sour your good humor and staunch your creativity. Respect your need to question everything because it is one of the keys to your success. The organ of Water is the kidneys, so be sparing with salty foods and take good care of your urinary system.

The Rooster (You)

Feb 4, 1933 to Feb 3, 1934: Water Rooster of the barnyard pond

Feb 4, 1945 to Feb 3, 1946: Wood Rooster crowing at dawn

Feb 4, 1957 to Feb 3, 1958: Fire Rooster of seclusion

Feb 4, 1969 to Feb 3, 1970: Earth Rooster of foraging fields

Feb 4, 1981 to Feb 3, 1982: Metal Rooster of steel cages

Feb 4, 1993 to Feb 3, 1994: Water Rooster of the barnyard pond

Feb 4, 2005 to Feb 3, 2006: Wood Rooster crowing at dawn

Feb 4, 2017 to Feb 3, 2018: Fire Rooster of seclusion

If your year pillar is ruled by You, the earthly branch of the Rooster, you are an individual of appearances, reality, and emotion. Finely dressed and with a taste for pageantry, the Rooster has a lively, outgoing manner and is an efficient and methodical soul. You understand the concept of delayed gratification—how to work hard today while looking ahead toward tomorrow's rewards. Confident, resilient, and industrious, those souls born with a year pillar of the Rooster apply themselves cheerfully to practical projects. Enthusiastic about details others may have overlooked, Roosters prefer to give the orders rather than take them. Roosters love to socialize and are at their best in a crowd. The assertive Rooster needs a strong and self-assured partner whom he or she can respect, such as the powerful Dragon, the handsome Snake, or the stable Ox.

Wood Rooster

The creative Wood element produces an imaginative and creative Rooster who is more efficient than most people. The adaptable Wood Rooster has a free and easy manner and a eye for color, style, and interior decorating. Confident that their way is the right way, Wood Roosters have an ability to improvise in difficult situations. If this is your sign, you have a rich imagination that you often put to good use, particularly if you work in the arts. Take refuge in nature in order to fulfill your need for liberty, space, and harmony. Your calm and collected demeanor makes you appear at ease; however, this self-assured attitude is a defensive mask behind which you skillfully hide your doubts and fears. The physical organ of Wood is the liver; so avoid self-medicating by drinking alcohol or overeating.

Fire Rooster

The impassioned Fire element makes for a firecracker of a Rooster who warms, burns, animates, transforms, and overthrows. Fire in the Rooster augments this sign's passion, audacity, argumentativeness, and rashness. The quixotic Fire Rooster needs to be surrounded by flattery and applause. Warrior, statesman, emperor, or revolutionary, the Fire Rooster runs after ideals that he or she can seldom grasp. Gifted with a perplexing and powerful personality, you will evolve within a special universe, far from others and run-of-the-mill situations. You are likely to be lucid and clairvoyant; however, Fire is also a symbol of passion and violence, so you'll need to control your anger and aggressiveness lest they get out of hand. Fire governs the heart and circulatory system, so reserve your strength and do not burn your energy recklessly. Be careful of overwork and excesses of every kind.

Earth Rooster

With its caverns and buried treasures, the practical Earth element is very harmonious for the Rooster. The Earth Rooster is more realistic than the others, but also more materialistic, cautious, and skeptical. Earth Roosters reach their goals as a result of continual diligent efforts. For this Rooster, the Earth element symbolizes a safe deposit box rather than a refuge for meditation. A hard and conscientious worker, you enjoy accumulating wealth and could be preoccupied with success, security, and appearances. You may have a tendency to bury your treasures (so to speak) away from indiscreet glances and prying eyes. The organ of Earth is the spleen, so be moderate with sweets, stay active, and watch a tendency to put on weight after middle age.

Metal Rooster

The structured and defining Metal element brings forth a Rooster who is the "sword that harvests." Organized, outspoken, and blunt, Metal Roosters implement plans of action and turn ideas into reality. They like to take command and organize everything, leaving little left to chance. They can also be rather fanatical about their work ethic, doing things correctly, and being punctual.

Their lack of tact can sometimes jeopardize fragile negotiations. If this is your sign, a little flexibility could benefit you, as could more tenderness, subtlety, and diplomacy. Relax, be more flexible, and take time to play a bit. The organ of Metal is the lungs, so be diligent to get enough fresh air, be careful of breathing difficulties, and take good care of your respiratory system.

Water Rooster

The intuitive, deep, and placid Water element gives birth to a calmer, more reflective Rooster. The Water element subdues and subverts this sign's native pride, turning it instead toward social causes. Water Roosters will often be found embroiled in community dilemmas as advocates of justice and/or as champions of improved social conditions. Water Roosters will succeed in any profession that demands self-assurance, nerve, and brilliance. Intelligent and skillful, they know how to convince and persuade. If you are one of the adaptable Water Roosters, you are able to create a special universe around you by setting up a comfortable, harmonious, and organized home. The organ of Water is the kidneys, so be sparing with salty foods and take good care of your kidneys and urinary system.

The Dog (Xu)

Feb 4, 1934 to Feb 4, 1935: Wood Dog on guard

Feb 4, 1946 to Feb 4, 1947: Fire Dog of dreams (sleep)

Feb 4, 1958 to Feb 4, 1959: Earth Dog of the mountain

Feb 4, 1970 to Feb 4, 1971: Metal Dog of gold bracelets

Feb 4, 1982 to Feb 4, 1983: Water Dog of deep oceans

Feb 4, 1994 to Feb 4, 1995: Wood Dog on guard

Feb 4, 2006 to Feb 4, 2007: Fire Dog of dreams (sleep)

Feb 4, 2018 to Feb 4, 2019: Earth Dog of the mountains

If your year pillar is ruled by Xu, the earthly branch of the Dog, you are a watchful worrier and champion of the little guy. Dogs are famous for complete loyalty toward their friends and loved ones, and intense ferocity toward the enemies of their loved ones. Anxiety, loyalty, and protectiveness characterize the magnanimous Dog personality. Devotion, generosity, and perseverance are the cornerstones of the anxious Dog's temperament. Earnest, sincere, and faithful to those they love, wary Dogs can have sharp tongues and a tendency to jump to conclusions. Cautious and serious regarding love, the Dog needs a trustworthy partner who has strong family sympathies and who appreciates the Dog's need for tenderness. Low on ego but high on their soapboxes, Dogs are known for their fair-minded humanitarianism. Just as a calm river and a violent torrent can spring from the same source, there are many different kinds of Dogs, but they all have worry and anxiety in common.

Wood Dog

The creative Wood element produces a more serene Dog who is a lover of harmony, beauty, and elegance. The Wood element brings a peacefulness to the Dog's sometimes anxious personality. Socially popular and highly intuitive, the Wood Dog is a seer and prophet. The Wood Dog is also a seducer who is able to convince, confuse, and attract. If you are a Wood Dog, your subtle emotions make you well-suited for the arts and other creative endeavors. However, as with all Dog natives, you likely hide a lack of self-confidence behind a calm and relaxed exterior. This is a defensive reaction, as your overwrought imagination is adept at imagining the worst possible outcome in every scenario. Your charm lies in your unaffected behavior and sincerity. Wood governs the liver, so avoid drinking alcohol.

Fire Dog

The impassioned Fire element makes for an energetic Dog who is quite capable of taking on a leadership position. Always on tenterhooks, perpetually agitated, and eternally unsatisfied, the Fire Dog is not easy to live with, however. Once they are convinced of their position, nothing can make them change their mind. Indeed, with their strong passions and sudden angers, some may think the Fire Dog impossible to please. Attracted to mysticism, Fire Dogs are known to cut themselves off from the outside world and focus exclusively on spiritual practices. Some Fire Dogs choose to live completely isolated for a time. Fire is the yang, positive, masculine day- force that animates, transforms, and quickens. For Dogs, Fire is the flame of energy and dynamism, a creative and stimulating force. If this is your sign, you are an exceptional person! Make full use of your great potential. Fire governs the heart and circulatory system, so guard against high blood pressure, toxic anger, and excessive worry.

Earth Dog

The practical Earth element brings into being a sensible Dog who has all paws planted firmly on terra firma. This immovable sentry is active and honest, a conscientious worker who is appreciated by superiors and subordinates alike. Earth Dogs are concerned with the here-and-now, and they obtain goals as a result of repeated and diligent efforts. If this is your sign, you are knowledgeable in your area of expertise. You are also shrewd and mature, and will give priority to the interest of the collective over your own. On the downside, you can be troubled by anxiety and a fear of commitment, but contact with nature soothes your fears and doubts. The organ of Earth is the spleen, so be moderate with sweets and watch a tendency toward weight gain.

Metal Dog

The structured and defining Metal element brings forth an organized Dog who can be austere and verbally merciless. If there is a chink in someone's armor, the Metal Dog will find it. Metal Dogs vacillate between beauty and material success on one hand; and spiritual preoccupations and death on the other. If you are a Metal Dog, you may be torn between worldly achievement and an internal, secret spiritual light. Metal Dogs are discerning and lucid, but cannot seem to avoid torturing themselves with burdens. Free yourself by jettisoning the iron collar of rules and regulations and the straightjacket of dogmas that bind you. The organ of Metal is the lungs, so be diligent to get enough fresh air, be watchful for breathing difficulties, and take good care of your respiratory system.

Water Dog

The intuitive, deep, and placid Water element gives birth to a devout and spiritually discerning Dog. Water soothes the inherent anxiety and dampens the aggressive impulses of this earthly branch. Natural warriors of righteous causes and the heroes in difficult dilemmas, Water Dogs can be found in foreign countries as missionaries, doctors, nurses, and teachers. They are defenders of the peace, determined leaders, and humanitarians of the highest order. Water Dogs are humane and benevolent benefactors who achieve their goals through dogged perseverance. Excessive emotionality and passions are often the result of this element and sign combination, as well. The organ of Water is the kidneys, so be sparing with salty foods and take good care of your kidneys and urinary system.

The Pig (Hai)

Feb 5 1935 to Feb 4, 1936: Wood Pig of travel and journeys

Feb 5, 1947 to Feb 4, 1948: Fire Pig cresting the mountain

Feb 5 1959 to Feb 4, 1960: Earth Pig of the monastery

Feb 5, 1971 to Feb 4, 1972: Metal Pig of fine jewelry

Feb 5, 1983 Feb 13 to Feb 4, 1984: Water Pig of the wide sea

Feb 5, 1995 to Feb 4, 1996: Wood Pig of travel and journeys

Feb 5, 2007 to Feb 4, 2008: Fire Pig cresting the mountain

Feb 5, 2019 to Feb 4, 2020: Earth Pig of the monastery

If your year pillar is ruled by Hai, the earthly branch of the Pig, you are considerate, long-suffering, and supremely honest. The unpretentious Pig makes a cheerful friend and sincere partner. Trusting Pigs are often betrayed or duped because of their faith in other people, but are eventually rewarded due to their sincerity and pure heart. Companionship, physical love, and emotional security are a must. These souls need an easy-going mate who talks out problems instead of shouting. Gentle yet strong-willed, Pigs are motivated by their conscience. They would never push themselves ahead at the expense of another.

Wood Pig

The creative Wood element produces a Pig who is a lover of peace, justice, and equality. This is an artistic Pig who loves travel and the splendor of the outdoors. Nature, the woods, and scenic nooks unknown to others are all favorite haunts of the Wood Pig. Those born with the Wood Pig as their year pillar prefer the country over the city, the arts over the world of business, and their freedom over wealth. A structured bureaucratic society is the epitome of everything Wood Pigs detest. They prefer to be relaxed, simple, and sometimes even a little careless. If this is your sign, you may feel ill at ease and cramped in a highly organized or rigid environment. The organ of Wood is the liver, so for optimum health it is best to limit alcoholic beverages and keep your emotions in perspective.

Fire Pig

The transforming Fire element makes for a Pig who is a reservoir of natural energy, audacity, and passion. The Fire Pig is more opinionated and outspoken, and much more of a fighter than other Pigs. Intellectually curious, the Fire Pig is on a never-ending quest for risk and novelty. This impulsive and big-hearted soul is a lover of mystery and sometimes a bit solitary. Fire Pigs can give of themselves while being utterly blind to the consequences. Lucid, clairvoyant, and emotional, Fire Pigs reject mediocrity and conventional ways of expressing themselves. Their bawdy sense of humor can be shocking in a charming kind of way. If this is your sign, you get around obstacles by relentlessly overthrowing them. Your Fire element also endows you with zeal and an enthusiasm for new ideas. The organ of Fire is the heart and circulatory system, so curb your tendency toward aggressiveness and impulsiveness, and try to keep your taste for dangerous enterprises in check.

Earth Pig

The no-nonsense Earth element brings into being a shrewd, sensible Pig who is concerned with realistic ideas and concepts. The Earth Pig tends to be an egotist, snug in his or her solitary lair. Male Earth Pigs in particular can resemble Mr. Spock in that they are calculating, logical, and careful. They will create detailed plans and projects, evaluating risks and weighing the pros and cons before making a decision. Their efforts are often devoted to accumulating wealth that they will then hide from the eyes of others. Female Earth Pigs appear to be submissive, but the reality is that they control from behind the scenes. This is a stay-at-home, cozy Pig who prefers warm refuges over the aggressions of the outside world. Earth Pigs in general tend to be distrustful and suspicious, and are haunted by a fear of being cheated. The organ of Earth is the spleen, so the Earth Pig should be moderate with sweets and watch a tendency toward inactivity and weight gain.

Metal Pig

The structured and defining metal element brings forth a self-confident Pig who does not seek solitude as other Pigs do, but rather walks in full daylight enjoying success and glory. Metal Pigs are energetic and ambitious, but their clear-sightedness can sometimes be painful. Metal Pigs are galvanized by the mysteries of the soul and of the subconscious. The Metal Pig is a scrupulous yet ambitious person who may sacrifice his or her private life for material success. If you are a Metal Pig, humor is your best friend and defense against tragedy and misfortune. Surround yourself with positive, upbeat people, and relax and give up chasing after inaccessible or "perfect" ideals. The organ ruled by the element of Metal is the lungs, so take good care of your respiratory system. Breathe deeply, seek the open air, sail a boat, or go climb a mountain.

Water Pig

The deep, calm, and composed Water element gives birth to a receptive and empathic Pig who knows how to listen. This is a mellow, reflective Pig who generally refrains from excess. Water Pigs are pacifists and humanists, and often have a fear of difficulties and confrontation. If this is your sign, a certain timidity and lack of self-confidence holds you back at times. Don't recede into the background—be less passive and take the risk! Helpful, sympathetic, and honest, you can be encroached upon if you are perceived as too passive, so don't get in the habit of giving more than you receive. The organ of Water is the kidneys, so look after your spine and urinary tract system. Remain active to avoid putting on weight during midlife, and drink plenty of water to hydrate your body.

Chapter 3
The Month Pillar

The second pillar of destiny is the month pillar. Like the year pillar, it is composed of two Chinese characters that depict the universal qi distinct to the month in which you were born. We can use the month pillar in our charts for a great deal of information and clarity. Using the software included, find your month pillar in the center of your Zi Wei Dou Shu chart. Find your monthly animal branch sign below and then continue on to find what life stage you are in.

If the animal sign in your month pillar is the Rat: You are sociable, dynamic, and a born leader. You are gifted in the art of debate and you have a talent for convincing others. You are a perpetual student—inquisitive and always yearning for answers. Inwardly you feel that you are destined for greatness, but don't be impatient to achieve your goals; a steady pace will insure success.

If the animal sign in your month pillar is the Ox: You are not the kind of person who will settle for second best. You are determined to succeed in this life and are not bothered by what others think. When the stresses of work build up, exercise is a good way to release them. When you make money you will keep it. Long-term romances will be fortunate.

If the animal sign in your month pillar is the Tiger: You are quite the individualist, a traveler who likes to travel the path least taken. Taking care of your home and family are very important to you, despite many ups and downs in love. You are noticed by superiors as a result of your shining abilities. Setting clear priorities and directions will help achieve your goals.

If the animal sign in your month pillar is the Rabbit: You are tolerant and sensitive, and dream of making a difference. You will most likely be tested many times, but patience and learning to understand your priorities makes you stronger. Duty to family and to responsibilities at work pull you in two opposite directions.

If the animal sign in your month pillar is the Dragon: You are direct and blunt. A natural leader by example and deed, you will enjoy a passionate love life, possibly with many different lovers. You will most likely find yourself in the public eye in some way.

If the animal sign in your month pillar is the Snake: You are productive and practical with the ability to improve on other people's ideas to make them more efficient. Much emphasis will be on your career, with your social life put secondary. Relationships will be tested, but eventually they will pass with flying colors.

If the animal sign in your month pillar is the Horse: You have the gift of gab and can talk to anyone about almost anything. You are able to make people believe every word you say. Over time, more responsibilities will emerge, some more serious than you might anticipate. Romance finds you, and your loved ones go out of their way to please you.

If the animal sign in your month pillar is the Goat: You are an introvert and very cautious until you slowly get to know someone; once you do, you are friends for life. You will provide your children with whatever they need and indulge them with the finest you can afford. Financial luck is indicated.

If the animal sign in your month pillar is the Monkey: You love life and love to have fun! You will make a good leader if you don't take criticism personally. You have a flair for the dramatic. Roadblocks are lifted and opportunities flow. Take care of financial responsibilities early on so that they don't come back to haunt you later on down the line.

If the animal sign in your month pillar is the Rooster: You are analytical, with keen observational skills. Your patience will be tested many times, but you will analyze your way through it. As responsibilities increase, frustration rises, so take time to wind down and relax frequently.

If the animal sign in your month pillar is the Dog: You have a strong sense of duty and make sure those who rely on you have a safe haven. Decision-making can be hard with too many variables in mind. Opportunities abound, but pick and choose carefully. You search diligently for a soulmate. Don't let heartache early on spoil your desire, as true love comes later for you.

If the animal sign in your month pillar is the Pig: You have incredible insight into what others feel, but you tend to keep your emotions to yourself. You can sometimes spend beyond your means and then suffer when it's time to pay. Try to heal yourself by confronting your past, and don't give more than you receive, as this could become a heavy burden.

After locating your month pillar in the center of the Zi Wei Dou Shu chart on the CD, find your life stage and your daymaster (example: if your day pillar is the Fire Horse, your element is yang Fire; if your day pillar is the Fire Rabbit, your element is yin Fire.) Then, move down through the animal signs underneath and stop at the one present in your month pillar. You will be comparing your daymaster element with the branch (animal sign) of your birth month. Note what life stage you are in (Childhood, Adolescence, Adulthood, Prime, Decline, Aging, Death, Dormancy, Void, Embryo, Pregnancy, or Birth) and look to the end of the chapter for the meaning.

If yang Wood is your daymaster element (Wood Rat, Wood Tiger, Wood Dragon, Wood Horse, Wood Monkey, or Wood Dog) and your Month pillar is in the sign of:

- ◈ The Rat, your life stage is Childhood.
- ◈ The Ox, your life stage is Adolescence.
- ◈ The Tiger, your life stage is Adulthood.
- ◈ The Rabbit, your life stage is Prime.
- ◈ The Dragon, your life stage is Decline.
- ◈ The Snake, your life stage is Aging.
- ◈ The Horse, your life stage is Death.
- ◈ The Goat, your life stage is Dormancy.
- ◈ The Monkey, your life stage is Void.
- ◈ The Rooster, your life stage is Embryo.
- ◈ The Dog, your life stage is Pregnancy.
- ◈ The Pig, your life stage is Birth.

If yin Wood is your daymaster element (Wood Ox, Wood Rabbit, Wood Snake, Wood Goat, Wood Rooster, Wood Pig) and your Month pillar is in the sign of:

- ◈ The Rat, your life stage is Aging.
- ◈ The Ox, your life stage is Decline.
- ◈ The Tiger, your life stage is Prime.
- ◈ The Rabbit, your life stage is Adulthood.
- ◈ The Dragon, your life stage is Adolescence.
- ◈ The Snake, your life stage is Childhood.
- ◈ The Horse, your life stage is Birth.
- ◈ The Goat, your life stage is Pregnancy.
- ◈ The Monkey, your life stage is Embryo.
- ◈ The Rooster, your life stage is Void.
- ◈ The Dog, your life stage is Dormancy.
- ◈ The Pig, your life stage is Death.

If yang Fire is your daymaster element (Fire Rat, Fire Tiger, Fire Dragon, Fire Horse, Fire Monkey, or Fire Dog) and your month pillar is in the sign of:

- ◈ The Rat, your life stage is Embryo.
- ◈ The Ox, your life stage is Pregnancy.
- ◈ The Tiger, your life stage is Birth.

- ◈ The Rabbit, your life stage is Childhood.
- ◈ The Dragon, your life stage is Adolescence.
- ◈ The Snake, your life stage is Adulthood.
- ◈ The Horse, your life stage is Prime.
- ◈ The Goat, your life stage is Decline.
- ◈ The Monkey, your life stage is Aging.
- ◈ The Rooster, your life stage is Death.
- ◈ The Dog, your life stage is Dormancy.
- ◈ The Pig, your life stage is Void.

If yin Fire is your daymaster element (Fire Ox, Fire Rabbit, Fire Snake, Fire Goat, Fire Rooster, or Fire Pig) and your month pillar is in the sign of:

- ◈ The Rat, your life stage is Void.
- ◈ The Ox, your life stage is Dormancy.
- ◈ The Tiger, your life stage is Death.
- ◈ The Rabbit, your life stage is Aging.
- ◈ The Dragon, your life stage is Decline.
- ◈ The Snake, your life stage is Prime.
- ◈ The Horse, your life stage is Adulthood.
- ◈ The Goat, your life stage is Adolescence.
- ◈ The Monkey, your life stage is Childhood.
- ◈ The Rooster, your life stage is Birth.
- ◈ The Dog, your life stage is Pregnancy.
- ◈ The Pig, your life stage is Embryo.

If yang Earth is your daymaster element (Earth Rat, Earth Tiger, Earth Dragon, Earth Horse, Earth Monkey, or Earth Dog) and your month pillar is in the sign of:

- ◈ The Rat, your life stage is Embryo.
- ◈ The Ox, your life stage is Pregnancy.
- ◈ The Tiger, your life stage is Birth.
- ◈ The Rabbit, your life stage is Childhood.
- ◈ The Dragon, your life stage is Adolescence.
- ◈ The Snake, your life stage is Adulthood.
- ◈ The Horse, your life stage is Prime.
- ◈ The Goat, your life stage is Decline.

◈ The Monkey, your life stage is Aging.

◈ The Rooster, your life stage is Death.

◈ The Dog, your life stage is Dormancy.

◈ The Pig, your life stage is Void.

If yin Earth is your daymaster element (Earth Ox, Earth Rabbit, Earth Snake, Earth Goat, Earth Rooster, Earth Pig) and your month pillar is in the sign of:

◈ The Rat, your life stage is Void.

◈ The Ox, your life stage is Dormancy.

◈ The Tiger, your life stage is Death.

◈ The Rabbit, your life stage is Aging.

◈ The Dragon, your life stage is Decline.

◈ The Snake, your life stage is Prime.

◈ The Horse, your life stage is Adulthood.

◈ The Goat, your life stage is Adolescence.

◈ The Monkey, your life stage is Childhood.

◈ The Rooster, your life stage is Birth.

◈ The Dog, your life stage is Pregnancy.

◈ The Pig, your life stage is Embryo.

If yang Metal is your daymaster element (Metal Rat, Metal Tiger, Metal Dragon, Metal Horse, Metal Monkey, or Metal Dog) and your month pillar is in the sign of:

◈ The Rat, your life stage is Death.

◈ The Ox, your life stage is Dormancy.

◈ The Tiger, your life stage is Void.

◈ The Rabbit, your life stage is Embryo.

◈ The Dragon, your life stage is Pregnancy.

◈ The Snake, your life stage is Birth.

◈ The Horse, your life stage is Childhood.

◈ The Goat, your life stage is Adolescence.

◈ The Monkey, your life stage is Adulthood.

◈ The Rooster, your life stage is Prime.

◈ The Dog, your life stage is Decline.

◈ The Pig, your life stage is Aging.

If yin Metal is your daymaster element (Metal Ox, Metal Rabbit, Metal Snake, Metal Goat, Metal Rooster, Metal Pig) and your month pillar is in the sign of:

◈   The Rat, your life stage is Birth.

◈   The Ox, your life stage is Pregnancy.

◈   The Tiger, your life stage is Embryo.

◈   The Rabbit, your life stage is Void.

◈   The Dragon, your life stage is Dormancy.

◈   The Snake, your life stage is Death.

◈   The Horse, your life stage is Aging.

◈   The Goat, your life stage is Decline.

◈   The Monkey, your life stage is Prime.

◈   The Rooster, your life stage is Adulthood.

◈   The Dog, your life stage is Adolescence.

◈   The Pig, your life stage is Childhood.

If yang Water is your daymaster element (Water Rat, Water Tiger, Water Dragon, Water Horse, Water Monkey, or Water Dog) and your month pillar is in the sign of:

◈   The Rat, your life stage is Prime.

◈   The Ox, your life stage is Decline.

◈   The Tiger, your life stage is Aging.

◈   The Rabbit, your life stage is Death.

◈   The Dragon, your life stage is Dormancy.

◈   The Snake, your life stage is Void.

◈   The Horse, your life stage is Embryo.

◈   The Goat, your life stage is Pregnancy.

◈   The Monkey, your life stage is Birth.

◈   The Rooster, your life stage is Childhood.

◈   The Dog, your life stage is Adolescence.

◈   The Pig, your life stage is Adulthood.

If yin Water is your daymaster element (Water Ox, Water Rabbit, Water Snake, Water Goat, Water Rooster, Water Pig) and your Month pillar is in the sign of:

◈   The Rat, your life stage is Adulthood.

◈   The Ox, your life stage is Adolescence.

◈   The Tiger, your life stage is Childhood.

◈   The Rabbit, your life stage is Birth.

- ❖ The Dragon, your life stage is Pregnancy.
- ❖ The Snake, your life stage is Embryo.
- ❖ The Horse, your life stage is Void.
- ❖ The Goat, your life stage is Dormancy.
- ❖ The Monkey, your life stage is Death.
- ❖ The Rooster, your life stage is Aging.
- ❖ The Dog, your life stage is Decline.
- ❖ The Pig, your life stage is Prime.

Embryo

If Embryo is your life stage, you are the youngest of souls and in the earliest stages of spiritual development. As such, you proceed through specific and recognizable stages of new beginnings in this life. According to legend, the fetus in the womb sees from one end of the universe to the other, including the unborn's own deep past and his or her ultimate destiny. However, during the birth process, you experienced total forgetfulness of all knowledge of your pre-birth existence. If you are born into this earliest of the karmic life stages, the purpose of your life is to recover this knowledge. Interested in all things new, you will possess a good sense of humor and enjoy helping people. Good luck surrounds you. Health is weak when young, but as you age, health improves. Those in this life phase like to know details and reasons for things and are optimistic about the future.

Pregnancy

If Pregnancy is your life stage, you are a very young soul. This will be a life of heightened spiritual awareness for you. During this lifetime, you will often notice symbols or signs in your daily life which will provide you with needed information. Born into this life stage, you experience vivid or prophetic dreams and often rely on your intuition or inner knowing. You will have many questions about these spiritual experiences and may not understand what is happening. You may find yourself wondering if others have experienced the same types of things, and question if your own experiences are true and accurate. Be accepting of the insights and information that these experiences provide. The physical form in which you find yourself during this lifetime will be the closest to the pure essence of you—your spiritual self. You are the only soul with your particular "brand" of personality. You've recently come into being, and have now crossed over into physical form. You need a lot of energy and strong support from family, friends, and environment. Hard work pays off for you and you will be known as an honest and social person who is satisfied with your existence and lifestyle.

Birth

If Birth is your life stage, you are a relatively young soul. Born at this time into physical form by human parents, you use your physical senses to take in the world around you. You are in a karmic stage of help and assistance to others. Happiness, kindness, honesty, gentleness, good relationships, and popularity with others are the gifts of this life to you. A quick learner and highly intelligent, you will live a long life and have many opportunities offered to you. Keep in mind that, spiritually speaking, you're still a baby and learning sounds, shapes, emotions, and even words. You don't quite know who you are yet. You're still learning the basics of life, such as right and wrong. You will be strongly attached to your parent(s) or guardian(s), as they were the first who provided your basic human needs. There will be gradual growth and enjoyment of many (what seem like) new activities for you. Those in this life stage are easily influenced by others both positively and negatively, and will need inspiration and assistance to develop and mature. You will always need a stable partner in life and in love.

Adolescence

If Adolescence is your life stage, you are a younger soul. You are extremely energetic and imaginative and many times act with impunity, doing as you please. You're very self-expressive and creative; this will generally be a happy life for you. This is where you begin school, spiritually speaking. If you find yourself experiencing the Adolescent stage of the 12 life cycles, you are in a rebellious stage with unconventional thinking. You may have strained relations with your family early on, and consider yourself powerless to change the status quo—that is, until that fateful day when a spiritual force steps in and convinces you to take action. Naturally (or supernaturally), your actions result in an almost miraculous improvement in family relations. You're in the puberty stage, spiritually, and are here to learn to clean up your own messes and focus on learning about relationships, developing, maturing, and leading. You will use your intelligence to succeed and use verbal skills to the max.

Adulthood

If Adulthood is your life stage, you are to some degree an experienced soul. You may be motivated early to start a relationship, get married, and/or have children. You have a strong sense of security and are now focused on the assets of others. You have the power to handle other people's belongings. It is quite possible that one of your relatives will leave you with an inheritance. In this life cycle, you are quite ambitious and passionate, sexual and quite intense. Symbolically you are a vulnerable but world-weary young hero(ine) facing down the realities of a harsh world—but only for a time, after which everything that's confusing and uncertain turns out to be safe and welcoming in the end. Optimism, faith in a power greater than yourself, and a certain resilience characterizes this life stage. You may find yourself wanting recognition and fame; however, you will do better behind the scenes in management or in any type of leadership role. An independent self-made person, you possess the potential for great prosperity and success in this life.

Prime

If Prime is your life stage, you are an experienced soul. There is an old saying that youth is wasted on the young, the implication being that although we are at our best physically in our youth, the young are still inexperienced and are not able to take advantage of their best years. This is not the case with you, as you have evolved to the point at which you are able to take advantage of all the benefits this life has to offer. At this stage, materialism is the greatest risk to spiritual development. If this is your life cycle, you will most likely pursue higher education and a traditional relationship, and attain an admired career. Much of your focus will be on relationships. You appreciate your own beauty as well as the beauty of others. You're finally at the stage at which you have the personal confidence to act on your own, and the freedom to act as your conscience dictates. There is a good probability for celebrity and success in some form. Be cautious of becoming overconfident or overbearing.

Decline

If Decline is your life stage, you are a very experienced soul. You will need a steady 9-to-5 job where the responsibilities end when the work day is completed. At this stage, your inner spiritual self is daily becoming more mature and acquiring strength and renewal. The older you are, the better you become; during middle age in particular, when you are no longer making foolish, youthful decisions and are no longer governed by youthful passions and indiscretions, you can finally be at your best. You are quite philosophical and work hard at your job. As you get close to retiring, you may feel better than you did in your 20s. Because you may feel that you were born old, you'll likely not go through a midlife crisis. At that time, you will finally be comfortable in your own skin. Your parents are likely to have had a strong influence in your life, for good or for bad, and their passing may be particularly hard on you. Your life situations tend to reach the top then turn back down again with some memorable peaks and valleys. You are a genuinely nice person, albeit a bit of a procrastinator, who needs a calm, steady life. This life stage has a passive influence. This could cause you to be hesitant to challenge authority. Take time for vacations with your family or spouse while you're young and enjoy old age, reflecting on these gratifying adventures. It has been said that the memories of a man in his old age are the deeds of a man in his prime.

Aging

If Aging is your life stage, you are an old soul. You will experience many changes in yourself and wear many hats during this lifetime. You are a multidimensional person in the process of physical, psychic, and spiritual transformation. Some dimensions of your life will grow and expand, while others will decline. Even during your youth, your reaction time may be slow, but your knowledge of world events and wisdom will be profound at times and greatly expanded. Even late in life, you will find that a new potential exists for physical, mental, and spiritual growth and development. Like a bristlecone pine that has no cells older than 30 years, you will experience great longevity. However, you need a gentle and peaceful work environment without stress or pressure, and a calm and steady life course to accomplish your goals.

Death

If Death is your life stage, you are indeed an old soul. Death is separation. During this life stage, you separate from the karmic patterns that have bound you and held you back. You shed crippling fears, old ghosts, and hang-ups that will not be carried with you to the next existence.

You are completing some very important soul-work. You are a rather retiring person, a worrier, and susceptible to lethargy at times. You need energy, exercise, and good nutrition to achieve. You may not have a traditional career, but a series of jobs that are only a means to be able to live the life you want. You will work to live rather than live to work. Choose a profession in the arts or literature, not in business or management. You may yearn for retirement at an early age. Although you are not particularly ambitious in the traditional sense, you won't tolerate being cheated financially and will insist on receiving what you deserve. This life cycle can create a lot of problems in relationships. It is recommended that you marry late in life.

Dormancy

If Dormancy is your life stage, you are a very old soul. Creatives, immortals, and famous philosophers find themselves born into this life stage. You are involved in a cycle in which growth, development, and even physical activity can be temporarily suspended. This helps you conserve spiritual energy. You instinctually know how to start protecting yourself *before* the onset of adverse conditions, and are able to enter into a recuperative phase afterward. This will happen when your life becomes unpredictable or when the climate of a relationship changes very suddenly. These constant adaptations can lead to high stress levels. As an introvert, you enjoy doing anything indoors; you may take pleasure in collecting things and saving money. You are most likely cautious, quiet, and honest, but need to be motivated and exposed to new ideas and ways of thinking. Your mind has been liberated from worldly things; you feel detached from "all that." You don't dwell on the past, but dream about the future. You'll likely be thinking about what your spouse or children will have received from you, and also about your future in the spiritual realm. Ultimately, you want to be a source of joy and hope, and share pearls of wisdom with your family and friends. In this life stage, you'll want to offer your (now formidable) spiritual guidance. You're ready to cross over into the hereafter.

Void

If Void is your life stage, you have completed the other stages at least once and are an ancient soul. *Kong* (Chinese, "emptiness" or "nothingness"; *ku* in Japanese) one of the teachings of the Buddha, essentially means that form is impermanent and, hence, nothing possesses enduring identity. Exploring and understanding this "emptiness of phenomena" cultivates insight that will lead to wisdom and inner peace for you. This is a particularly important insight for those born into this karmic life cycle. Challenges for you can include emptiness, worry, impatience, hastiness, and an inability to complete projects. Poor planning can make you susceptible to being cheated or duped by others. Focus on being calm, careful, and mindful, or many problems and obstacles will surface. If you find yourself born into this life phase, symbolically you have crossed over into the spiritual realm. You realize that you are one in a sea of infinite souls, and there are endless universal possibilities. You now have the power to control your spiritual journey or assist the journeys of others. This is also where you realize the importance of the physical journey. The cycle is complete and you can begin it all over again, starting with rebirth.

Chapter 4
The Day Pillar

The day pillar, or daymaster, is perhaps the most important pillar of your birth chart. In Ba Zi, the heavenly stem (top element) of the day is called the daymaster. In a Ba Zi analysis, this daymaster is referenced against the birth year, month, and hour pillar to reveal your destiny and life path. The top element stem represents you—your spirit and your qi. The bottom animal sign is your marriage/partnership branch. Using the software included, find your day pillar in the center of your Zi Wei Dou Shu chart and write it here: _____.

The element of your daymaster represents a specific energy. There are a total of 10 stems, or elements—five elements expressed twice, once in a positive yang form and once in a negative yin form.

The 10 Heavenly Stems

1. Jia Yang Wood: trees
2. Yi Yin Wood: milled timber
3. Bing Yang Fire: lightning
4. Ding Yin Fire: candle or incense
5. Wu Yang Earth: hills
6. Ji Yin Earth: pottery/stoneware
7. Geng Yang Metal: ore
8. Xin Yin Metal: kettle
9. Ren Yang Water: saltwater
10. Gui Yin Water: fresh water

55

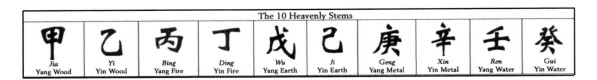

The 10 Heavenly Stems									
甲	乙	丙	丁	戊	己	庚	辛	壬	癸
Jia Yang Wood	*Yi* Yin Wood	*Bing* Yang Fire	*Ding* Yin Fire	*Wu* Yang Earth	*Ji* Yin Earth	*Geng* Yang Metal	*Xin* Yin Metal	*Ren* Yang Water	*Gui* Yin Water

Within each of the 12 earthly branches (animal signs), there are one or more hidden stems, or elements, that will also become part of your chart equation.

The 12 Earthly Branches

1. Zi Rat Water: North
2. Chou Ox Earth: North/Northeast
3. Yin Tiger Wood: East/Northeast
4. Mao Rabbit Wood: East
5. Chen Dragon Earth: East/Southeast
6. Si Snake Fire: South/Southeast
7. Wu Horse Fire: South
8. Wei Goat Earth: South/Southwest
9. Shen Monkey Metal: West/Southwest
10. You Rooster Metal: West
11. Xu Dog Earth: West/Northwest
12. Hai Pig Water: North/Northwest

The 12 Earthly Branches and Their Hidden Elements											
Yang Water	Yin Earth	Yang Wood	Yin Wood	Yang Earth	Yin Fire	Yang Fire	Yin Earth	Yang Metal	Yin Metal	Yang Earth	Yin Water
Rat	Ox	Tiger	Rabbit	Dragon	Snake	Horse	Goat	Monkey	Rooster	Dog	Pig

These elements are able to combine or clash with other elements in a chart and it is this kind of interaction that allows an astrologer to tell the story of your life. Each chart is as unique as the person. Interpretations come from the other elements in the chart and how they act in relation to your daymaster, or self element. For example, the daymaster element can be supported or destroyed by other elements. Also, the day pillar elements and animal branch signs may or may not be harmonious with those in the adjoining pillars.

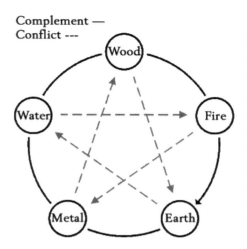

Complement —
Conflict - - -

The element that is the same as your daymaster is its "friend" or "companion" element. This element represents your friends, colleagues, and siblings. The element that your daymaster produces is its "intelligence" or "wisdom" element. This harmonious element will bring fame and recognition to you. The element that your daymaster is produced by is its "parent" or "talent" element. Although this element is generally favorable, it can be either nurturing or smothering, depending on whether the yin/yang polarity is the same as your daymaster or not. The element that controls your daymaster is its "proper discipline" or "ambition/career" element. This element will represent the husband for a female. For women, the spouse element is the same as the power element, which also represents control and status. The element that the daymaster controls is its "wealth" or "windfall" element. This element will represent the wife for a male. For men, the spouse element is the same as their wealth element. The element that produces your daymaster element is its "support" or "parent" element. This will be the element that nourishes and provides resources for you.

According to the month (season) in which you were born, your daymaster element will be rated as strong or weak. This has nothing to do with the strength or weakness of your character. Elements that are weak in a chart become lucky when supplemented, and elements that are strong (overpowering) in a chart are unlucky and should be minimized. When we talk about the relative strength and weakness of daymasters, we are talking about universal energy, tangible and intangible. If your daymaster element is Wood, it will be strongest if you were born in spring, and weakest in the fall. If your daymaster element is Fire, it is strongest if you were born in the summer, and weakest in the winter. If your daymaster element is Earth, it is strongest if you were born in between seasons or in late summer, and weakest during the winter/spring transition. If your daymaster element is Metal, it is strongest if you were born in the fall, and weakest during the spring. If your daymaster element is Water, it is strongest if you were born in the winter, and weakest during the summer.

Find your daymaster sign on pages 58 to 60 and read its description.

Element	Sign	Stem	Branch	Polarity
Wood	Rat	Jia	Tze	Yang Wood
Wood	Ox	Yi	Chou	Yin Wood
Wood	Tiger	Jia	Yin	Yang Wood
Wood	Rabbit	Yi	Mao	Yin Wood
Wood	Dragon	Jia	Chen	Yang Wood
Wood	Snake	Yi	Si	Yin Wood
Wood	Horse	Jia	Wu	Yang Wood
Wood	Goat	Yi	Wei	Yin Wood
Wood	Monkey	Jia	Shen	Yang Wood
Wood	Rooster	Yi	You	Yin Wood
Wood	Dog	Jia	Xu	Yang Wood
Wood	Pig	Yi	Hai	Yin Wood

Element	Sign	Stem	Branch	Polarity
Fire	Rat	Bing	Tze	Yang Fire
Fire	Ox	Ding	Chou	Yin Fire
Fire	Tiger	Bing	Yin	Yang Fire
Fire	Rabbit	Ding	Mao	Yin Fire
Fire	Dragon	Bing	Chen	Yang Fire
Fire	Snake	Ding	Si	Yin Fire
Fire	Horse	Bing	Wu	Yang Fire
Fire	Goat	Ding	Wei	Yin Fire
Fire	Monkey	Bing	Shen	Yang Fire
Fire	Rooster	Ding	You	Yin Fire
Fire	Dog	Bing	Xu	Yang Fire
Fire	Pig	Ding	Hai	Yin Fire

Element	Sign	Stem	Branch	Polarity
Earth	Rat	Wu	Tze	Yang Earth
Earth	Ox	Ji	Chou	Yin Earth
Earth	Tiger	Wu	Yin	Yang Earth
Earth	Rabbit	Ji	Mao	Yin Earth
Earth	Dragon	Wu	Chen	Yang Earth
Earth	Snake	Ji	Si	Yin Earth
Earth	Horse	Wu	Wu	Yang Earth
Earth	Goat	Ji	Wei	Yin Earth
Earth	Monkey	Wu	Shen	Yang Earth
Earth	Rooster	Ji	You	Yin Earth
Earth	Dog	Wu	Xu	Yang Earth
Earth	Pig	Ji	Hai	Yin Earth

Element	Sign	Stem	Branch	Polarity
Metal	Rat	Geng	Tze	Yang Metal
Metal	Ox	Xin	Chou	Yin Metal
Metal	Tiger	Geng	Yin	Yang Metal
Metal	Rabbit	Xin	Mao	Yin Metal
Metal	Dragon	Geng	Chen	Yang Metal
Metal	Snake	Xin	Si	Yin Metal
Metal	Horse	Geng	Wu	Yang Metal
Metal	Goat	Xin	Wei	Yin Metal
Metal	Monkey	Geng	Shen	Yang Metal
Metal	Rooster	Xin	You	Yin Metal
Metal	Dog	Geng	Xu	Yang Metal
Metal	Pig	Xin	Hai	Yin Metal

Element	Sign	Stem	Branch	Polarity
Water	Rat	Ren	Tze	Yang Water
Water	Ox	Gui	Chou	Yin Water
Water	Tiger	Ren	Yin	Yang Water
Water	Rabbit	Gui	Mao	Yin Water
Water	Dragon	Ren	Chen	Yang Water
Water	Snake	Gui	Si	Yin Water
Water	Horse	Ren	Wu	Yang Water
Water	Goat	Gui	Wei	Yin Water
Water	Monkey	Ren	Shen	Yang Water
Water	Rooster	Gui	You	Yin Water
Water	Dog	Ren	Xu	Yang Water
Water	Pig	Gui	Hai	Yin Water

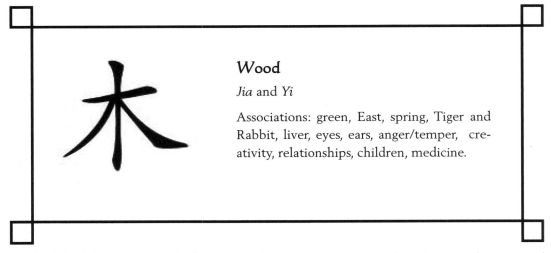

Wood

Jia and *Yi*

Associations: green, East, spring, Tiger and Rabbit, liver, eyes, ears, anger/temper, creativity, relationships, children, medicine.

The Wood element parallels the season of spring and represents the rising sun, the eastern direction, tall cylindrical shapes, and the color green. It corresponds to the liver, medicine, diseases, and the senses of sight and hearing. Wood element people renew their strength in the morning hours and are invigorated by the wind. The feng shui direction assigned to the Wood element is East, representing family, creativity, relationships, and the slender, cylindrical forms of columns and towers.

The Wood element represents the period from birth to age 12, a time of rapid mental and physical development, imagination, creativity, simplicity, and compassion. Like the great sequoia tree, the nature of Wood is to move upward, spread outward, and expand toward the light. Its temperate nature is concerned with establishing goodwill, furthering the arts, and pursuing beauty.

Wood element people have high-minded values and believe in the dignity of every human being. They understand the value of teamwork and excel in organizing extensive and complex projects. Like their daymaster element, those with a Wood daymaster know how to expand, achieve cooperation, and persuade others. They are progressive in their thinking and futuristic in their goals. The Wood element endows you with a natural presence and sense of propriety; however, Wood is also flammable and bestows a touchy temper. This is why the emotion associated with Wood is anger. The Wood element blesses you with idealism, imagination, a love of family, and many artistic gifts. It is closely tied to the liver and gallbladder, and the senses of sight and hearing.

- ◈ Predominant senses: sight and hearing.
- ◈ You produce/assist/help/feed: the Fire element.
- ◈ You are produced/assisted/enabled by: the Water element.
- ◈ Wood traits: kindness, generosity, creativity, expansion, but also anger, apathy, hot temper.
- ◈ Dangers: disease, rot, jaundice, insomnia, liver ailments.
- ◈ Blessings: relationships, children, imagination, creativity, future vision.

 You are **yang Wood Jia** if your daymaster is the Wood Rat, Wood Tiger, Wood Dragon, Wood Horse, Wood Monkey, or the Wood Dog. Jia Wood people are forward, stubborn, and constant, just like a tree growing slowly and surely straight up to reach the sunlight. Jia Woods have strong willpower; in the face of adversity they don't give up easily. They devise and plan their actions carefully, always moving toward a well-thought-out goal. The Jia Wood person is akin to the soaring California redwood, the solid oak tree, or the strong cherry tree. Jia Wood people are upright, dependable types whose greatest weakness is a lack of tact. You like to call a spade a spade each and every time. You are progressive and keen on self-cultivation, but like the slow-growing tree, you take a long time to achieve your goals of self-improvement. Jia Woods are late bloomers and often look younger as they grow older. Jia Woods are generally good at networking and have superior people skills. Many Jia Woods were thrust into responsibilities at an early age and can have trouble adapting to conflicting rules. You have a certain way of doing things and may resist changing your familiar ways.

The Jia Wood man is a dependable fellow, a shoulder to cry on and someone you can always rely on for support. You can talk, and he'll listen. The Jia Wood man is always there for you, although you shouldn't expect him to be terribly useful in getting things done. He will be much better at just listening. The Jia Wood man is more pragmatic than romantic, and you should certainly not expect him to understand subtleties in matters of the heart. In short, you may have to be blunt with him—or even do the proposing yourself! Jia Wood men are the least amenable to any sort of change, so forget about modifying him. Say "I do" rather than "I will redo him."

The Jia Wood woman can be quite stubborn and practical, and like her male counterpart, is unconcerned with the nuances and subtleties of romance. This is not to say she doesn't like being wined and dined; she just prefers it if you are upfront about your intentions. Persistence is the key to successfully winning her heart, as is an initial friendship. She will not play hard to get or be deliberately coy, but it takes a lot to arouse her interest. You must be prepared to show a lot of persistence and staying power. The enlightened Jia Wood woman is not entirely beyond change, but don't expect it to be a quick process.

If you are yang Wood Jia:

◈ Your sudden, unexpected wealth/windfall element is yang Earth (Wu).

◈ Your entitled, earned wealth/property element is yin Earth (Ji).

◈ Your happiness/guardian/proper care element is yin Water (Gui).

◈ Your beneficial, positive change/angel element is yin Metal (Xin).

◈ Your unfavorable/conflict/unbecoming/harmful element is yang Metal (Geng)

Because your daymaster element is yang Wood (Jia), the element of Wood represents you as well as your companions, spouse, and any rivals you might have. Wood element years of the same polarity as your daymaster (yang Wood 2004, 2014) compliment and assist you, but Wood element years of the opposite polarity (yin Wood 2005, 2015) may bring competition, rivals, or challengers. The element of Earth represents your finances. This element also represents your father. Yang Earth years (2008, 2018) bring unexpected or sudden wealth, and yin Earth years (2009, 2019) bring earned wealth. The element of Water represents your mother. It also represents all caretakers, mentors, and people who support or protect you. Yin Water years (2003, 2013) bring great happiness for you, and yang Water years (2002, 2012) bring a satisfied mind. The element of Fire represents your offspring as well as your ideas (your brainchildren). Both yang and yin Fire years (2006, 2007, 2016, 2017) will allow your optimum creativity and expression. The element of Metal represents your career or vocation. This is a difficult element for you. Yang Metal years (2000, 2010) bring unfavorable change, while yin Metal years (2001, 2011) bring difficult yet beneficial change.

If your daymaster is the Wood Rat, you are attractive and passionate, ready at a moment's notice to socialize and to transform your social milieu. Diligent, curious, and blessed with an inquisitive mind, you like to find out how things work. You are inclined to be carefree, but may have trouble with intimacy and experience a tumultuous love life.

If your daymaster is the Wood Tiger, you are a good judge of character, street-smart, and understand the importance of teamwork. Noble, protective and popular with just about everyone, you change professions and employment frequently. The Wood Tiger will appear relaxed and at ease, but this is a mask behind which he or she hides an anxious nature. The stage attracts you and the limelight awaits you.

If your daymaster is the Wood Dragon, you have a dual nature—dynamic and courageous on one hand, and seductive and appeasing on the other. Imaginative and talented, you are able to improvise when faced with chaotic or unexpected events. This Dragon possesses the gift of creative invention and is attracted to nature and symbols of beauty. This is a practical Dragon who is less prone to having a heated temper, and whose feet are firmly planted on the ground.

If your daymaster is the Wood Horse, you are a cheerful and cooperative team player. Changes and innovations capture your vivid imagination, and you possess a quick and disciplined mind. You are a progressive modern thinker and the most social of all the Horse element combinations.

Amusing, a good conversationalist, and attracted to theater, you are a natural public speaker as well as a sports aficionado.

If your daymaster is the Wood Monkey, you maintain high standards for yourself and others. You are resourceful and enthusiastic, but may have trouble slowing down or pacing yourself. The Wood Monkey is gregarious, socially adept, and quick-witted. Personal expression and a sense of humor are essential to you and you are an active participant in life. Your curious mind excels at solving difficult problems and finding an easier way to do things. You are almost always able to find funds and resources.

If your daymaster is the Wood Dog, you are affectionate, passionate, and known for your strong convictions. This is the team player of the Dog family. Idealistic and eager to learn, the Wood Dog is popular and forms strong bonds with others. This is a charming, personable Dog who defends his or her values with tenacity and vigor. Watchful and nurturing, Wood Dogs can organize major projects and manage large groups of people with ease. They excel in motivating others.

You are **yin Wood Yi** if your daymaster is the Wood Ox, Wood Rabbit, Wood Snake, Wood Goat, Wood Rooster, or Wood Pig. Yi Wood grows toward the sun like a creeping vine or blade of grass. Yi Woods are adaptable and shrewd in their dealings with people, and although they may appear indecisive, they know precisely what they want and how to get it. Yi Wood people make good business owners as well as formidable competitors. Learned, intelligent, logical, and an original thinker, you may become absorbed in abstract trivia, proving your own theories, or counter-attacking criticism. Yin Woods enjoy spending time alone in order to understand the world, clarify their thoughts, and prepare answers to difficult questions. You always look for opportunities to learn, but it is knowledge for knowledge's sake, not necessarily knowledge that you will put to any practical use. Yi Wood is symbolized by ivy, creeping vines, flowers, grass, small plants, and ferns. Yi Woods are consummate networkers; they entwine themselves with other people, ideas, and projects. Unenlightened yin Woods can be manipulative and are not above using those around them to get what they desire. Yin Woods have an innate understanding of the concept of leverage, and possess first-rate survival instincts. Dirt rarely sticks to them, thanks to their inherent charm and their penchant for ensuring they have enough wiggle room to get out of a jam.

The term "femme fatale" best describes the yin Wood woman. Once you succumb to her charms and she has you under her influence, you may find it difficult to escape. The yin Wood lady enmeshes herself with her man through a combination of charm, understanding, sexuality, and just the right dash of intellectual challenge to keep him interested. Possessing a chameleon-like nature, the yin Wood lady frequently and rapidly changes personality and appearance, thereby keeping her partner interested. She also has a knack for making him feel good about decisions she has made for him! Romancing a yin Wood female requires regular professions of undying devotion, large amounts of affection, and endless displays of loyalty. She likes to feel as if her mate is her knight in shining armor and her love is still to be won.

The yin Wood man is a marathon sort of guy, with a slow but sure hand. Charming, well-mannered, and polite, this smooth gentleman has been blessed with the gift of gab. The problem with him is that he can be capricious and fickle; when presented with many choices, he may have difficulty settling down with one partner. A fear of commitment is not uncommon amongst yin Wood males. That is not to say that he can't commit, but don't expect it to be easy to get him to agree to take the relationship to the next level. The yin Wood man will always keep his options open. Alas, reasoning won't work with the yin Wood man, but giving him an ultimatum might be just the thing if you want him badly enough.

If you are yin Wood Yi:

◈   Your sudden, unexpected wealth/windfall element is yin Earth (Ji).

◈   Your entitled, earned wealth/property element is yang Earth (Wu).

◈   Your happiness/guardian/proper care element is yang Water (Ren).

◈   Your beneficial, positive change/angel element is yang Metal (Geng).

◈   Your unfavorable/conflict/unbecoming/harmful element is yin Metal (Xin).

Because your daymaster element is yin Wood (Yi), the Element of Wood represents you as well as your companions, spouse, and any rivals you might have. Wood element years of the same polarity as your daymaster (yin Wood 2005, 2015) compliment and assist you; however, Wood element years of the opposite polarity (yang Wood 2004, 2014) may bring competition, rivals, or challengers. The element of Earth represents your finances. This element also represents your father. Yin Earth years (2009, 2019) bring 'unexpected' or sudden wealth, and yang Earth years (2008, 2018) bring earned wealth. The element of Water represents your mother. It also represents all caretakers, mentors, and people who support or protect you. Yin Water years (2003, 2013) bring great happiness for you, and yang Water years (2002, 2012) bring a satisfied mind. Water is an auspicious element for you, as it nurtures and supports your Wood element daymaster. The element of Fire represents your offspring as well as your ideas (your brainchildren). Both yang and yin Fire years (2006, 2007, 2016, 2017) will allow optimum creativity and expression. The element of Metal represents your career or vocation. This is a difficult element for you. Yin Metal years (2001, 2011) bring unfavorable change, while yang Metal years (2000, 2010) bring difficult yet beneficial change. Limit this element and everything connected to it.

If your daymaster is the Wood Ox, you possesses a relentless determination that assures success in this life. Blessed with authority and natural presence, this is the most artistic of the Oxen. Music, creative writing, and poetry all come naturally to the Wood Ox. Your greatest obstacle is not understanding those who think differently than you, and petty jealousies from less talented individuals. The Wood Ox has great mechanical ability, so working with your hands will bring good luck.

If your daymaster is the Wood Rabbit, you possesses poetic gifts and will be attracted to the fine arts. Gardening and landscaping will please your sense of beauty and harmony while fulfilling your need for space and freedom. The Wood Rabbit is an outwardly shy, highly intuitive, and deep-feeling soul. This is the gentle seducer who avoids restraints and obligations. Wood Rabbits are collectors of art, antiques, and other objects of beauty.

If your daymaster is the Wood Snake, you crave quiet, stability, and plenty of privacy. This is a sympathetic and earnest individual who shares their philosophical ideas with all who care to listen. This Snake has a strong need for independence and can successfully take on large projects.

The aesthetic nature of Wood blesses this Snake with a love of other cultures, lands, and customs. Wood Snakes are possessive and very protective of their home and family circle.

If your daymaster is the Wood Goat, you are romantic, agreeable, and well-liked. This is a courteous Goat with a good sense of humor. The Wood Goat in your day pillar makes you sentimental and eager to please those you love. This is a nurturing Goat who has a soft heart toward stray animals and compassion for friends down on their luck. The Wood Goat is supremely generous and always gives freely of his or her resources.

If your daymaster is the Wood Rooster, you are thoughtful and more tactful than other Roosters. Open-minded, ambitious, and happiest amongst a social group sharing lively conversation, Wood Roosters are passionate and often susceptible to excesses of all types. You must use clear-sightedness to avoid getting carried away or pushed over the edge into obsessions or extremes. You will gain balance and more self-assurance in midlife, which tends to be your best years.

If your daymaster is the Wood Pig, you are a calm, stable, and an all-around decent person. A well-balanced individual who loves to be close to nature, you may express yourself through a career in one of the earth sciences. Possessing eerie intuition and influence, you tend to be passive and cannot live without physical love. The Wood element may encourage you to overindulge in both food and drink, so be moderate.

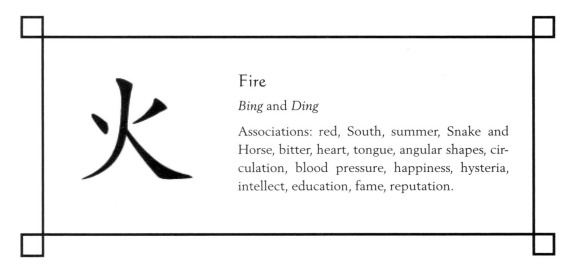

Fire

Bing and *Ding*

Associations: red, South, summer, Snake and Horse, bitter, heart, tongue, angular shapes, circulation, blood pressure, happiness, hysteria, intellect, education, fame, reputation.

The Fire element parallels the season of summer and represents the noonday sun, the southern direction, pointed shapes, and the color red. It corresponds to the heart, the blood, and the circulatory system. Fire element people renew their strength in the peak of each day at noon, and are invigorated by their keen sense of touch. The feng shui direction assigned to the Fire element is South, representing intellect, reputation, fame, the pointed angles of triangles, and the sharp edges of mountain peaks. The Fire element represents the period from ages 13 to 24, the adolescent time of dynamic passion, energy, aggression, and leadership. The nature of Fire is to consume, to resolve, and to bring about an outcome. The Fire element will multiply inborn talents and energies and impart gifts of leadership, passion, and assertiveness. Those with a Fire daymaster rarely have trouble making decisions; they are decisive and masterful, and attract others with their strong and radiant personalities. The Fire element arouses, changes, and converts.

Fire element souls have an abundance of energy that may cause impatience when pursuing goals. The movement of Fire is rapid and can consume one's energies if it is not balanced with relaxation and moderation. The Fire element represents the ability to be decisive, to lead, and to act spontaneously without forethought. It endows you with a natural presence; however, Fire can also be uncompromising and demanding of others. Always fervent and passionate, those with a Fire daymaster possess a sparkling wit and an enthusiasm that inspires others. This is why the emotion associated with Fire is happiness. The Fire element blesses you with a sense of humor and the ability to use comic relief when necessary. It is closely tied to the heart, the tongue, blood pressure, and circulation.

◈   Your predominant sense: touch.

◈   You produce/assist/help/feed: the Earth element.

◈   You are produced/assisted/enabled by: the Wood element.

◈   Fire traits: optimism, generosity, happiness, enthusiasm, but also impatience, an inability to compromise, prudishness, and hysteria.

◈   Dangers: fire and combustion, circulation, blood pressure, heart.

◈   Blessings: education, intellect, fame, leadership.

 You are **yang Fire Bing** if your daymaster is the Fire Rat, Fire Tiger, Fire Dragon, Fire Horse, Fire Monkey, or Fire Dog. Yang Fire is symbolized by a burning furnace or raging forest fire. Bing Fire people are the conquering heroes of the 10 daymasters. Strong, assertive, and lovers of a challenge, Bing Fires are natural leaders, champions of causes, and righters of wrongs. The driving force behind this personality is a fear of weakness or being dominated. Generous, vivacious, and as warm and passionate as the sun itself, Bing Fire produces people who have no hidden agenda and do not hold grudges. They are upright and noble in their actions, but can also be proud and self-centered, as well. Bing Fire is the fire of the sun—warming, radiant, and essential to the growth of all living things. Bing Fire people are magnanimous, generous, and giving, and will have a cause that they support or contribute to generously. Like the sun that rises in the east and sets in the west, Bing Fire people are very routine-driven until they hit a plateau. Life is never dull with Bing Fires, as they are fiercely independent. The key to their happiness is to give them their own space to shine, literally and figuratively.

The Bing Fire woman is the personification of the modern independent female. She is rarely in a hurry to marry and may find herself ill-suited to a traditional relationship. Bing Fire ladies who wish to marry should settle down only after they have fulfilled their life dreams. The Bing Fire female becomes bored easily and craves excitement, new thrills, and amazing experiences. Diversity and novelty are vital for her psychological well-being, and her partner must be able to keep things fresh and interesting for her. Travel is always a good idea, preferably on a more or less regular basis. If her partner always keeps life interesting for her and gives her space, they stand a good chance of having a successful relationship. At the very least, she will keep the home fires—and his love life—burning.

The Bing Fire man is warm, generous, and fun to be around. Like his Fire sisters, he, too, needs his own space and independence, which sometimes makes him reluctant to commit. There is also a tendency to be a bit too fervent and passionate, and to surround himself with like-minded people. A relationship with a Bing Fire man is a very sensual one, and often the connection is on every level—emotional, physical, and spiritual. However, be warned that his passion has another side. The Bing Fire man can be quite aggressive in his approach and is not above emotional bullying to achieve his goals. Uncompromising and demanding, the Bing Fire male is akin to a burning furnace or a raging forest Fire in his methodology. In order to keep things interesting, it is essential to keep his interest in the bedroom and arrange plenty of one-on-one time together.

If you are yang Fire Bing:

◈   Your sudden, unexpected wealth/windfall element is yang Metal (Geng).

◈   Your entitled, earned wealth/property element is yin Metal (Xin).

◈   Your happiness/guardian/proper care element is yin Wood (Yi).

◈   Your beneficial, positive change/angel element is yin Water (Gui).

◈   Your unfavorable/conflict/unbecoming/harmful element is yang Water (Ren).

Because your daymaster element is yang Fire Bing, the element of Fire represents you as well as your companions, spouse, and any rivals you might have. Fire element years of the same polarity as your daymaster (yang Fire 2006, 2016) compliment and assist you; however, Fire element years of the opposite polarity (yin Fire 2007, 2017) may bring competition, rivals, or challengers. The element of Earth represents your offspring as well as your ideas (your brainchildren). Both yang and yin Earth years (1998, 1999, 2008, 2009, 2018, 2019) will facilitate optimum creativity and outward expression. The element of Water represents your career or vocation. This is a very difficult element for you, as water extinguishes and controls your Fire element daymaster. Yang Water years (2002, 2012) bring unfavorable change, while yin Water years (2003, 2013) bring beneficial change. The Element of Wood represents your mother. It also represents all caretakers, mentors, and people who support or protect you. As Wood is the "parent" element to Fire, yin Wood years (1995, 2005, 2015) bring happiness and nurturing. The element of Metal represents your finances. This element also represents your father. Yang Metal years (2000, 2010, 2020) bring a windfall of unexpected or sudden wealth, and yin Metal years (2001, 2011, 2021) bring earned or expected wealth.

If your daymaster is the Fire Rat, you are enthusiastic regarding new projects, but must guard against having too many irons in the fire at one time. You are determined and self-disciplined, with strong moral principles and high-minded thinking. As an eternal student of the universe, you thirstily absorb knowledge just as a sponge soaks up water. Consequently, you are well-versed in a wide variety of subjects. The Fire Rat is assertive by nature and capable of self-confident leadership as well as offering prudent advice.

If your daymaster is the Fire Tiger, you may find it hard to delay gratification; patience isn't necessarily your strong point. However, you have been blessed with extraordinary leadership aptitude. Fire Tigers are volatile and passionate in life and in love. Your charm is that you are always up for a new adventure. You are action oriented and passionate! Rather nomadic by nature, you will choose frequent changes of environment and will rarely be content staying any one place too long. You are the most independent member of the Tiger's pride.

If your daymaster is the Fire Dragon, you have a tremendous desire to succeed and are more ambitious than other Dragons. You are articulate and knowledgeable about everything from politics to Shakespeare. No one knows from day to day what you will be up to: "unpredictable" describes you to a T. Mysterious, a natural thespian, and a born leader, you will be happiest being in the public eye in some way. You are strong-willed and tend to rely on your own judgment without taking others' views into account. Humility and patience may be difficult for you as it is admiration that you seek.

If your daymaster is the Fire Horse, you are the most ardent and impetuous of all Horse element combinations. You may make your mark early in life and exhibit your talents in astonishing ways. You have been endowed with superior wisdom, but perseverance may be difficult. You display above-average qualities of leadership and can easily rally others to your causes. With your heightened need for social interaction, you will tend to gravitate toward outdoor team sports. You belong to the palace of sexuality, so the pursuit of romantic love will be a dominant theme throughout your life.

If your daymaster is the Fire Monkey, you are a problem-solver and a self-starter. Competitive and popular, you have a wide variety of interests and friends from diverse backgrounds. Energetic and animated, you are convincing, resourceful, and highly complex. The Fire element imparts great vitality and good health to you, but could also consume much of your energy. Your fertile imagination produces an ingenious, albeit suspicious personality who will always look for a quicker and easier way to do things.

If your daymaster is the Fire Dog, you have no problem expressing yourself and connect easily with others. You may choose to go into politics or the entertainment industry. Opinionated, dynamic, and radiant with energy, you may seem a bit too animated to outsiders, who are always surprised at how outspoken you are. Your friendly personality conceals a self-effacing and anxious spirit. Possessing great charm, you stand your ground and are severe only when diplomacy has failed.

 You are **yin Fire Ding** if your daymaster is the Fire Ox, Fire Rabbit, Fire Snake, Fire Goat, Fire Rooster, or Fire Pig. Yin Fire is symbolized by soft candlelight, twinkling stars, and the illumination of the full moon. Ding Fire people are naturally influential and motivate those around them with an inspired sense of humor. They are meticulous and detail-oriented, but due to their helpful nature, they can forget about their own needs and be

susceptible to burnout. Those with a yin Fire daymaster are inspirational, wise, conscientious, idealistic, and hardworking. A bit perfectionistic at times, they are bothered when things are not done the right way (read: their way). When frustrated, they may become critical of others and of themselves. Their underlying motivation is to avoid anger and avoid being wrong or criticized. However, few things or people in this life are perfect, so life is rarely easy for them. Like the tiny flame that can either flare up into a great fire or burn down into embers, Ding Fire people can either rise to the occasion or hide in the shadows, waiting for the right opportunity to shine again. Ding Fire people can be temperamental, fickle, sensitive, and prickly at times, but they are always thinking about others first. They often need to be reminded that they must sometimes come first. Whether male or female, the Ding Fire person will always hold his or her mother in great regard.

If you wish to seduce a Ding Fire lady, make sure you are on good terms with her mother. If her mother likes you, all will go well when it comes to dating a Ding Fire woman. The Ding Fire lady is usually a night owl so nocturnal activities usually appeal to her, especially late-night romantic diners, movies, or stargazing. She is strongly attracted to self-improvement, alternative ideas, and education, so make cultural and intellectual activities and conversations part of your life together. An art gallery, the theatre, or even a wine-tasting outing might be just what she had in mind. The Ding Fire female is not likely to share her life with a rude, crude, or uncouth man, so be courteous, be on time, and don't pressure her. These are the keys to her heart.

Like his Ding Fire sisters, the Ding Fire male has a very close bond with his mother. Prideful, and concerned with his image and reputation, he dislikes being challenged or shown up in front of others. Self-knowledge and personal cultivation is very important to him, so it is crucial that you are able to keep up with him in this regard. The Ding Fire male usually has an extensive library and enjoys reading. He loves learning and considers himself something of an intellectual. His partner may be very beautiful, but if she isn't able to hold an intelligent conversation with him, the long-term prospects for the relationship are not good. He searches for a mature woman who is sensible and nurturing.

If you are yin Fire Ding:

◈ Your sudden, unexpected wealth/windfall element is yin Metal (Xin).
◈ Your entitled, earned wealth/property element is yang Metal (Geng).
◈ Your happiness/guardian/proper care element is yang Wood (Jia).
◈ Your beneficial, positive change/angel element is yang Water (Ren).
◈ Your unfavorable/conflict/unbecoming/harmful element is yin Water (Gui).

Because your daymaster element is yin Fire Ding, the element of Fire represents you as well as your companions, spouse, and any rivals you might have. Fire element years of the same polarity as your daymaster (yin Fire 2007, 2017) compliment and assist you, while Fire element years of the opposite polarity (yang Fire 2006, 2016) can bring competition, rivals, or challengers. The element of Earth represents your offspring as well as your ideas (your brainchildren). Both yang and yin Earth years (1998, 1999, 2008, 2009, 2018, 2019) will facilitate optimum creativity and outward expression. The element of Water represents your career or vocation. This is a very difficult element for you, as water extinguishes and controls your Fire element daymaster. Yin Water years (2003, 2013) bring difficult or unfavorable changes for you, while yang Water years (2002, 2012) bring beneficial or needed change. The element of Wood represents your Mother. It also represents all caretakers, mentors, and people who support or protect you. Yang Wood years (1994, 2004, 2014) bring happiness for you, as Wood is your Fire daymaster's "parent" element. The element of Metal represents your finances. This element also represents your father. Yin Metal years (2001, 2011) bring a windfall of unexpected or sudden wealth, while yang Metal years (2000, 2010) bring earned or expected wealth.

If your daymaster is the Fire Ox, you are a conqueror and may be drawn to politics or perhaps even the military. You are talented with your hands and highly creative. You also have tremendous reserves of energy, which can make you impatient to reach your goals. Delegate some responsibilities to others, avoid becoming exhausted, and respect your body's limits. The Fire Ox is fiercely individualistic yet feels a strong sense of filial duty. Although you are highly family oriented, you will always be the king or queen of your castle.

If your daymaster is the Fire Rabbit, you have a tendency to keep your distance, especially if you feel rejected or excluded. Although you personify the essence of detachment, the Fire element releases a boldness in you that can overcome this natural reticence. The Fire Rabbit has a deep, profoundly spiritual side and will always burn with an inner flame. Fire enhances your sense of touch vis-à-vis your most intimate relationships. You are a natural healer, counselor, or reiki master who knows the wisdom of gaining strength through accepting one's weakness.

If your daymaster is the Fire Snake, you are a sensual, compassionate, and contemplative individual. You earn respect and win support from others with your firm yet calm manner. Those with this daymaster are healthy, vital, and confident enough to get any job done. The Fire Snake tends to be outgoing and energetic, and enjoy sports and "woodsy" outdoor activities. You possess an excellent sense of humor, will enjoy a wide circle of friends, and could live to a very old age.

If your daymaster is the Fire Goat, you are blessed with extraordinary artistic talents. A natural writer, poet, and artisan, you are expressive and passionate and form close bonds with other people. Generous to a fault and charismatic amongst your peers, you inspire other people with your art. You are as charming as you are self-indulgent and manipulative.

If your daymaster is the Fire Rooster, you are lively, intense, and energetic. Always the first one to jump on a task that needs doing, you may have difficulty staying on one subject. Indeed, you are known to have many projects in the works at one time. The Fire Rooster is self-assured and determined, as well as expressive and brutally candid with his or her observations. The Fire element imparts great vitality and a highly competitive nature. Mercurial, zealous, and efficient, you are strong-willed and capable of being either enchanting or unbearable.

If your daymaster is the Fire Pig, you are fun-loving, self-assured, alluring, opinionated, adventuresome, and radiant with energy. You may be very fortunate financially due to a combination of ambition and purity of heart. Fire also bestows leadership abilities and bravery; many Fire Pigs choose to work as firefighters, police officers, or EMTs.

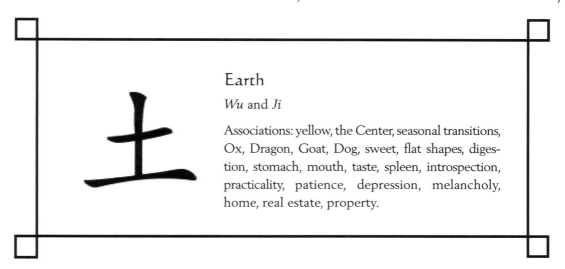

Earth

Wu and *Ji*

Associations: yellow, the Center, seasonal transitions, Ox, Dragon, Goat, Dog, sweet, flat shapes, digestion, stomach, mouth, taste, spleen, introspection, practicality, patience, depression, melancholy, home, real estate, property.

The Earth element parallels the periods between the seasons, the last days of each season, the Center, flat shapes, and the color yellow. It corresponds to the digestive system, the mouth, and the spleen. Fire element people renew their strength in the late afternoon and during the periods between seasons, and are invigorated by their keen sense of taste. The feng shui direction assigned to the Fire element is the Center, which represents practicality, endurance, and flat, square shapes.

The Earth element represents the period of life from ages 25 to 36, the young adult period characterized by stability, reliability, productivity, and common sense. The nature of Earth is to stabilize, to keep whole, and to preserve. The Earth element is symbolic of the mother's protected womb of peace and safety. Those with an Earth daymaster are practical and sensible. They have excellent organizational abilities and are competent leaders and executives. Stability, practicality, and reliability characterize those influenced by the Earth element. Its natives are capable of making wise and sensible decisions, and tend to be conservative and serious. Earth element natives are firmly anchored to their family, their partnerships, and their homeland. The Earth element keeps both your feet firmly planted on the ground and gives you the innate tenacity that allows you to complete arduous tasks. However, Earth daymasters can also produce obstinate and unbendable individuals. The emotion associated with Earth is melancholy/depression, which may make you seem distant or unapproachable. Like the rocks that make up a wall or the soil that produces food, Earth element people are traditional, firm, and persistent. The Earth is closely tied to the stomach and the mouth.

◈ Predominant sense: taste.

◈ You produce/assist/help/feed: the Metal element.

◈ You are produced/assisted/enabled by: the Fire element.

◈ Earth traits: introspection, practicality, centeredness, and responsibility, but also obsession, worry, embroilment, and depression.

◈ Dangers: collision, falling, hyperactivity.

◈ Blessings: family, estate, house, homeland.

You are **yang Earth Wu** if your daymaster is the Earth Rat, Earth Tiger, Earth Dragon, Earth Horse, Earth Monkey or Earth Dog. Wu Earth is symbolized by mountains, rocks, boulders, and passageways. Wu Earth people are as solid, immovable, and unwavering as the mountains. They make trustworthy, loyal, and dependable friends. Simple and down-to-earth, Wu Earths are quiet and prefer solitude. Once they have made up their mind, they can be quite stubborn in carrying out their decisions. The Wu Earth personality is a solid one, often slow to take action and of few words. They are ponderous, quiet types who often need to be motivated to take action. Procrastination is a pesky problem with Wu Earths. Superb at keeping secrets, the Wu Earth person is the soul of discretion. When they are feeling effusive, however, they are chatty, jolly, fun people to be around. Sometimes accused of being hedonistic and wanting the best of everything, this yang Earth personality may become materialistic and inclined to buy new toys. Their major fears are deprivation and boredom, and their compulsions involve avoiding pain and having more of everything.

The Wu Earth lady is usually curvaceous with an air of mystery that surrounds her. Mature, appealing, and not one to be taken lightly, she may be slow to act unless she's on a mission, at which point there is little that can stop her. It takes a lot to provoke a Wu Earth woman—unless she finds out you've been cheating on her! Communication isn't her strong point, so getting through to her can be a challenge. She is stubborn and difficult to dissuade once she has made a decision, so if she's laid down the law to you, don't expect her to change her mind easily. Outdoorsy, thrill-type activities usually appeal to her, but she often needs some initial prodding to get out there. Once she does, she'll soon see the fun in some whitewater rafting or rock climbing.

The Wu Earth male personifies the strong silent type. Like his sister Wu Earth, he often has a great deal of mystery surrounding him. His past is mysterious and his thoughts are deep. The Yang Earth male can also be extremely stubborn. He's also a procrastinator who doesn't usually like to participate in physical sports or a lot of activity; he prefers to keep his feet planted firmly on the ground. He loves nothing more than having a day to himself, reading a book or working on his prized model collection. The Wu Earth male has trouble expressing his deep feelings; it takes him a long time to collect his thoughts, much less write them down on paper. His actions speak louder than his words, so take your cues from what he does rather than what he says.

If you are yang Earth Wu:

◈   Your sudden, unexpected wealth/windfall element is yang Water (Ren).

◈   Your entitled, earned wealth/property element is yin Water (Gui).

◈   Your happiness/guardian/proper care element is yin Fire (Ding).

◈   Your beneficial, positive change/angel element is yin Wood (Yi).

◈   Your unfavorable/conflict/unbecoming/harmful element is yang Wood (Jia).

Because your daymaster element is yang Earth Jia, the element of Earth represents your artistic expression as well as your companions, spouse, and any rivals you might have. Yang Earth years (2008, 2018) bring friendships and new companions, but yin Earth years (1999, 2009, 2019) can bring contenders or competition. The element of Water represents your finances as well as your father. Yang Water years (2002, 2012) bring unexpected or sudden wealth, and yin

Water years (2003, 2013) bring earned or expected wealth. The element of Wood represents your career or vocation. This is a difficult element for you, as the Wood element saps the nutrients from your Earth daymaster. Yang Wood years (2004, 2014) bring difficult or unfavorable change, while yin Wood years (2005, 2015) bring beneficial change. The element of Fire represents your mother as well as all caretakers, mentors, and people who support or protect you. Yin Fire years (2007, 2017) bring a satisfied mind for you, and yang Fire years (2006, 2016) bring happiness, as Fire is the "parent" element to your Earth daymaster. The element of Metal represents you as well as your ideas (your brainchildren). Both yang and yin Metal years (2010, 2011, 2020, 2021) will facilitate optimum creativity and expression.

If your daymaster is the Earth Rat, you have remarkable willpower and a nurturing, down-to-earth temperament. Sensible and alert, you also have a tendency to worry about security and finances. The Earth element makes you especially prudent, crafty, and subtle. Always keep yourself busy to keep from dwelling on problems or becoming mired in life's dramas.

If your daymaster is the Earth Tiger, you like to nurture helpless things such as babies, stray animals, and sad friends down on their luck. Deeply conscientious and humanitarian in spirit, you embrace a practical approach in everything you undertake. The Earth Tiger is not as hot-headed as other Tigers, and possesses a more mature temperament. This daymaster personifies a fair-minded leader, counselor, or judge.

If your daymaster is the Earth Dragon, you enjoy accumulating wealth and financial speculation. A conscientious and hard worker, the Earth Dragon takes on chores and problems that others find impossible to conquer. Prudent and suspicious, you probably have eyes in the back of your head and miss nothing. This is a nurturing soul who is always willing to help out in a crisis and fiercely protective of family and loved ones.

If your daymaster is the Earth Horse, you probably enjoy speculation, sales, or real estate. A conservative realist by nature, you know how to advance prudently and skeptically. Your methodical manner would make you an excellent manager. You may have a tendency to be possessive and are very security conscious.

If your daymaster is the Earth Monkey, you are motivated by a need to expand and a desire for increasing possessions. Well-informed, benevolent, and kind, you are also pragmatic and realistic. Although you hide your fears about the future behind a stoic face, most of your enterprises will be blessed due to your intuition, your perfectionism, and your good head for money.

If your daymaster is the Earth Dog, you jealously protect your home and loved ones. Although you are an extremely proud person, you can be counted on to be a fair and impartial mediator. Your powerful need for recognition and appreciation makes you capable of devoting yourself entirely to a cause or to achieving your ambitions. You are patient in the face of difficulty but may be taken advantage of due to an exceedingly generous nature.

 You are **yin Earth Ji** if your daymaster is the Earth Ox, Earth Rabbit, Earth Snake, Earth Goat, Earth Rooster, or Earth Pig. Ji Earth is symbolized by the soft, rich, nourishing soil in which we grow our food. Nurturing, tolerant, and resourceful, Ji Earths are also avid and materialistic. This daymaster produces a dependable, likable, engaging person who makes a good friend. Ji Earth's instinct is to protect, nurture, and develop. Rejection, lonesomeness, and condemnation from an authority figure are especially troubling to Ji Earths. They follow the rules and prefer the approval of others. Yin Earths can also be secretive due to Earth's ability to keep things hidden. This makes them natural confidants and confessors.

Tolerant and occasionally guilty of being too giving, Ji Earth people have many hidden talents and abilities which often come to the forefront gradually and organically, just as a seed grows into a plant. Ji Earths often have an inborn aptitude for handling money and strong entrepreneurial inclinations. On the negative flipside, they can sometimes have trouble with their finances, as well.

The monogamous Ji Earth female is focused and disciplined in life and in love. Ji Earth women are generally in favor of marriage, family, and commitment. They seem to thrive in a committed relationship. Even when she is attached, however, the Ji Earth lady will always have her secrets. It is important to respect her private side and trust that she will eventually emerge and share her secrets with you when she is ready. Ji Earth ladies love a good project that they can pour their nurturing inclinations into, be it reforming your table manners, turning your old wardrobe upside down, or talking you into fixing the broken garage door.

The Ji Earth man is usually quiet and unassuming, but there is often a great talent within him that is waiting to emerge and blossom. They are often very attractive to women because of their trustworthy demeanor. The Ji Earth man is comforting to have around during a crisis. He is seldom bossy; rather, he will endeavor to guide you to find your own solutions to a problem. This is a man who should not be pressured into a relationship that he is not ready for. The Ji Earth man can crumble under this kind of pressure. Be gentle, be kind, and be a good listener—he'll repay the favor many times over.

If you are yin Earth Ji:

◈ Your sudden, unexpected wealth/windfall element is yin Water (Gui).

◈ Your entitled, earned wealth/property element is yang Water (Ren).

◈ Your happiness/guardian/proper care element is yang Fire (Bing).

◈ Your beneficial/positive change/angel element is yang Wood (Jia).

◈ Your unfavorable/conflict/unbecoming/harmful element is yin Wood (Yi).

Because your daymaster element is yin Earth Ji, the element of Earth represents you as well as your companions, spouse, and any rivals you might have. Yin Earth years (1999, 2009, 2019) bring friendships and new companions, but yang Earth years (2008, 2018) can bring "contenders" and competition. The element of Water represents your finances and your father. Yang Water years (2002, 2012) bring earned or expected wealth, while yin Water years (2003, 2013) bring unexpected or sudden wealth. The element of Wood represents your career or vocation. This is a difficult element for you, as your Earth element daymaster is depleted of nutrients by the Wood. Yang Wood years (2004, 2014) bring beneficial change, while Yin Wood years (2005, 2015) bring difficult or unfavorable change. The element of Fire represents your mother as well as all caretakers, mentors, and persons who support or protect you. Yin Fire years (2007, 2017) bring a satisfied mind, and yang Fire years (2006, 2016) bring happiness and nurturing. The element of Metal represents your offspring and your ideas (your brainchildren). Both yang and yin Metal years (2010, 2011, 2020, 2021) will see your optimum creativity and expression.

If your daymaster is the Earth Ox, you are a deep thinker who tends to be a loner. Loyal, steadfast, and stoic, your highest priorities are family, monogamy, and duty. The Earth itself serves as your refuge; it entices you to close the door on the human race and pursue meditation, relaxation, and solitude. Enduring and persistent, slow and sure, you are a marathon runner in this life. You pace yourself and therefore have staying power in any endeavor, be it a relationship, a job, or a project.

If your daymaster is the Earth Rabbit, you are quiet, reasonable, and hard to read. Introverted and extremely private, you are respected and held in high esteem by others. You are known for your excellent powers of logic and your preference for solid and reliable pursuits. The Earth element endows you with foresight and a capacity for organization. Conservative, wise, and sensible in financial matters, the Earth Rabbit daymaster reveals a diplomat and a peacemaker.

If your daymaster is the Earth Snake, you are a secure and cozy Snake who loves elegance and the material comforts of life. You posses an uncanny ability to turn inward and retreat from the outside world. You are a deeply feeling individual who is, for the most part, relaxed, at times even lethargic. In fact, you may be prone to "hibernation" and could choose a reclusive life of spirituality and contemplation.

If your daymaster is the Earth Goat, you are financially fortunate and have a taste for luxury and the finer things in life. Sympathetic, honest, and well-liked, you can, however, exhibit unpredictable moods and mental processes. Inconsistent and unconventional, the Earth Goat daymaster reveals an artistic and deep-thinking soul who lives in a world of dreams, fantasy, and whimsy. Detached and distracted, you may not be as outgoing as you would like; you could even suffer from social anxiety at times.

If your daymaster is the Earth Rooster, you are realistic, pragmatic, and shrewd. You have the uncanny ability to build upon the work of others, improving on it and adding the finishing touches. You have a profound perspective on life and are able to see the big picture. Persistent and persevering, you pursue success and security, and are always intent on presenting a positive appearance. You know how to save the fruits of your labor and will bury your treasures safely away from prying eyes.

If your daymaster is the Earth Pig, you enjoy socializing with a close circle of trusted friends. You are imaginative, but shrewd and perfectly realistic. You enjoy all the comforts and pleasures of life—good food, good drink, and good company. You are sensual and soft-spoken, but inwardly strong and self-sufficient. You may express your artistic leanings and talents through practical and pragmatic avenues such as computers. Although you may seem submissive, you control from behind the scenes.

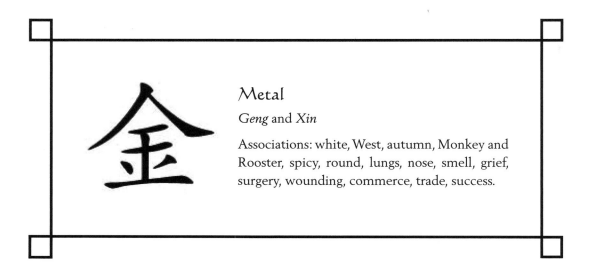

Metal

Geng and *Xin*

Associations: white, West, autumn, Monkey and Rooster, spicy, round, lungs, nose, smell, grief, surgery, wounding, commerce, trade, success.

The Metal element parallels the fall season and represents the late-day setting sun, the western direction, round shapes, and the color white. It corresponds to the lungs, the nose, and the respiratory system. Metal element people renew their strength in the early evening hours, and are invigorated by their keen sense of smell. The feng shui direction assigned to the metal element is West, which represents commerce, success, trade, and the roundness of coins, arches, hills, and domes.

The Metal element represents the period from ages 36 to 48, the middle age of life characterized by fixed values, strength of will, and fluency of speech. The nature of Metal is to define and to strengthen, and those with a Metal daymaster will work their way to the top because of these qualities. The Metal element symbolizes clear thinking, sincerity, and accuracy. Metal element people have the gift of structure and the ability to interface skillfully with the outside world. Those born into the Metal element set and follow their goals with fervor and passion. Metal is determined and fixed, positioning and holding by creating a foundation and a base. The Metal element can also add rigidity, stubbornness, and a reluctance to compromise to a sign. Fiercely independent, solitary, and blessed with a great strength of purpose, Metal element people tend to speak candidly and bluntly. The emotion associated with Metal is grief, which can turn into self-pity if taken to an extreme. Whether you are a yang metal sword that slays foes or a delicate yin metal clasp of a silver necklace, the Metal element blesses you with great strength of will. Metal element people are somber and strong loners. The Metal element is closely tied to the lungs, the nose, and the respiratory system.

◈ Predominant sense: smell.

◈ You produce/assist/help/feed: the Water element.

◈ You are produced/assisted/enabled by: the Earth element.

◈ Metal traits: structure, clarity, commerce, and trade, but also grief, self-pity, and callousness.

◈ Dangers: wounds, respiratory disease, flu.

◈ Blessings: success, wealth, relaxation, and entertainment.

You are **yang Metal Geng** if your daymaster is the Metal Rat, Metal Tiger, Metal Dragon, Metal Horse, Metal Monkey, or Metal Dog. Yang metal is symbolized by iron ore, knives, swords, and axes. Geng Metal people come into this world as a blank slate ready to be written upon by the hand of the universe. Through discipline, focus, and even hardship, they emerge as solid, sharp personalities with a strong drive to succeed at all costs. Perfectionism is their need and responsibility is their creed. Geng Metal people place a high premium on justice, equality, and loyalty. Though they may complain bitterly about a decision or situation, they are also willing to roll up their sleeves and do something about it. Geng Metals have a tough constitution and will usually outtalk and outperform most of their competitors. Loyal, stubborn, and most definitely persistent, they will defend their home, their country, and those they care for to the death. Able to endure hardships that would crush weaker spirits, Geng Metals are sharp, determined, strong-willed, and straightforward. They do not admit failure easily and define themselves by their strong sense of justice and fair play.

The Geng Metal female is a go-getter. Confident, ambitious, and inspiring to others, she can also become overly competitive due to a powerful need to succeed. Always wanting to come out on top, she attempts to impress others as a protective mechanism to avoid failure and rejection. She can probably outdrink, outrun, and outwit you—and anyone else, for that matter. Despite all this, she is still quite feminine, but don't be fooled by her pretty exterior: beneath the surface she's solid steel. Subconsciously she believes that her personal worth is determined by her achievements. She will frequently be found in professions that are held in high esteem, such as the healing arts, emergency work, social services, or perhaps championing the rights of children or animals. Although she will prove to be the most stubborn woman you have ever loved, she will also be endearingly loyal to you.

The Geng Metal man has a tough constitution and you will need to be able to go the distance with him. Vigorous, brave and decisive, he possesses an imposing kind of authority. He loves a challenge and never shrinks from hardships. Additionally, he upholds justice and has a high tolerance for external pressures. However, his thirst for challenges can make him seem rather imposing and off-putting to others. He is driven by a need to succeed and to outshine rivals at all costs. He wants nothing more than to feel useful to you and able to do things for you, so never overdo the "strong, independent woman" role. The going is always tough at first with the Geng Metal male, but once he warms to you, it will be more than worth your trouble.

If you are yang Metal Geng:

◈ Your sudden, unexpected wealth/windfall element is yang Wood (Jia).

◈ Your entitled, earned wealth/property element is yin Wood (Yi).

◈ Your happiness/guardian/proper care element is yin Earth (Ji).

◈ Your beneficial/positive change/angel element is yin Fire (Ding).

◈ Your unfavorable/conflict/unbecoming/harmful element is yang Fire (Bing).

Because your daymaster element is yang Metal Geng, the element of Metal represents you as well as your companions, spouse, and any rivals you might have. Yang Metal years (2000, 2010, 2020) bring friendships and new companions; however, yin Metal years (2001, 2011, 2021) can bring "contenders" and drain resources. The element of Earth represents your Mother. As Earth is your "parent" element, Earth element years (2008, 2009, 2018, 2019) bring caretakers, mentors, and persons who support or protect you; However, they can also bring over-involvement, maternal smothering, and/or oppressive care. All in all, the Earth element brings nurturing and a satisfied mind. The element of Water represents your biological offspring as well as your ideas (your brainchildren). Both yang and yin Water years (2002, 2003, 2012, 2013) will allow optimum creativity and expression. The element of Wood represents your finances. This element also represents your father, symbolizing financial support to the family. Yang Wood years (2004, 2014) bring unexpected or sudden wealth, while yin Wood years (2005, 2015) bring earned or expected wealth. The element of Fire represents your career or vocation. This is a difficult element for you as it conflicts with your Metal daymaster. Yang Fire years (2006, 2016) bring difficult or unfavorable change, while yin Fire years (2007, 2017) bring beneficial change.

If your daymaster is the Metal Rat, you are very success-oriented, with strong monetary instincts and the ability to save for a rainy day. You are an emotional but shrewd socialite who knows how to use the system to get ahead. You can also be adamant and even rigid in expressing your opinions, argumentative when provoked, and quick-witted. Your sharp tongue, backed by an impressive vocabulary, is capable of winning any verbal disagreement.

If your daymaster is the Metal Tiger, you have much ambition and are fascinating to those around you. Glamorous and distinctive in appearance, magnetism is your specialty and you stand out in any crowd. Although your goals may change from time to time, the Metal element bestows perseverance and structure. Unbending and bold in expression, you must learn to compromise with those who are in a position to benefit you in order to succeed.

If your daymaster is the Metal Dragon, you are sharp-tongued, argumentative, and a natural-born performer. Capable, cunning, and particularly shrewd in business matters, you have excellent financial sense. You are attracted to spiritual pursuits and may choose to isolate yourself for periods of solitary contemplation. You are an energetic and decisive individual who excels at instructing others, facing confrontation, and handling conflicts.

If your daymaster is the Metal Horse, you are impartial, honest, and an ardent idealist. Humanitarian in nature, with very high standards for both yourself and others, you act quickly and decisively. You will readily take on a crusade or worthy cause. With your magnetic personality, you can go far with career ambitions. Effective, decisive, and an expert in your field of interest, you are the dynamic cutting blade of the Horse family.

If your daymaster is the Metal Monkey, you will strive for high positions. You are gifted in putting plans into action, and will usually be involved with the nuts and bolts of putting an idea together. Independent, solitary, and smart, you may become frustrated by failure and can be impatient with your life progress. Boredom is your greatest enemy, whereas your ability to manipulate ideas and language is your greatest ally.

If your daymaster is the Metal Dog, you are a paradox: an idealistic realist who is torn between a desire for material success on one hand, and an equally strong desire for spiritual reflection on the other. If there is a chink in someone's armor or a flaw in someone or something, you will spot it immediately. An independent thinker who follows your own path, you are success-oriented and steady in your determination to succeed. Your happiness is to be found in harmonizing the two sides of yourself.

 You are **yin Metal Xin** if your daymaster is the Metal Ox, Metal Rabbit, Metal Snake, Metal Goat, Metal Rooster, or the Metal Pig. Yin Metal is symbolized by fine jewelry, gold, silver, clasps, needles, rings, and bracelets. Xin Metal people enjoy praise, so much so that they are easy targets for flattery. They have an acerbic tongue that can be as sharp as a needle and cut like a knife. Xin Metals make formidable enemies, have excellent memories, and can hold a grudge for a surprisingly long time. Despite a brusque exterior, those with a Xin Metal daymaster are very sensitive, in touch with their feelings, and true to themselves. They become moody, withdrawn, and critical if they are overloaded with stress. They have no tolerance for fools, and an even lower tolerance for laziness. They need an intellectual equal and place a high value on those with whom they are mentally in synch. Xin Metals make good managers and compelling teachers. They are good at spotting details that others have missed. Xin Metals enjoy problem-solving and need to be intellectually challenged. They are also always up for a good debate or discussion; they need a partner with whom they can converse and banter ideas freely. A silent, withdrawn, or taciturn partner will result in boredom and disinterest.

The Xin Metal woman can be a challenge to handle. "Ice princess," "disdainful," and "arrogant" are some of the terms that come to mind. She demands intellectual stimulation and places a high premium on a partner being her equal, if not better than herself. She needs to respect her partner and will not compromise on this matter. The Xin Metal woman can drink, play poker, and recite off-color jokes with the best of them, all while managing to present an image of propriety and purity. A "proper" romance is integral to succeeding with a Xin Metal woman—wine and dine her, put a little glamour and showmanship in your wooing technique, display some intelligence in your romantic strategy, and, most importantly, be an old-fashioned gentleman. If you get all this together, she may consent to come down from her pedestal. Until then, don't waste your time. If you should cross the Xin Metal woman, be prepared for World War III. She is a first-rate plotter and schemer who serves her revenge cold.

The Xin Metal man is energetic, competitive, ambitious, and driven. He learns quickly, has fast reflexes, and his principles are based on his preferences. Personal benefits take precedence over any benefits to others. He usually has a hero complex, so whatever you do, play the damsel in distress and make him feel as though he is your rescuer. Interestingly, the Xin Metal Man has a distinct feminine side and forms close friendships with women. He is also most likely very close with his mother and female relatives. He is fussy about small things, has many opinions, and is usually effusive and talkative. Nuance, subtlety, and good taste are extremely important to the Xin Metal man, and he loathes pretentious, fake, or affected people. The Xin Metal man likes to be intellectually challenged and enjoys a good debate. A distant or retiring woman really doesn't cut it with a Xin Metal male. But remember, Mr. Xin Metal hates to be wrong, so challenge, excite, and debate with him, but never belittle him. In the end, make him feel as though he comes out on top.

If you are yin Metal Xin:

◈ Your sudden, unexpected wealth/windfall element is yin Wood (Yi).

◈ Your entitled, earned wealth/property element is yang Wood (Jia).

◈   Your happiness/guardian/proper care element is yang Earth (Wu).

◈   Your beneficial/positive change/angel element is yang Fire (Bing).

◈   Your unfavorable/conflict/unbecoming/harmful element is yin Fire (Ding).

Because your daymaster element is yin Metal Xi, the element of Metal represents you as well as your companions, spouse, and any rivals you might have. Yin Metal years (2001, 2011) bring friendships and new companions, but yang Metal years (2000, 2010) can bring "contenders," competitors, or drain resources. The element of Wood represents your finances as well as your father. Yang Wood years (2004, 2014) bring earned or expected wealth, while yin Wood years (2005, 2015) bring unexpected or sudden wealth. The element of Earth represents your mother as well as all caretakers, mentors, and persons who support or protect you. However, as the Earth is your "parent" element, it may also bring smothering or oppressive care of some sort. Yang Earth years (2008, 2018) bring happiness and nurturing for you. Yin Earth years (2009) also bring happiness but can feel a bit stifling. The element of Water represents your offspring as well as your ideas (your brainchildren). Both yang and yin Water years (2002, 2003, 2012, and 2013) will allow optimum creativity and expression. The element of Fire represents your career or vocation. This is a difficult element for you, as Metal is destroyed by Fire. Yin Fire years (2007, 2017) bring unfavorable change, while yang Fire years (2006, 2016) bring difficult yet beneficial change. Minimize the Fire element whenever possible.

If your daymaster is the Metal Ox, you are immersed in duty and not easily swayed, even in the face of hardships, drawbacks, or initial failures. Some may think you rigid and even severe at times. You are ambitious, success-oriented, and unwavering in your determination. This strong combination of sign and element as daymaster reveals an individual who is financially fortunate, constant, and true to his or her word. You have a flair for adapting and reshaping what is already well-established.

If your daymaster is the Metal Rabbit, you have an intense need for privacy and possess a lone wolf–style of problem solving. Clever, sly, and blessed with many artistic talents, you are street smart and savvy in the ways of the world. You are intelligent and sensitive, and have a deeply romantic core, but you must learn which battles to lose in order to win your wars. Let the little things go but stick firmly to your position in truly important matters. You will enjoy a small but very loyal group of friends.

If your daymaster is the Metal Snake, you are capable of creating great wealth, as you possess strong financial instincts and an inborn caution. You keep your counsel and prefer to work independently. Blessed with emotional intelligence and a deeply sensitive core, you have the ability to influence the outcome of virtually any situation. You are quiet and confident, and have a love and appreciation for literature and the fine arts, and especially music.

If your daymaster is the Metal Goat, you are a curious mixture of compromise and stubbornness, dependence, and self-sufficency. This duality may seen like an inconsistency to others. You hide the heart of a warrior beneath an easygoing, artistic exterior. The Metal Goat as daymaster reveals an energetic and shrewd individual who is not as harmless as he or she looks. You stand a good chance of becoming financially fortunate, and may receive a sudden windfall or inheritance at some point in your life.

If your daymaster is the Metal Rooster, you are powerfully candid, have a gift for captivating an audience, and have been blessed with shrewd and sharp powers of deduction. Analytical and a hard worker, you may find it difficult to compromise. Although you can feel unappreciated at times, nothing could be further from the truth, as your family, friends, and colleagues rely on your powers of observation and resourcefulness.

If your daymaster is the Metal Pig, you are truly one of the kindest and most decent people alive. You are pragmatic and prefer a predictable "sure thing" over risky ventures. Able to completely scrutinize a situation or troubleshoot a problem with your analytical eye, you enjoy success, but remain realistic in your expectations. You may be perceived as rigid because you can throw away a good situation when it does not conform to your expectations.

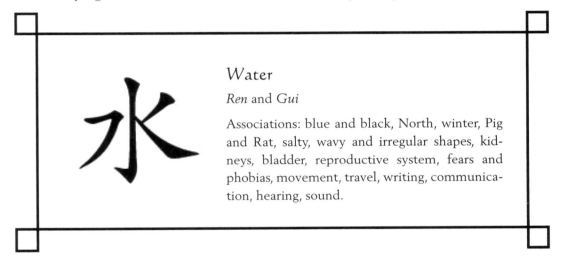

Water

Ren and *Gui*

Associations: blue and black, North, winter, Pig and Rat, salty, wavy and irregular shapes, kidneys, bladder, reproductive system, fears and phobias, movement, travel, writing, communication, hearing, sound.

The Water element parallels the season of winter and represents nighttime, the Northern direction, irregular shapes, and black and dark blue colors. It corresponds to the kidneys, bladder, and reproductive system. Water element people renew their strength in the dark of the night, and are invigorated by their keen sense of hearing. The feng shui direction assigned to the Water element is North, which represents travel, writing, and communication. The Water element is often represented with wavy lines and irregular shapes, which, in turn, represent flowing emotions.

The Water element represents the final period in the 60-year cycle between the ages of 48 and 60, a time characterized by reflection, sensitivity, and persuasiveness. Water's nature is similar to feelings and emotions; it descends, seeks out, and fills low places, especially the hearts of the downtrodden and the needy. Those with a Water daymaster are guided by their feelings and a need to communicate. It endows them with a lucid and quick mind. However, Water can also be chaotic because it does not have its own form and is dependent on the shape of the vessel that contains it. Water element people know how to persuade others and manipulate their environment. The Water element also brings the gift of empathy and gives them a calm and sedate nature. Water element people view life objectively and are sought after for their advice. The Water element blesses its natives with a deep spiritual nature and ability to thrive in social contexts. Those with Water daymasters possess extraordinary intuition and function as a kind of spiritual barometer. Water element people speak insightfully and bluntly. They are also fiercely independent, solitary, and blessed with great strength of purpose. The emotion associated with Water is fear, which can sometimes turn into pesky phobias. The Water element blesses you with great psychic powers and deep feelings. Whether you are a yang Water raging ocean or a yin Water trickling mountain creek, you probably suffer from personal issues, anxieties, and doubts. The Water element is closely tied to the kidneys, bladder, and reproductive system.

◈ Predominant sense: hearing.

◈ You produce/assist/help/feed: the Wood element.

◈ You are produced/assisted/enabled by: the Metal element.

◈ Water traits: deep feelings, clairvoyance, wisdom, and communication, but also excessive emotion, fears, and phobias.

◈ Dangers: flooding, drowning.

◈ Blessings: Communication, travel, movement, writing.

 You are **yang Water Ren** if your daymaster is the Water Rat, Water Tiger, Water Dragon, Water Horse, Water Monkey, or Water Dog. Yang Water is symbolized by vast oceans, great lakes, and rapid rivers. Ren Water people prefer freedom of movement and a carefree lifestyle, and strongly dislike pressure and confrontations. They are extroverted, optimistic, resourceful, and artistic lovers of poetry and dance. They also make excellent businesspeople. Like a rushing river, Ren Waters are frequently on the go. Movement and activity are important for their emotional and physical well-being. As the saying goes, still waters run deep, and it is sometimes difficult to "read" the Ren Water person. Dynamic and focused, Ren Waters can be myopic when they have their mind set on something or someone. Inconsistent and temperamental, their moods tend to swell and recede like the tide. Compassionate, attentive, empathic, and warm, Ren Water persons sometimes care too much, and may suffer from giving more than they receive. These are the good Samaritans of the 10 heavenly stems. Unfortunately, they may become so concerned about advocating and spreading love and goodwill that they overlook the nuts-and-bolts practicalities of helping. Ren Waters almost always have good intentions; however, their hidden compulsion is neediness—a need to be needed, appreciated, and loved—but they often avoid recognizing those needs.

The Ren Water female is a challenging to understand and to please. Demanding, sometimes snappish, and disdainful of weakness, she tends to have high expectations of her partner. Love is always confusing for the Ren Water woman. Should she select a dominant, influential man who rebuffs her testy demeanor, or a romantic, sweet man who is always available and ready to carry out her wishes? Truthfully, she would love to have both available for her, depending on her mood du jour.

The Ren Water male is the classic strong, silent type. Never one for small talk or meaningless verbal banter, the Ren Water man says what he means and means what he says. His affections will be expressed in tangible ways such as gifts or financial assistance. Although he is not verbally effusive with his declarations of passion, he is highly sentimental and will enjoy the little gestures and romantic things that you do. The Ren Water man will almost always be a successful businessman, manager, or entrepreneur, but he'll probably be just as married to his job as he is to you. Nurture and facilitate his career and you will endear yourself to him forever!

If you are yang Water Ren:

◈ Your sudden, unexpected wealth/windfall element is yang Fire (Bing).

◈ Your entitled, earned wealth/property element is yin Fire (Ding).

◈ Your happiness/guardian/proper care element is yin Metal (Xin).

◈ Your beneficial/positive change/angel element is yin Earth (Ji).

◈ Your unfavorable/conflict/unbecoming/harmful element is yang Earth (Wu).

Because your daymaster element is yang Water Ren, the element of Water represents you as well as your companions, spouse, and any rivals you might have. The Water element endows you with communication skills and makes for a deep and intuitive personality. The yearning to travel and to explore may be strong, as well. Yang Water element years (2002, 2012) bring companions, helpers, and cooperative associations, but yin Water years (2003, 2013) may bring competitors or rivals. The Element of Wood represents your offspring as well as your ideas (brainchildren). Both yang and yin Wood years (2004, 2005, 2014, 2015) will facilitate your optimum creativity and outward expression. The element of Fire represents your finances. This element also represents your father. Yang Fire years (2006, 2016) bring a windfall of unexpected or sudden wealth to you, and yin Fire years (2007, 2017) bring good luck with earned wealth. The element of Metal represents your mother. It also represents all caretakers, mentors, and persons who support or protect you. Yin Metal years (2001, 2011, 2021) bring nurturing and happiness for you, while yang Metal years (2000, 2010, 2020) may feel smothering or oppressive. The element of Earth represents your career or vocation. This can be a difficult element for you, as the Earth element traps your Water daymaster. Yang Earth years (1998, 2008, 2018) can bring crisis or unfavorable change, while Yin Earth years (1999, 2009, 2019) bring beneficial or good change. This will be especially true in matters of work or business.

If your daymaster is the Water Rat, you are deeply emotional, know how to communicate, and can easily influence a crowd. You are an open-minded individual, always looking for new ideas and experiences. Sensitive and capable of empathizing with others, communication, learning, and travel are all important to you. With a fine vocabulary and vivid imagination, you may excel in language, writing, or journalism.

If your daymaster is the Water Tiger, you are self-motivated, with a great desire to communicate, teach, and lead. You are a natural intermediary and may be drawn to public relations. Humanitarian, empathic, and morally upright, you have been blessed with sensible insight into human nature and a "sixth sense." Those with a Water Tiger daymaster are exquisitely insightful and may choose to pursue positions of spiritual leadership.

If your daymaster is the Water Dragon, you are humane and an excellent judge of the truth. You would excel in any type of career involving public affairs, social relations, or public speaking. Always open to new ideas and experiences, you have a true gift for seeing things objectively and creating a foundation to build upon in all that you do. Your urge to communicate may be expressed in a love of travel and embracing different cultures. Outgoing, fluent, and a first-rate conversationalist, you may chart your course to exotic locations. Careers that involve theatrics and playing to an admiring audience suit you best.

If your daymaster is the Water Horse, you are always seeking new ideas and experiences. You advance your own ideas by influencing the opinions and thoughts of others. Open-minded, objective, and friendly, you possess an insatiable need for movement, communication, and decisive action. You have a love of the outdoors and may lean toward team sports. You follow the latest trends and want to be the first to learn of and pass on news.

If your daymaster is the Water Monkey, you rarely take yourself too seriously and are generally full of humor and good cheer. The Water element imparts a great need to communicate with others. You cannot tolerate boredom, routine, or stagnation of your keen mind; you need to be challenged and stimulated mentally. Watch a tendency to be suspicious, and to leverage a response using your gifts of influence and persuasion. Your ability to manipulate language, ideas, and tricky situations is uncanny.

If your daymaster is the Water Dog, you are empathetic, tenderhearted, and capable of great sacrifice. Talented and intuitive, you could be very persuasive for the right cause. Others see you as kind, compassionate, and loyal. You are an exceptionally scrupulous and virtuous individual whose principal quality is devotion. Occasionally lacking self-confidence, you are very emotional and need a lot of encouragement and emotional support from others to assuage your fears, worries, and self-doubts.

 You are **yin Water Gui** if your daymaster is the Water Ox, Water Rabbit, Water Snake, Water Goat, Water Rooster, or Water Pig. Yin Water is symbolized by pools, small ponds, gentle rain, dew, and foggy mist. Gui Water people are upright, gentle, and kind. In addition to being humble and polite, they are also reliable, down-to-earth, disciplined, and helpful. With their strong sense of responsibility, Gui Waters are nurturing, inherently soft-hearted, and childlike. They are innocent and can be naive regarding the realities of life despite their age. Gui Waters are inherently fickle, never able to stay in one place for too long and flitting from interest to interest. This daymaster reveals the heart of a pacifist; accepting, patient, unpretentious, open, and a genuinely nice person. The risk with Gui Waters is that they may become too submissive or accommodating to others— sometimes to their own detriment. Gaining peace at any price and a fear of conflict prevents you from speaking up for yourself at times.

Gui Water females can be temperamental. In a relationship, they look to their partner to provide them with clarity and confidence. The Gui Water woman has trouble making up her mind and will look to her partner for relationship decisions. Her interests are as changeable and fluid as her element; today's fancy may or may not be tomorrow's passion. The Gui Water woman needs a career with a lot of diversity. A job that requires travel would suit her well.

The Gui Water male has a reputation as a ladies' man. He likes to keep his options open and may string along several women at one time. He thoroughly enjoys an abundance of female attention. He may be loathe to settle down and become a confirmed bachelor, or a perpetual adolescent who endlessly plays the romantic field. With his hand on the pulse of society, he may have intuition and psychic powers that are not readily apparent. His ever-changing interests (which he will expect you to wholeheartedly support) are varied and unconventional at times.

If you are yin Water Gui:

◈ Your sudden, unexpected wealth/windfall element is yin Fire (Ding).

◈ Your entitled, earned wealth/property element is yang Fire (Bing).

◈ Your happiness/guardian/proper care element is yang Metal (Geng).

◈ Your beneficial/positive change/angel element is yang Earth (Wu).

◈ Your unfavorable/conflict/unbecoming/harmful element is yin Earth (Ji).

Because your daymaster element is yin Water (Gui), the element of Water represents you as well as your companions, spouse, and any rivals you might have. The Water element endows you with communication skills and makes for a deep and intuitive personality. The yearning to travel and to explore may be strong, too. Yang Water element years (2002, 2012) bring competitors and rivals, while yin Water years (2003, 2013) bring companions, helpers, and cooperative associations. The element of Wood represents your offspring as well as your ideas (your brain-children). Water is the "parent" element that produces Wood, so both yang and yin Wood years (2004, 2005, 2014, 2015) will facilitate your optimum creativity and expressivity. The element of Fire represents your finances as well as your father. Yang Fire years (2006, 2016) bring good luck with earned wealth, and yin Fire years (2007, 2017) bring a windfall of unexpected or sudden wealth. The element of Metal is favorable and represents your Mother. It also represents all caretakers, mentors, and persons who support or protect you. All things connected to the Metal element will be lucky and bring happiness to you. Both yin and yang Metal years (2001, 2002, 2011, 2012) bring nurturing and proper guidance, as Metal is the parent element to your Water daymaster. The element of Earth represents your career or vocation. This is a difficult element for you, as the Earth "traps" and controls your Water daymaster. Yin Earth years (2009, 2019) can bring unfavorable or discordant change, but yang Earth years (2008, 2018) bring beneficial, albeit uncomfortable, change.

If your daymaster is the Water Ox, you have a way with words and a talent for achieving goals in an indirect way. With your knack for accurately gauging future outcomes and using the talents and resources of others, you are persuasive and able to wear away even the most resistant detractor with your quiet yet constant efforts. You are intuitive and stealthy, and prefer to infiltrate rather than dominate.

If your daymaster is the Water Rabbit, you are a deep thinker and possesses enhanced intuition bordering on the psychic. Sensitive and well-liked, your vulnerable feelings can be soothed by liberal doses of luxury and the finer things in life. You are also a gifted judge of character. You value sincerity and despise deception, and are eagerly sought out for your good taste and advice.

If your daymaster is the Water Snake, you are objective, compassionate, and an excellent student of human nature. You are charismatic, capable, and insightful, possessing an intuitive radar. A natural-born empathy, you have a well-developed capacity for feeling the pain of and empathizing with others. You enjoy a multitude of interests and have friends from very diverse backgrounds.

If your daymaster is the Water Goat, you are a peace-loving artist and creative savant. Humanitarian yet shrewd to the ways of the world, you possess remarkable street-smarts. You need a healthy amount of emotional support; in fact, dependence on others is a definite risk you run with this daymaster. You may be a poet, writer, artist, or performer. Seductiveness is your forte, but unfortunately, patience is not.

If your daymaster is the Water Rooster, you are fond of social activity and never hesitate to share your opinions with others. Candid, outspoken, and resourceful, you are energetic and possess a sarcastic yet enjoyable sense of humor. You enjoy the arts and anything recreational (the more people present the better). Proficient in the use of the written word and a commanding speaker, you possess a strong personality and will always find a more efficient way to complete any task.

If your daymaster is the Water Pig, competition is of little interest to you; what you seek is peace and tranquility. You are shy and quiet, yet able to express yourself eloquently. Hardworking, longsuffering, and loyal, you may have felt constrained somehow during your early life. You are a very private person, and have a horror of airing your dirty laundry in public. Sweet, gentle, and pure of heart, you prefer to live within a safe and comfortable world of love and affection.

Chapter 5
The Hour Pillar

The fourth and last pillar of destiny is the hour pillar. Similar to the year, month, and day pillars, the hour pillar is composed of two Chinese characters that depict the cosmic qi distinct to the time you were born. Each year, month, day, and hour has its own energy. The energy, or qi, that surrounds you as you take your first breath is your destiny. For example, 12 noon is very different from 12 midnight: noon is very "yang" and full of life, whereas midnight is very "yin," quiet, and still. Each animal sign or branch influences a two-hour period of each 24-hour day. It not only modifies and shades your personality, but also represents your offspring, your creative ideas, and your career. Using the software included, find your hour pillar in the center of your Zi Wei Dou Shu chart.

Birth Hour Pillars

11 p.m.–1 a.m.	Rat 鼠	子	Tze
1 a.m.–3 a.m.	Ox 牛	丑	Chou
3 a.m.–5 a.m.	Tiger 虎	寅	Yin
5 a.m.–7 a.m.	Rabbit 兔	卯	Mao
7 a.m.–9 a.m.	Dragon 龍	辰	Chen
9 a.m.–11 a.m.	Snake 蛇	巳	Si
11 a.m.–1 p.m.	Horse 馬	午	Wu
1 p.m.–3 p.m.	Goat 羊	未	Wei
3 p.m.–5 p.m.	Monkey 猴	申	Shen
5 p.m.–7 p.m.	Rooster 雞	酉	You
7 p.m.–9 p.m.	Dog 狗	戌	Xu
9 p.m.–11 p.m.	Pig 豬	亥	Hai

The Hour of the Rat

The charming and intelligent Rat rules the energies during the late-night hours between 11 p.m. and 1 a.m. You are outgoing, sociable, and cautious with money. The essence of the Rat is concealment, which indicates an extra cautious and eclectic personality. You have been blessed with writing talent, acute intelligence, and formidable social charm. Rat hours are in harmony with pillar branches of the Dragon, Monkey, and Ox, and clash with pillars of the Horse and Goat.

If your hour pillar is the Rat and your daymaster stem (element) is:

◈ Yang Wood, it indicates intelligence, metaphysical interests, writing talent, fame, and high achievement.

◈ Yin Wood, it indicates ingenuity used to find an easier way to do things; shortcuts are key to your success.

◈ Yang Fire, it indicates stubbornness or narrow thinking, which can waste your resources. Family provides inheritance.

◈ Yin Fire, you use force to ensure success. You are also ambitious, flamboyant, and physically competitive.

◈ Yang Earth, you achieve success through diligence and hard work. You are also stingy with resources.

◈ Yin Earth, it indicates sudden financial windfalls that are spent on your social life, as well as multiple marriages.

◈ Yang Metal, you are a good communicator, but speech can get you into trouble. You have a strong drive to succeed.

◈ Yin Metal, you are materialistic, but interested in the arts and romance. You have a steady family life, but encounter health and emotional problems.

◈ Yang Water, your proclivity for speculation, gambling, and inadvisable money deals make partnerships difficult.

◈ Yin Water, you are independent and competitive, and will have leadership positions. You like to be in charge.

The Hour of the Ox

Those born during the hours of the solitary and serious Ox, 1 a.m. to 3 a.m., are blessed with the gift of endurance. You are restrained, cautious, and steady. Hardworking and strong-willed, you are a natural authority and a powerful speaker. This hour pillar promotes self-confidence, willpower, and authority. Ox hours are in harmony with pillar branches of the Snake, Rooster, and Rat, but clash with the pillars of the Goat and Horse.

If your hour pillar is the Ox and your daymaster stem (element) is:

◈ Yang Wood, you are a good communicator, but speech can get you into trouble. You have a strong drive to succeed.

◈ Yin Wood, you are materialistic, but interested in the arts and romance. You have a steady family life, but also health and emotional problems.

◈ Yang Fire, your speculation, gambling, and shady money deals make partnerships difficult.

◈ Yin Fire, you are independent and competitive and will have leadership positions. You like to be in charge.

◈ Yang Earth, it indicates intelligence, metaphysical interests, writing talent, fame, and high achievement.

◈ Yin Earth, you have a talent for finding easier ways to do things; shortcuts are the key to your success.

◈ Yang Metal, your stubbornness or narrow thinking can waste resources. Your family provides an inheritance.

◈ Yin Metal, you use force to ensure success. You are ambitious, flamboyant, and physically competitive.

◈ Yang Water, you achieve success through diligence and hard work. However, you are stingy with resources.

◈ Yin Water, it indicates sudden financial windfalls, but they get spent on social life. Also, multiple marriages.

The Hour of the Tiger

The adventurous Tiger rules the energies during the dark pre-dawn hours of 3 a.m. to 5 a.m. You are more outgoing, more action-oriented, and more impulsive than the other signs. You have a noble heart, but you intend to win in this life. This hour pillar produces a self-assured, almost majestic individual. These Tiger hours will influence you to be more self-reliant, more adventurous, and more passionate. Tiger hours are in harmony with the pillar branches of the Horse, Dog, Rabbit, and Pig, but clash with the pillars of the Monkey and the Snake.

If your hour pillar is the Tiger and your daymaster stem (element) is:

◈ Yang Wood, you use force to ensure success. You are also ambitious, flamboyant, and physically competitive.

◈ Yin Wood, it indicates stubbornness or narrow thinking, which can waste resources. Family provides inheritance.

◈ Yang Fire, it indicates sudden financial windfalls, but they get spent on social life. Also, multiple marriages.

◈ Yin Fire, you achieve success through diligence and hard work. Stingy with resources.

◈ Yang Earth, you are materialistic, but love the arts and romance. Steady family life, but health and emotional problems.

◈ Yin Earth, you are a good communicator, but speech can get you into trouble. High drive to succeed.

◈ Yang Metal, you are independent and competitive, and will have leadership positions. You like to be in charge.

◈ Yin Metal, your speculation, gambling, and money deals make partnerships difficult.

◈ Yang Water, you have a talent for finding an easier way to do things. Shortcuts are the key to success.

◈ Yin Water, it indicates intelligence, metaphysical interests, writing talent, fame, and high achievement.

The Hour of the Rabbit

The virtuous Rabbit rules the energies during the dawn hours between 5 a.m. and 7 a.m. You are more moderate, reflective, diplomatic, and discreet than other people. You have excellent manners and strong artistic instincts. You may collect art or antiques. The earthly branch of the Rabbit contributes a kind of detachment to your personality. You will require more privacy, tranquility, and peace than other people. Rabbit hours are in harmony with the pillar branches of the Goat, Pig, Snake, and Dog, but clash with the pillars of the Rooster and Dragon.

If your hour pillar is the Rabbit and your daymaster stem (element) is:

◈ Yang Wood, your stubbornness or narrow thinking can waste resources. Family provides inheritance.

◈ Yin Wood, you use force to ensure success. You are ambitious, flamboyant, and physically competitive.

◈ Yang Fire, you achieve success by diligence and hard work. Stingy with resources.

◈ Yin Fire, it indicates sudden financial windfalls, but they get spent on social life. Multiple marriages.

◈ Yang Earth, you are a good communicator, but speech can get you into trouble. High drive to succeed.

◈ Yin Earth, you are materialistic, but love the arts and romance. You have a steady family life, but health and emotional problems.

◈ Yang Metal, your speculating, gambling, and money deals make partnerships difficult.

◈ Yin Metal, you are independent and competitive and will have leadership positions. You like to be in charge.

◈ Yang Water, it indicates intelligence, metaphysical interests, writing talent, fame, and high achievement.

◈ Yin Water, you have a talent for finding an easier way to do things. Shortcuts are the key to your success.

The Hour of the Dragon

The powerful Dragon rules the energies during the energetic morning hours between 7 a.m. and 9 a.m. You have been given strength, determination, and added ambition. You are also unpredictable, opinionated, very outspoken, and extremely lucky. You possess exceptionally good health and a vital physical energy. Dragon hours are in harmony with the pillar branches of Rat, Monkey, Snake, and Rooster, and clash with the pillars of the Rabbit and Dog.

If your hour pillar is the Dragon and your daymaster stem (element) is:

◈ Yang Wood, you are materialistic, but love the arts and romance. Steady family life, but health and emotional problems.

◈ Yin Wood, you are a good communicator, but speech can get you into trouble. High drive to succeed.

◈ Yang Fire, you are independent and competitive and will have leadership positions. You like to be in charge.

◈ Yin Fire, your speculating, gambling, and money deals make partnerships difficult.

◈ Yang Earth, you always find an easier way to do things. Shortcuts are the key to success.

◈ Yin Earth, it indicates intelligence, metaphysical interests, writing talent, fame, and high achievement.

◈ Yang Metal, you use force to ensure success. You are ambitious, flamboyant, and physically competitive.

◈ Yin Metal, your stubbornness or narrow thinking can waste resources. Family provides inheritance.

◈ Yang Water, you experience sudden financial windfalls, but they are spent on your social life. Multiple marriages.

◈ Yin Water, your success comes by diligence and hard work. Stingy with resources.

The Hour of the Snake

The wise and philosophical Snake rules the mid-morning hours between 9 a.m. and 11 a.m. You are intuitive, reflective, and private. Stealthy, mystical, and patient for the right moment to make your mark, your strength, knowledge, and physical form gather strength gradually. You are the quintessential power behind the throne. Snake hours are in harmony with the pillars branches of the Ox, Rooster, Dragon, and Monkey, and clash with pillars of the Pig and Tiger.

If your hour pillar is the Snake and your daymaster stem (element) is:

◈ Yang Wood, you have sudden financial windfalls, but they are spent on your social life. Multiple marriages.

◈ Yin Wood, you achieve success by diligence and hard work. Stingy with resources.

◈ Yang Fire, you are materialistic, but love the arts and romance. Steady family life, but health and emotional problems.

◈ Yin Fire, you are a good communicator, but speech can get you into trouble. High drive to succeed.

◈ Yang Earth, you are independent and competitive and will have leadership positions. You like to be in charge.

◈ Yin Earth, your speculating, gambling, and bad money deals make partnerships difficult.

◈ Yang Metal, you always find an easier way to do things. Shortcuts are the key to your success.

◈ Yin Metal, it indicates intelligence, metaphysical interests, writing talent, fame, and high achievement.

◈ Yang Water, you use force to ensure success. You are ambitious, flamboyant, and physically competitive.

◈ Yin Water, your stubbornness or narrow thinking can waste resources. Family provides inheritance.

The Hour of the Horse

The athletic Horse rules the midday hours of 11 a.m. to 1 p.m. You have a high level of energy and need to be in continuous motion. You are decisive, a gifted orator, and a natural public speaker. This hour pillar makes you extremely self-confident and attracted by all that glitters. You will need an exciting direction to go in, preferably something adventurous, daring, and/or future-oriented. Horse hours are in harmony with the pillar branches of the Tiger, Dog, and Goat, but clash with the pillars of the Rat and Ox.

If your hour pillar is the Horse and your daymaster stem (element) is:

◈ Yang Wood, you achieve success by diligence and hard work. Stingy with resources.

◈ Yin Wood, you have sudden financial windfalls, but they get spent on social life. Multiple marriages.

◈ Yang Fire, you are a good communicator, but speech can get you into trouble. High drive to succeed.

◈ Yin Fire, you are materialistic, but drawn to the arts and romance. Steady family life, but health and emotional problems.

◈ Yang Earth, your speculating, gambling, and money deals make partnerships difficult.

◈ Yin Earth, you are independent and competitive and will have leadership positions. You like to be in charge.

◈ Yang Metal, it indicates intelligence, metaphysical interests, writing talent, fame, and high achievement.

◈ Yin Metal, you have a talent for finding an easier way to do things. Shortcuts are the key to your success.

◈ Yang Water, stubbornness or narrow thinking can waste your resources. Family provides inheritance.

◈ Yin Water, you use force to ensure success. You are ambitious, flamboyant, and physically competitive.

The Hour of the Goat

The whimsical and artistic Goat rules the early afternoon hours between 1 p.m. and 3 p.m. You have a strong sense of propriety, an artistic spirit, and a sweet nature. You are tolerant, easygoing, and receptive, but also dramatic, dependent, and dreamy in a fantasy-prone kind of way. You resist schedules and prefer the easy life. Goat hours are in harmony with the pillar branches of the Rabbit, Pig, and Horse, but clash with the pillars of the Ox and Rat.

If your hour pillar is the Goat and your daymaster stem (element) is:

◈ Yang Wood, you are a good communicator, but speech can get you into trouble. High drive to succeed.

◈ Yin Wood, you are materialistic, but love the arts and romance. Steady family life, but health and emotional problems.

◈ Yang Fire, your speculating, gambling, and shady money deals make partnerships difficult.

◈ Yin Fire, you are independent and competitive and will hold leadership positions. You like to be in charge.

◈ Yang Earth, it indicates intelligence, metaphysical interests, writing talent, fame, and high achievement.

◈ Yin Earth, you have a talent for finding an easier way to do things. Shortcuts are the key to your success.

◈ Yang Metal, stubbornness or narrow thinking can waste resources. Family provides inheritance.

◈ Yin Metal, you use force to insure success. You are ambitious, flamboyant, and physically competitive.

◈ Yang Water, you achieve success through diligence and hard work. Stingy with resources.

◈ Yin Water, you will have sudden financial windfalls, but they are spent on social life. Multiple marriages.

The Hour of the Monkey

The mischievous Monkey rules signs born in the late afternoon hours between 3 p.m. and 5 p.m. You are charming, shrewd, and jovial on the surface, yet secretly suspicious underneath. Your profound powers of persuasion and irrepressible personality give you an aptitude for entrepreneurial ventures. Your amusing sense of humor gains you popularity and favor. Your natural wit and comedic timing can take you far. Monkey hours are in harmony with the pillar branches of the Rat, Dragon, Rooster, and Snake, but clash with the pillars of the Tiger and Pig.

If your hour pillar is the Monkey and your daymaster stem (element) is:

- Yang Wood, you are independent and competitive and will have leadership positions. You like to be in charge.
- Yin Wood, your speculating, gambling, and money deals make partnerships difficult.
- Yang Fire, you always find an easier way to do things. Shortcuts are your key to success.
- Yin Fire, it indicates intelligence, metaphysical interests, writing talent, fame, and high achievement.
- Yang Earth, you use force to ensure success. You are also ambitious, flamboyant, and physically competitive.
- Yin Earth, your stubbornness or narrow thinking can waste resources. Family provides inheritance.
- Yang Metal, you will have sudden financial windfalls, but they get spent on your social life. Multiple marriages.
- Yin Metal, you achieve success by diligence and hard work. Stingy with resources.
- Yang Water, you are materialistic, but love the arts and romance. Steady family life, but health and emotional problems.
- Yin Water, you are a good communicator, but speech can get you into trouble. High drive to succeed.

The Hour of the Rooster

The disciplined Rooster rules the early evening hours of 5 p.m. to 7 p.m. You know how to apply yourself and have the ability to defer gratification, tolerating tedious everyday work in order to enjoy future rewards. Both flamboyant and extroverted, you are efficient and can get much done in minimal time. You have been blessed with a lively and outgoing manner; verbally, you are very direct and no-nonsense. You are concerned with your appearance and are always fashionably dressed. Rooster hours are in harmony with the pillar branches of the Ox, Snake, Monkey, and Dragon, but clash with the pillars of the Rabbit and Dog.

If your hour pillar is the Rooster and your daymaster stem (element) is:

◈ Yang Wood, your speculating, gambling, and money deals make partnerships difficult.

◈ Yin Wood, you are independent and competitive and will have leadership positions. You like to be in charge.

◈ Yang Fire, it indicates intelligence, metaphysical interests, writing talent, fame, and high achievement.

◈ Yin Fire, you use ingenuity to find an easier way to do things. Shortcuts are key to success.

◈ Yang Earth, your stubbornness or narrow thinking can waste resources. Family provides inheritance.

◈ Yin Earth, you use force to insure success. You are ambitious, flamboyant, and physically competitive.

◈ Yang Metal, you achieve success by diligence and hard work. Stingy with resources.

◈ Yin Metal, you experience sudden financial windfalls, but they are spent on your social life. Multiple marriages.

◈ Yang Water, you are a good communicator, but speech can get you into trouble. High drive to succeed.

◈ Yin Water, you are materialistic, but love the arts and romance. Steady family life, but health and emotional problems.

The Hour of the Dog

The watchful and wary Dog energy rules the hours between 7 p.m. and 9 p.m. You are a guardian—a watchful, loyal, dutiful individual who is also anxious at times. Although you possess a bit of the pessimistic Dog outlook on life, you are capable of great sacrifice for the right cause. Your magnanimous nature is non-materialistic, reasonable, and fair-minded. You will quickly assess any situation and take up the gauntlet for others if necessary. Dog hours are in harmony with the pillar branches of the Tiger, Horse, Pig and Rabbit. They clash with the pillars of the Dragon and Rooster.

If your hour pillar is the Dog and your daymaster stem (element) is:

◈ Yang Wood, you are materialistic, but love the arts and romance. Steady family life, but health and emotional problems.

◈ Yin Wood, you are a good communicator, but speech can get you into trouble. High drive to succeed.

◈ Yang Fire, you are independent and competitive and will have leadership positions. You like to be in charge.

◈ Yin Fire, your speculating, gambling, and ill-advised money deals make partnerships difficult.

◈ Yang Earth, you are always able to find an easier way to do things. Shortcuts are your key to success.

◈ Yin Earth, it indicates intelligence, metaphysical interests, writing talent, fame, and high achievement.

◈ Yang Metal, you use force to insure success. You are ambitious, elegant, and creative.

◈ Yin Metal, your tough, resilient personality conceals a tender core. Your stubbornness or narrow thinking can waste resources. Family provides inheritance.

◈ Yang Water, you'll have sudden financial windfalls, but they will be spent on your social life. Multiple marriages.

◈ Yin Water, you achieve success by diligence and hard work. Stingy with resources.

The Hour of the Pig

The obliging and truthful Pig energy rules the late evening hours of 9 p.m. to 11 p.m. You have an honest and accommodating personality that is resigned to the way the world is. The Pig in your hour pillar reveals a peaceful, reclusive, and sensitive person, but you can be sociable and self-indulgent, as well. You are a solitary yet caring person who is a touch vulnerable and naïve. You have the ability to acquire fine treasures and worldly goods. Pig hours are in harmony with the pillar branches of the Goat, Rabbit, Dog, and Tiger, but clash with the Snake and Monkey.

If your hour pillar is the Pig and your daymaster stem (element) is:

◈ Yang Wood, your ingenuity is used to find an easier way to do things. Shortcuts are the key to your success.

◈ Yin Wood, it indicates intelligence, metaphysical interests, writing talent, fame, and high achievement.

◈ Yang Fire, you use force to insure success. You are also ambitious, elegant, and creative.

◈ Yin Fire, your stubbornness or narrow thinking can waste resources. Family provides inheritance.

◈ Yang Earth, you will have sudden financial windfalls, but they will get spent on your social life. Multiple marriages.

◈ Yin Earth, you achieve success by diligence and hard work. Stingy with resources.

◈ Yang Metal, you are materialistic, but love the arts and romance. Steady family life, but health and emotional problems.

◈ Yin Metal, you are a good communicator, but speech can get you into trouble. High drive to succeed.

◈ Yang Water, you are independent and competitive and will have leadership positions. You like to be in charge.

◈ Yin Water, your speculating, gambling, and money deals make partnerships difficult.

Is your hour pillar compatible with the other pillars in your chart? Does it clash with or form any special patterns with your birth month, birth day, or birth year pillars? We'll see in the next chapter!

Chapter 6
Compatibilities Between Pillars

When certain signs group together, they can be favorable or unfavorable. For example, a combination such as the Dog, Tiger, and Horse reveals ambition and motivation, whereas the combination of the Ox and Goat can signal inner struggles and conflict. This chapter is concerned with the combinations that are compatible. Write down your Four Pillars here:

Hour:_____   Day:_____

Month:_____   Year:_____

The Three Crosses

The three crosses contain two sets of opposite signs. Although an opposition between signs is usually unfavorable, when all four signs (two pairs of opposites) team up together in a chart, they become favorable in specific ways. If you have three out of the four signs in the cross, or if two signs are missing, there can be problems. Do you have any of these combinations in your chart?

The peach blossoms: Rat, Rabbit, Horse, and Rooster

Power and fame are indicated here. This group signifies balance through tension. Because all four of these signs are peach blossoms, you are at extremely high risk for all kinds of vices, from gambling to obsessive love. This combination can thrust you to the top of love's mountain or slay you in the valley of heartbreak. These four signs found together in a chart bring with them torrid

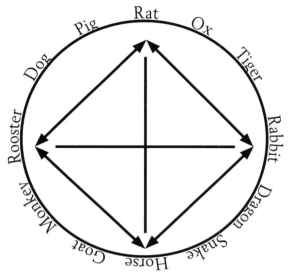

love affairs and unforgettable romances. For example, the chart of a beautiful ex-model turned local entertainer on her fifth marriage, born June 15, 1945 at 12:09 a.m. local time, with all four peach blossoms in her chart, shows that she probably struggles with relationships and various addictions.:

Hour	Day	Month	Year
Fire	Wood	Water	Wood
Rat	Rabbit	Horse	Rooster

If one sign is missing from these four, this can cause problems, as well:

◈ If Rat is absent, you have trouble keeping track of money and may spend impulsively.

◈ If Rabbit is absent, you have problems with health, home, or children.

◈ If Horse is absent, you have problems with mobility, movement, and physical weakness.

◈ If Rooster is absent, you suffer from unwarranted anxiety and an inability to relax.

The literary cross: Ox, Dragon, Goat, Dog

Literary and artistic potential and endeavors are indicated here. Some of the great masters of music had these four signs in their chart. For example, the chart of a composer and multitalented musician born on April 8, 1973 at 2:17 p.m. local time shows all four literary signs:

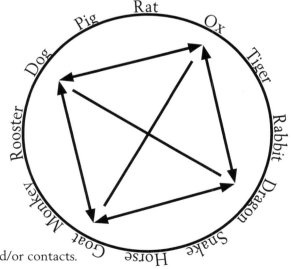

Hour	Day	Month	Year
Metal	Wood	Fire	Water
Goat	Dog	Dragon	Ox

Do you have one sign that is missing from these four?

◈ If Ox is absent, you lack perseverance or stamina.

◈ If Dragon is absent, you are hesitant to try new things.

◈ If Goat is absent, you lack family ties and/or contacts.

◈ If Dog is absent, you have difficulty adjusting or adapting.

The four steeds: Tiger, Snake, Monkey, Pig

Also known as the four winged horses, these are the energies of movement, change, travel, and reevaluation. This movement can either be by choice (to walk in) or by force (to be pulled in). Travel and immigration are indicated. This group signifies continuous journeys and perhaps even a nomadic life. Having all four steed signs in a chart can be exhausting, draining, and depleting. For example, a computer specialist who travels all over the country on work assignments, born September 5, 1959 at 10:34am local time, shows all four steed in her chart:

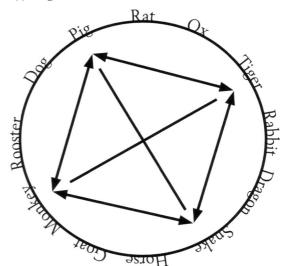

Hour	Day	Month	Year
Metal	Metal	Water	Earth
Snake	Tiger	Monkey	Pig

Do you have one sign that is missing from these four?

◈ If Tiger is absent, you lack assertion or authority.

◈ If Snake is absent, you have legal problems.

◈ If Monkey is absent you lack verbal skills or manual dexterity.

◈ If Pig is absent, you have problems settling down.

Compatible Combinations

In-kind

"In-kind" combinations are two signs in sequence which team up to complete one of the six life palaces. Each sign is coupled together with the sign found directly before or after it. The six in-kind palaces are:

1. Rat/Ox—creative expression

2. Tiger/Rabbit—progress/success

3. Dragon/Snake—spirituality

4. Horse/Goat—sexuality/reproduction

5. Monkey/Rooster—career/vocation

6. Dog/Pig—home and hearth

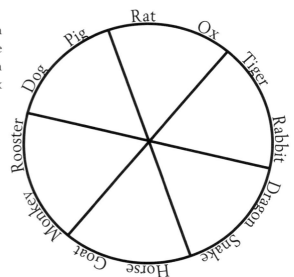

Palace #1 creative expression—Rat (begins)/Ox (completes):

The Rat and Ox make up the life palace of creativity and artistic expression. When the Rat and Ox are found together in a chart, it reveals an extremely creative individual. It also shows a person who is family-oriented and wishes to create a kind of personal sanctuary around him- or herself.

Palace #2 progress/success—Tiger (force)/Rabbit (persuasion):

Part boisterous Tiger, part understated Rabbit, if these two signs are found together in your chart, they will greatly assist you in developing and fostering your personal talents. The Rabbit accomplishes by diplomacy and the Tiger develops by force.

Palace #3 spirituality—Dragon (magician)/Snake (sage):

The magical Dragon and the mystical Snake make up the life palace of spirituality. If these two signs are found together in your chart, you will have a deep, otherworldly side. The possessive Snake and autonomous Dragon allow you to rise above the mundane and soar to new esoteric heights.

Palace #4 sexuality/reproduction—Horse (yang masculine)/Goat (yin feminine):

The Horse and the Goat comprise the life palace of sexuality. These two form opposite sides of the same coin and make for a powerfully magnetic and sensual personality. If these signs are found together in your chart, you will have a perfect balance of male, yang force and female, yin force, thus attracting many admirers.

Palace #5 Career/vocation—Monkey (versatility)/Rooster (efficiency):

The Monkey and Rooster comprise the life palace of career and vocation. These two signs together in a chart reveal cleverness, dexterity, and a shrewd, quick wit. The Rooster promotes you via competence, and the Monkey, via craftiness. This pairing in a chart brings success in business.

Palace #6 home and hearth—Dog (creates)/Pig (finishes):

When the earnest Dog and affectionate Pig are found teamed up in a chart, one will find a lover of home and family. Together they reveal a loyal and romantic individual whose allegiance is to his or her family, spouse, and/or children.

Trine signs

These four groups form very favorable combinations in a chart. They are: the pillars of creativity (Rat/Dragon/ Monkey); the pillars of trade and commerce (Ox/Snake/Rooster); the pillars of ambition (Tiger/Dog/Horse); and the pillars of home and family (Rabbit/Goat/Pig).

The pillars of creativity—concealment, unpredictability, irrepressibility:

If you have a Rat, Dragon, and Monkey combination present, you could well be an inventive genius, able to make your ideas work and bring drawing-board concepts into tangible reality. Ideas become possibilities,

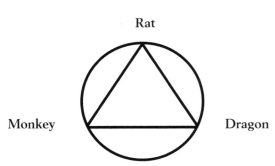

which are then transformed into actuality. This combination makes for an intense and enthusiastic personality. You will tend toward restlessness and will definitely accomplish what you set out to do. Impetuous and easily frustrated, you possess a triple dose of potent, positive, masculine yang energy.

The pillars of trade and commerce—endurance, accumulation, application:

If you have an Ox, Snake, and Rooster combination present, you have a natural business sense and the ability to persevere until the end. You could become extremely wealthy as a result of your business savvy and consistent staying power. This combination also makes for a fixed and rigid personality with strong opinions and views. You will be a genius

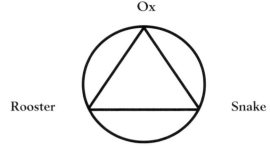

at meticulous planning, and understand the wisdom of deferred gratification. Stable and long-lasting, you are ruled by deep, dark, negative, feminine yin energy.

The pillars of ambition—decisiveness, nobility, watchfulness:

If you have a Tiger, Horse, and Dog combination present, you are a highly motivated go-getter, most likely an entrepreneur of some type. You are active and determined to succeed at any price, and will aim for the top in your chosen field. This combination of signs in a chart also reveals a humanitarian who excels in verbal communication and is a gifted speaker.

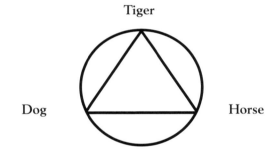

Relationships and personal connections are your highest priority; you seek a soulmate in this life. Idealistic, influential, and upright, you are ruled by potent, positive, masculine yang energy.

The pillars of home and family—detachment, propriety, resignation:

If you have a Rabbit, Goat, and Pig combination present, you are destined to live a happy and contented life. A fruitful career and cozy home are just some of the rewards with this peaceful, empathic, and lucky combination. Family will always come first for you. This combination of signs in a chart reveals a quest for all things spiritual and beautiful in

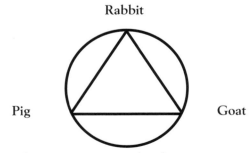

this life. You are artistic, refined, and well-mannered. You also possess a more placid temperament than others, and recoil from strife and ugliness. Reflective and gentle, you are ruled by deep, dark, negative, submissive, feminine yin energy.

Best Sign Combinations

Powerful, strong, and very harmonious, these six sign combinations are the luckiest of the lucky to find in your chart. They are: Rat/Ox, Pig/Tiger, Dog/Rabbit, Rooster/Dragon, Monkey/Snake, and Goat/Horse.

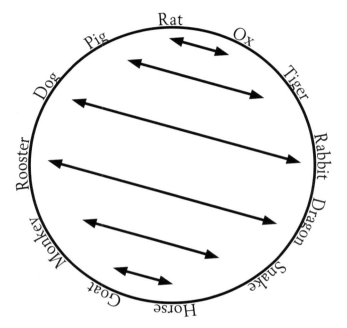

Rat/Ox:

The combination of these compatible signs in a chart is very lucky and produces a very sentimental and vulnerable person. These two signs form the foundation for a family- and security-oriented life. The Ox provides you with stability, consistency, and practicality, while the Rat bestows clever ideas and the ability to exhibit these ideas by way of tangible projects.

Pig/Tiger:

The combination of these compatible signs in a chart is very lucky and produces an affectionate, forthright person. These two signs form the foundation for a life filled with grand accomplishments and success in friendships and in love. The Tiger provides you with the ability to work through nearly any difficulty, and the Pig imparts a great need for affection and physical comforts.

Dog/Rabbit:

The combination of these compatible signs in a chart is very lucky. It produces a tenderhearted person who will have the well-being and personal growth of others in the forefront of his or her heart and mind. You are a selfless type of person who gives the best of yourself to others and will make many personal connections in this lifetime. The devoted Dog makes you watchful, and the detached Rabbit reveals your faithfulness as a friend.

Rooster/Dragon:

The combination of these compatible signs in a chart is very lucky and produces an independent person who will always retain his or her own outside interests. The Rooster provides you with spunk and enterprise, and the Dragon bestows drama and the ability to hold the interest of others. You could be very successful on the stage or podium, and will be eye-catching in any type of uniform or costume.

Monkey/Snake:

The combination of these compatible signs in a chart is very lucky and produces an intense, physically attractive individual who has an equal measure of both guile and allure. The Snake provides you with a deep philosophical side, while the Monkey gives you the ability to transform raw materials into something beautiful. You could be very successful in any kind of career that requires you to be convincing, such as sales.

Goat/Horse:

The combination of these compatible signs in a chart is very lucky and produces a person who is both decisive and creative. These two signs form the base for a life filled with debate, oration, and public speaking. The Horse is the personification of the yang, masculine day-force, and the Goat is the very essence of the yin, feminine night-force. If these two signs connect in your chart, you could be very successful in any career that concerns human sexuality or reproduction.

Multiple Signs

If your chart contains two, three, or all four of its pillars in the same branch animal sign, the traits of the sign are enhanced even further. For example, a firefighter born on October 31, 1958, at 7:30 p.m. local time, shows a triple Dog pillar:

Hour	Day	Month	Year
Earth	Metal	Water	Earth
Dog	Snake	Dog	Dog

And an extraordinarily beautiful young fashion designer born on May 19, 1989, at 9:15 a.m. local time, shows a triple Snake pillar:

Hour	Day	Month	Year
Earth	Earth	Earth	Earth
Snake	Rabbit	Snake	Snake

In the chart that follows, you can mix and match the animal branches in your four pillars chart and evaluate the degree of compatibility between pillars.

	Rat	Ox	Tiger	Rabbit	Dragon	Snake	Horse	Goat	Monkey	Rooster	Dog	Pig
Rat	2											
Ox	1	4										
Tiger	4	3	5									
Rabbit	5	3	4	2								
Dragon	2	4	3	5	2							
Snake	5	2	6	2	4	3						
Horse	5	6	2	4	3	4	2					
Goat	6	5	4	2	4	4	1	2				
Monkey	2	4	5	3	2	1	4	3	2			
Rooster	4	2	3	5	1	2	3	4	3	5		
Dog	4	4	2	1	5	3	2	5	3	6	3	
Pig	3	4	1	2	3	5	3	2	6	4	3	2

Key:

1 = Outstanding! The most auspicious of sign combinations. Lucky to find in any chart.

2 = Excellent, harmonious combination of two signs. They will create a positive effect.

3 = Good combination of complimentary signs.

4 = Fair or mediocre combination of signs.

5 = Poor combination of signs and a difficult clash in energy.

6 = Bad combination of signs with severe conflict between them.

In the next chapter, we will explore the more difficult or clashing combinations between pillars, squares, oppositions, and other combatant combinations.

Chapter 7
Incompatibilities Between Pillars

Oppositional combinations involve signs that are locked in combat with one another. These are the worst-of-the-worst combinations that cause frustrations, delays, and other difficulties. Sometimes these difficult sign combinations are placed in our charts for a reason—for personal growth, for example. Combatant signs paired together in a combatant vibration will exhibit the darker side of the sign's nature. We can choose to conquer the conflict once and for all or deal with it at another time. The type of difficulty and obstacle can be determined by the qualities of the signs themselves and the life pillars where they are found.

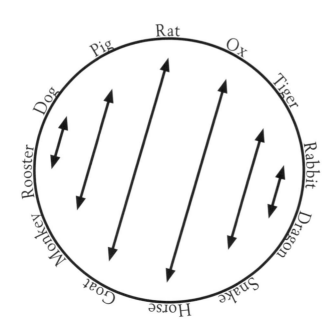

Pillars of Conflict

Rat/Goat:

These two signs found together in your chart indicate difficulties. Hyperactivity fights against sloth, and the results can be inharmonious to say the least. Part of you is a thrifty, neat perfectionist, while the other half is a messy spendthrift with a penchant for shopping. You may fluctuate between interests and can view your world in radically different ways depending on your mood. Someone with a conflicted Rat in his or her chart can be covert and secretive, and will deflect or mislead if it is to his/her advantage. He or she may also be difficult to please, demanding, and highly critical of others. Someone with a conflicted Goat in his or her chart can be irresponsible, undisciplined, and unreliable. He/she could easily squander a small fortune or run up astronomical bills. He/she may complain bitterly when matters don't go his or her way.

Ox/Horse:

When these two signs are found together in your chart, idealism meets dispassion and neither part of you can easily reconcile with the other. Part of you feels a duty to the family circle, while the other part wishes to escape all confinements and responsibilities. You experience conflicts over choices between home and hearth on one hand, and outside activities on the other. Someone with a conflicted Ox can be overly stern and display a terrible temper. He or she hates to be contradicted, especially in front of others, and can be subject to explosive outbreaks of anger. He/she does not enjoy being teased and can hold grudges for a long time. Someone with a conflicted Horse can be infatuate, hotheaded, and incredibly selfish. He/she may be tactless and ruthless, and believe that this world and everything in it belongs to him/her.

Tiger/Snake:

When these two signs are found together in your chart, impatience meets reserve, and fast butts heads with slow. Part of you always feels pushed to go faster than you are comfortable with. Conflicts occur internally between waiting and acting. One facet of you is externally focused while the other remains internally centered. Endless pondering can cause you to miss opportunities. Someone with a conflicted Tiger is careless, obstinate, and rebellious. His/her pride gets him/her in trouble frequently. He/she is reckless and oppositional, and tends to make foolish or hasty decisions. Someone with a conflicted Snake can be overly covert and secretive, and vacillate between being extravagant and stingy. He/she is likely possessive and jealous, yet a shameless philanderer and hedonist. Laziness and procrastination are some of this person's most irritating personality traits.

Rabbit/Dragon:

When these two signs are found together in your chart, good manners meet boorishness. Part of you is refined and mannerly, while the other side is crass and outspoken. This can cause you embarrassment and create many tensions in your relationships. You experience difficulties with friendships, family relations, and especially lovers. Someone with a conflicted Rabbit can be overly aloof, secretive, and petty. He or she may run away when being forced to choose sides or make difficult choices. He/she is likely commitment-phobic, and may relish the role of philanderer.

Someone with a conflicted Dragon can be short-tempered, demanding, and cruelly candid. A soul of extremes, he/she channels intense energy negatively, which can cause great destruction. The tendency to be unfaithful is one of his/her most unattractive traits.

Monkey/Pig:

When these two signs are found together in your chart, the trickster meets the naïve, and the con man combines with the duped victim. This combination creates a great deal of conflict within the conscience. One side of you wants to be truthful and forthright, while the other part can't help pulling the wool over people's eyes. Someone with a conflicted Monkey is manipulative, opportunistic, and status-seeking. He/she hides a low opinion of others behind an outward friendliness. He/she has a complicated and dubious personality which, when skewed, becomes trickery, arrogance, and self-interest. Someone with a conflicted Pig is passive, self-indulgent, and uncompetitive. He/she has a passive-aggressive personality and can use it as an excuse to avoid making decisions. His/her search for earthly pleasures can blind him/her and lead him/her down a carnal path to fetishes and perversions of all types.

Dog/Rooster:

This is an especially antagonistic combination. When these two signs are found together in your chart, egotism combines with insecurity. One side of you is thin-skinned to criticism, and the other is the instigator of such criticism (usually in the form of some pretty caustic verbal barbs). You will have your feelings hurt frequently because you can dish out critique better than you can take it. Someone with a conflicted Dog is agitated, secretive, and paranoid. Conflicted Dog pillars can reveal a "prophet of doom" mentality; many times these individuals are condescending and moralistic. They are also prone to obsessive, dysfunctional relationships with troubled partners. Someone with a conflicted Rooster is vain, hairsplitting, and downright cruel. He/she may have a sadistic streak and suffer from vanity and obsession with his/her appearance. He/she may also tend to focus on perfection and be highly critical of others.

Pillars of Opposition

These signs are in direct opposition and repel each other due to clashes in essential qi. The six oppositions are: Rat/Horse, Ox/Goat, Tiger/Monkey, Rabbit/Rooster, Dragon/Dog, Snake/Pig.

Rat/Horse:

When both of these opposite signs are found together in your chart, it points to tensions. A dual nature means that you have a need for security along with a conflicting need for independence.

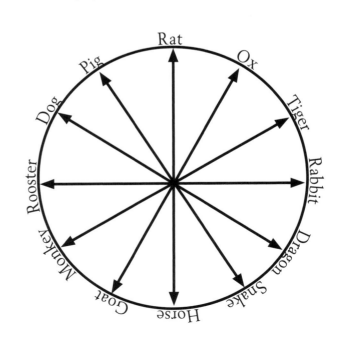

Love relationships are tumultuous; initially they seem to be made in heaven, but can end in disappointment and bitterness.

Ox/Goat:

When both of these opposite signs are found together in your chart, it points to tensions. These two signs are polarized opposites with radically different temperaments and opinions. Having both present in your chart can make you feel as though you are in a mental prison of sorts. Artistic and laid-back Goats thrive in a casual atmosphere, whereas Oxen are regulated, organized, and controlled. The Ox side of your personality continually fights with the unpredictable, capricious Goat. The pillar that is involved will determine the life area or phase that will be most affected by this combination.

Tiger/Monkey:

There will be trust issues in some form when the Tiger and Monkey comprise two of your four pillars. Depending on which pillars are affected, you mistrust others, but are capable of playing tricks and conning others. The tug-of war between ethics and desires can wreck havoc on your personality. A know-it-all attitude contributed by the Monkey, combined with the Tiger's bravado to express it readily, tends to provoke other people. If these two signs are placed in your day and hour pillars, antagonism in your marriage or primary relationship and between you and your children may plague you. This combination of signs almost always reveals an extremely independent person who opts to spend a lot of time away from their home base. Constant change, travel, and danger are in store for you throughout your life.

Rabbit/Rooster:

These two oppositions are also peach blossoms or love signs. When found together in a chart, they can indicate problems and conflicts in romantic relationships. Compatibility with another person may always seem just out of your reach. The Rooster's aggressive verbal style mixed with the sensitive Rabbit's feelings produces an individual who can dish out criticism, but has trouble taking it. This very inauspicious combination of opposite signs reveals an individual who is cocky and self-assured one minute, and aloof and withdrawn the next. You likely have a virtuous moral character, yet progress is limited due to your self-punishing and constraining personality. Best results can be achieved by commandeering the Rooster's resourcefulness and the Rabbit's creativity in order to find temperance in a personality that gravitates toward extremes.

Dragon/Dog:

When both of these opposite signs are found together in your chart, it points to bitterness, antagonism, and great stress. This case of two polarized opposites clashing produces an individual who is brutally honest and candid to a fault. Love relationships are particularly affected, with many bumps, dramas, traumas, and sticky situations along the way. As it is in the Rooster/Rabbit combination, the outspoken Dragon aspect criticizes with impunity, but has trouble accepting the same criticism due to the hypersensitive Dog side of the personality. This is not someone you should ever deliberately anger or engage with in a verbal sparring match. The greatest hurdle to jump for this individual will be to quell the conflict that rages between a sense of duty on one hand, and indifference on the other. If this is your combination, you need to remember that being involved doesn't necessarily mean that you are solely responsible for the outcome.

Snake/Pig:

With this combination, the childlike honesty of the Pig clashes rather abruptly with the elastic conscience of the Snake. Although both sides of the personality are generally agreeable and deeply feeling, the Snake's dishonesty and opportunism clashes with the honest Pig. In addition, the Snake's penchant for penny-pinching causes great stress for the self-indulgent Pig side of the personality. One part of the person scrimps and saves, only to go on an extravagant shopping binge a week later. This person's taste for luxury may be extreme, and over-indulgence in material pleasures is almost assured.

Pillars of Arguing, Fighting, and Penalties

Finding pillars doubled up, side-by-side, or in any combination of these four signs can presage serious maladjustment problems.

◈ Two Horses yields sharply defined gender roles and an extreme personality.

◈ Two Roosters is a warning sign to avoid dependence on alcohol or drugs.

◈ Two Pigs yields a person who is selfish, partisan, and judgmental.

◈ Two Dragons betokens personal rivalries, as well as an overconfident, rash, and antagonistic personality.

Here is an example of a difficult and conflicted chart for a yin female born on December 15, 1967, at 2:30 a.m. local time:

Hour	Day	Month	Year
Offspring	Spouse	Parents	Self
Water	Water	Water	Fire
Ox	Ox	Rat	Goat

Not only are there multiple sign clashes and oppositions present, but the elements in the chart are fighting one another. Not surprisingly, this lady is not a happy camper. Her list of life crises would take pages to chronicle. Domestic violence, parental alienation, trouble with the law, relationship problems/divorce, and chronic health problems lead the list. Her birth year pillar (self) of the Fire Goat is fighting the element of the Water Ox in her day pillar (marriage, spouse) and month pillar (parents). The branch animal sign of her Goat year is in opposition to her day pillar and hour pillar (both Oxen), as well. This reveals oppositions with spouse and offspring, but even more severe conflicts during childhood with her parents. In fact, she was a rebellious runaway teen who balked against her parents' rules and control. In addition, the Water element is too heavy in her chart, indicating emotional issues and imbalances such as depression, mania, anxieties, and phobias. This imbalance of the Water element is also the source of her desire to be free of commitments, obligations to, and dependence on other people.

However, the grass is a little greener on the other side of her chart. Looking for balance and what is positive in a chart, even when it looks bleak, is important. Although this person has had difficulty adjusting and will likely continue to have difficult relationships, her parents, her spouse(s), and her offspring will experience harmony amongst themselves. The Rat in her parents pillar and the Ox in both her day and hour pillars reveal good rapport between her parents and offspring, as well as between her parents and her spouse. Her children and her ex do, in fact, have a favorable connection.

Chapter 8

Lucky and Unlucky Elements

In Chapter 4, we discovered the daymaster and the significance of the element of your day of birth. Elements that create, produce, and support your daymaster element are considered lucky. Here are some examples:

◈ If your daymaster element is Wood, Fire and Water are usually auspicious; Metal is not.

◈ If your daymaster element is Fire, Wood and Earth are usually auspicious; Water is not.

◈ If your daymaster element is Earth, Metal and Fire are usually auspicious; Wood is not.

◈ If your daymaster element is Metal, Water and Earth are usually auspicious; Fire is not.

◈ If your daymaster element is Water, Metal and Wood are usually auspicious; Earth is not.

Another way of determining your lucky and unlucky elements is to add up the elemental "weights," or scores, in your birth chart. The elements with the lowest score or weight will be your lucky ones. To do this, give yourself 100 points for each element you find in your four pillars. In addition, each of the 12 animal signs has a main element and hidden elements. For the sake of simplicity, we will only use the main element of each sign: Rat = Water, Ox = Earth, Tiger = Wood, Rabbit = Wood, Dragon = Earth, Snake = Fire, Horse = Fire, Goat = Earth, Monkey = Metal, Rooster = Metal, Dog = Earth, and Pig = Water. For the following chart with a Water Ox daymaster, we would calculate the elemental weights thusly:

Hour	Day	Month	Year
Water	Water	Water	Fire
Ox	Ox	Rat	Goat

Wood = 0   Fire = 100   Earth = 300   Metal = 0

Water: 100 X 3 for the top stems, and 100 for the Rat branch = 400

In this instance, Wood and Metal are the lucky elements. Adding them to this person's life and environment will be most auspicious. Water and Earth are too heavy in this chart and, therefore, unlucky, so minimizing them will be beneficial.

Lucky Elements

If Wood is your lucky element:

◈ The Eastern cardinal direction is lucky.

◈ Live in a home that faces east.

◈ Choose a bedroom on the east side of your home.

◈ Keep the eastern windows open with breezes coming from this direction.

◈ Forested properties are most auspicious.

◈ Orient your body with your head toward the East (Wood) while sleeping for optimum health.

◈ A wooden bed is recommended.

◈ Your lucky color is green; wear it often.

◈ When decorating your office and home, choose forest greens, evergreen plants, potted trees, palms, green silk plants, and bamboo clusters.

◈ Driving a green vehicle brings you luck and protection.

◈ The springtime is your lucky season; major plans and decisions are more likely to succeed at this time.

◈ The early morning sunrise hours are auspicious and most productive for you.

◈ When arranging your desk or study area, sit facing east, if possible.

◈ Friends and romantic partners with a higher Wood element score, and those born into Wood years, will be your best companions.

◈ Seek outdoor activities associated with the Wood element.

◈ Choose a career associated with the Wood element: writing, publishing, paper products, art, clothing/textiles, architectural design, home construction, furniture design, horticulture, landscaping, forestry, gardening, education, teaching, counseling, child care, pharmacy/medical.

If Fire is your lucky element:

◈ The Southern cardinal direction is lucky.

◈ Live in a home that faces south.

◈ Choose a bedroom on the south side of your home.

◈ Keep the southern windows open with breezes coming in from this direction.

◈ Orient your body with your head toward the South (Fire) when sleeping for optimum health.

◈ A wooden bed is recommended.

◈ Your lucky color is red; wear it often.

◈ When decorating your office or home, use a red, maroon, and/or rose color scheme, and include candles and other sources of heat and light.

◈ Driving a red car brings you luck and protection.

◈ The summer or hot season is lucky for you. Schedule important events and decisions at this time, especially during the hot midday hours.

◈ When arranging your desk or work area, sit facing south, if possible.

◈ Friends and romantic partners with a higher Fire element score, and those born into Fire years, will be your best companions.

◈ Seek activities associated with the Fire element.

◈ Spicy foods are good for you.

◈ Choose a career that corresponds with the Fire element: electrician, electrical engineer, solar and nuclear energy, combustibles (fuel, gas, petroleum), volcanology, firefighting, television, radio, the fine arts, publishing, motion pictures, scriptwriting, the cosmetic industry, fundraising, public relations.

If Earth is your lucky element:

◈ The cardinal Center is lucky for you.

◈ Live in a home that is in the center in some way—perhaps in the center of a complex or in the middle of a development.

◈ Choose a bedroom in the central area of your home.

◈ Your lucky colors are earth tones and yellow; wear them often, particularly for important meetings.

◈ When decorating your office or home, use jade gemstones, and use a palette of earth tones and yellow.

◈ Driving a tan, yellow, or brown car brings you luck and protection.

◈ The transitions between the seasons and late summer are your lucky times. Schedule important events and make decisions at this time.

◈   Friends or romantic partners with a high Earth element score, and those born into earth years, will be your best companions.

◈   Some sweet foods are good for you.

◈   For your health, you need a certain amount of moisture; wet and rainy weather actually benefits you.

◈   Take good care of your digestive system and joints, especially your knees and back.

◈   Choose a career associated with the Earth element: feng shui, geology, anthropology, running a pawnshop or an antique store, any of the service professions, the food industry, accounting, law, funeral/mortuary services, farming, land development, landscaping, pottery/statuary, animal care/veterinary services.

If Metal is your lucky element:

◈   The Western cardinal direction is lucky for you.

◈   Live in a home that faces west.

◈   Choose a bedroom on the west side of your home.

◈   Keep the western windows open, with breezes coming in from this direction.

◈   Orient your body with your head facing west while sleeping for optimum health.

◈   A metal bed is recommended.

◈   Your lucky colors are white and silver; wear them often.

◈   When decorating your home or office, use metal statues, wind chimes, vases, urns, and all kinds of ironwork. Choose a white and silver color scheme.

◈   Driving a white or silver car brings you luck and protection.

◈   The fall is your lucky season. Major plans and decisions are more likely to succeed at this time.

◈   When arranging your desk or office, sit facing west, if possible.

◈   Friends and romantic partners with a higher Metal score, or those born into a Metal year, will be your best companions.

◈   Wearing jewelry, especially sterling silver, is very auspicious for you.

◈   Spicy foods are good for you.

◈   For optimum mental health, laugh and surround yourself with cheerful people as much as possible. Choose comedies when selecting movies for entertainment, never horror.

◈   Take good preventative care of your respiratory and digestive systems.

◈   Seek leisure activities associated with the Metal element: martial arts, fencing, shooting, hunting, working out in a gym.

◈   Choose a career associated with the Metal element: banking, finance, stocks/bonds, jeweler, canned food products, mining, automobile and aircraft manufacturing, law enforcement, computers, singing, acting, composing music, museum curator, martial arts, gun shop owner, ballistics, weapons expert, security systems, video and audio recording and equipment, the military, law.

If Water is your lucky element:

◈ The Northern cardinal direction is lucky.

◈ Live in a home that faces north.

◈ Choose a bedroom on the north side of your home.

◈ Keep the northern windows open with breezes coming from this direction.

◈ Waterfront properties are most auspicious.

◈ Orient your body with your head toward the North (Water) while sleeping for optimum health.

◈ A metal bed or a waterbed is recommended.

◈ Your lucky colors are black and dark blue; wear them often.

◈ When decorating your home or office, incorporate fountains and artwork featuring bodies of water, and use a dark blue color scheme.

◈ Driving a black or dark blue car brings you luck and protection.

◈ Wintertime or the cold season is your lucky season; major plans and decisions are more likely to succeed at this time.

◈ The hours between 9 p.m. and 1 a.m. are auspicious and most productive for you.

◈ When arranging your desk or study area, sit facing north, if possible.

◈ Friends and romantic partners with a higher Water score, and those born into Water years, will be your best companions.

◈ Seek leisure activities associated with the Water element: swimming, boating/sailing, diving, waterskiing, ice skating, going to the beach, and fishing.

◈ A little salty food is good for you and allows you to retain potassium, calcium, and other electrolytes.

◈ For optimal mental health, don't dwell on your fears and anxieties. Avoid horror genres when choosing movies and books.

◈ For best physical health, sometimes you need cold and/or wet (humid) weather.

◈ Take extra care of your excretory and reproductive systems.

◈ Wearing any kind of jewelry brings you luck.

◈ Choose a career associated with the Water element: fishing, shipping, owning a tea house or restaurant, magician, philosopher, oceanographer, swimming/diving, moving, travel, public relations, diplomat/peacemaker, psychology, humanitarian efforts.

Unlucky Elements

If Wood is your unlucky element:

◈ Avoid making major decisions during the springtime.

◈ Avoid living in a home that faces east or has a main entrance on the east side.

◈ Don't choose a bedroom on the east side of the house.

◈ Keep eastern windows closed.

◈ Avoid winds or air coming from the east.

◈ Don't orient your body with your head toward the east while sleeping.

◈ When arranging your office or desk, avoid sitting facing east.

◈ The color green is unlucky for you; avoid wearing it.

◈ In the office, avoid using green folders, a green mug, green pens and pencils, and evergreen plants.

◈ Keep plants and foliage to a minimum when decorating your home.

◈ Do not drive a green car or one with a green interior.

◈ Sour foods are not good for you.

◈ For your mental health, avoid anger like the plague.

◈ For your health, limit your exposure to excessively windy/breezy weather.

◈ Take extra-good care of your nervous system, liver, and gall bladder.

◈ Watch for sprains and strains in your arms and legs.

◈ Avoid careers associated with the Wood element, as they tend to be unproductive or frustrating for you.

If Fire is your unlucky element:

◈ The Southern cardinal direction is unlucky for you.

◈ Avoid living in a home that faces south and using southern-facing entrances.

◈ Summertime or the hot season is unlucky for you. Postpone important events and decisions until the cooler months.

◈ Years and months of the Snake (June) and Horse (July) can be difficult for you.

◈ Don't schedule important meetings between 10 a.m. and 1 p.m.

◈ Don't choose a bedroom on the South side of the house.

◈ Dry Southern winds can dry your mucous membranes and cause bronchitis.

◈ Don't orient your head toward the south while sleeping.

◈ Don't sit facing the south while working.

◈ Avoid wooden beds.

◈ Don't wear red, and avoid using a red, maroon, or rose color scheme in your home and office.

◈ Don't drive a red car.

◈ Spicy foods are not good for you.

◈ Avoid careers linked to the Fire element.

If Earth is your unlucky element:

◈ The central area of your home and office are not auspicious for you.

◈ Do not choose a bedroom in the central area of your home.

◈ Avoid wearing yellow, brown, or tan, and jade gemstones or jewelry.

◈ Avoid earth tones and yellow when decorating your house.

◈ Don't drive a tan, yellow, or brown car.

◈ Sweet foods are not good for you.

◈ The periods between seasons are your difficult times.

◈ For your health, avoid exposure to excessively wet and rainy weather. Guard against fungus and mold allergies.

◈ Take good care of your digestive system and joints, especially your knees and back.

◈ Avoid careers associated with the Earth element.

If Metal is your unlucky element:

◈ The Western cardinal direction and area of your home is not auspicious for you.

◈ Do not live in a home that faces the west or use west-facing entrances.

◈ Keep western side window(s) closed.

◈ Do not choose a bedroom on the west side of the house, or orient your body with your head toward the west while sleeping.

◈ Avoid sleeping in a metal bed.

◈ Dry weather and arid westerly winds dry your mucous membranes and can cause bronchitis.

◈ Avoid using white and silver when decorating your bedroom, office, and study areas.

◈ Avoid using ironwork and metal elements around your home or office.

◈ Avoid wearing white or silver for important meetings.

◈ Do not drive a white or silver vehicle.

◈ Fall could be your most difficult season.

◈ Your least productive hours are between 5 p.m. and 7 p.m.

◈ Avoid living in geographical areas that are excessively dry.

◈ Be cautious around machinery and metal objects, including knives and weapons.

◈ Avoid professions associated with the Metal element.

If Water is your unlucky element:

◈ Wintertime or the cold season is your difficult period.

◈ The months of Pig (November) and Rat (December) can be touchy; you must guard against illness during these times.

◈ The Northern cardinal direction is not good for you.

◈ Do not use the northern entrances to your home.

◈ Do not choose a bedroom or study area on the north side of your home.

◈ Do not orient your head to the north when sleeping.

◈ Avoid a metal bed or a waterbed.

◈ Do not wear black or dark blue very often, if at all.

◈ Avoid a black or dark blue color scheme for your home and office.

◈ Do not drive a black or dark blue vehicle.

◈ Salty foods are not good for you, so try to limit them.

◈ For optimum health, do not dwell on fears or allow yourself to worry excessively.

◈ Avoid living in geographical areas that are excessively wet or cold.

◈ Be cautious while engaging in water sports and around lakes, oceans, streams, and ice.

◈ Avoid careers associated with the Water element.

Part II

Zi Wei Dou Shu: The Emporer/King of Stars

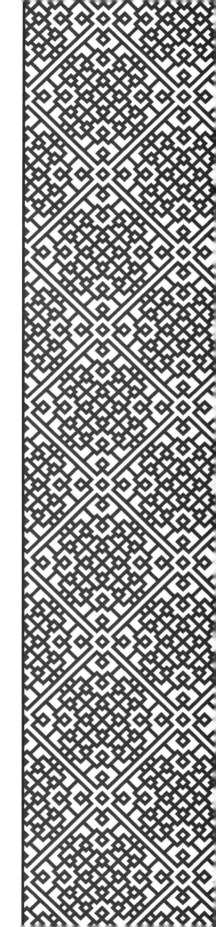

Chapter 9

What Is Zi Wei Dou Shu?

There is a great disparity between Eastern and Western cultures in how our earthly existence is viewed. Traditionally, Westerners do not believe that fate and luck can be pre-determined. It is widely believed that achievement is by choice, fortitude, and diligence, and that even those from meager beginnings can rise to the highest pinnacles. The idea of set limitations or a predetermined fate is frowned upon or labeled as superstition. However, consider how many intelligent people you have known who, despite their education, talents, and countless opportunities, never rise above a certain level. Conversely, think of all the rather dull, lazy, and/or painfully incompetent people who always happen to be in the right place at the right time, and who catapult to the top, seemingly without effort.

For the ancient Chinese, fate, or *ming shu*, was a reality. They believed that each of us is born with our own abilities and limitations, and it is by acknowledging and accepting these limitations that we can walk upon a life path leading to success rather than to frustration. They also believed that our fate is determined at birth. Our *xian tian*, or inherent temperament, is set and cannot be changed. It is what we start out with in life, our natural endowment, so to speak. The birth chart is akin to a schematic or owner's manual for an intricate machine. Your personal specifications, model number, operating instructions, and potential hazards are just some of the enlightenments included. The manufacturer has designed our "default" specifications, such as our birth date and time, our parents, our siblings, our ethnicity, and so on. These are all fixed and cannot be changed.

However, there are aspects of your life that can be changed through luck, or *yun*. Yun is that which we have control over through our efforts and character. In the West, luck is similar to chance in that it is random and can only be understood or manipulated by using statistics and probability. Therefore, if luck is random, it is also unpredictable. The Chinese concept of luck, however, is different in that it is cyclical and predictable. In this respect, it is similar to the orbits of the planets. An orbit is not a random movement, but passes through space and time in a specific predictable pattern. This makes it knowable. Likewise, if we know the status of our luck at any particular time, we can base our actions and our choices on how strong or weak it is. Understanding our strong points, our weaknesses, our potential, and our limitations is a move in an empowering direction. The art of fortune-telling originated from the desire to understand an unknowable world. It allowed the ancients to gain a semblance of control over seemingly haphazard natural occurrences. It is no wonder that the art of divination has become an integral part of the Chinese culture.

Over many millennia, the Chinese people created, documented, and correlated five major arts and philosophies. To understand the Zi Wei Dou Shu chart, you must begin by understanding and distinguishing these five major arts:

1. *Shan Shu* is the cultivation of an area of interest while living in seclusion. *Shan* (literally, "mountain") refers to practices that were carried out traditionally in the mountains. This included all religious beliefs and practices (Buddhism, Confucianism, and Taoism), cloistered meditation, and Zen. Areas of study such as qigong, martial arts, and white tiger/jade dragon sexual cultivation, are included in Shan Shu.

2. *Yi Shu* refers to the practice of Traditional Chinese Medicine (TCM), which includes acupuncture, reflexology, and spiritually guided life-force energy expressed physically. Also included in Yi Shu is the study and use of traditional Chinese herbs, tonics, and remedies. Other holistic practices, such as macrobiotics and the pursuit of physical longevity are included in Yi Shu, as well.

3. *Xiang Shu* is the practice of face-reading and palmistry. It also includes feng shui, the Chinese art of placement. Feng shui (literally, "wind and water") is about controlling our luck by observing and manipulating our environment and the objects in it, using the knowledge of yin and yang and the five elements.

4. *Bu Shu* is the art of divination through omens, signs, and oracles. This earliest means of interpreting the will of heaven was by reading cracks on animal bones or tortoise shells. It dates from around 2,600 BC or even earlier. The interpretations are represented by the 64 I-Ching hexagrams grouped into the eight sections of the Ba Gua. The I-Ching, or Book of Changes, is one of the oldest of the classic Chinese texts. Used as a system of divination by casting yarrow stalks or coins, the I-Ching remains the most timeless of the Bu Shu arts.

5. *Ming Shu* (literally, "magical calculations") consists of the various means for predicting the future, most notably astrology. Ming Shu centers on the dynamic yin/yang balance of opposites and all life events (both helpful and harmful) as a process. By analyzing character traits and potentials using the year, month, day, and time of birth, we can predict and understand events. This is what Ming Shu and, really, all forms of fortune-telling are about.

The Zi Wei Dou Shu chart is a profound form of Ming Shu. Although Zi Wei is the highest form of astrology and divination, it is an art form that anyone with dedication can master. There is a certain karmic element in Chinese astrology: what we are now is a result of what we were in a past life, and where we end up in the next life will be a result of what we make of this present life and what baggage we bring with us. That being said, success in life is, by and large, based on five areas of influence or importance:

1. Ming: Our fate, which is set at birth and cannot be changed, but can be known.

2. Yun: Our luck, which is predictable, but fluctuates with time.

3. Feng shui: Our environment, which may be manipulated to reach higher levels than what our fate and luck would allow.

4. Dao de: Our virtue and character, which brings good karma and goodwill.

5. Du shu: Our education and effort, the grunt work of life.

The Zi Wei Dou Shu chart is undoubtedly the Dewey decimal system of humanity and the universe! We will learn this amazing system by becoming familiar with the Zi Wei chart and its life palaces in the chapters to come.

Chapter 10
The Life Palaces

The Zi Wei Dou Shu chart shows each decade of life in detail, as various stars move in and out of 12 life houses, or "palaces." Everyone is born with a certain *ming* (socioeconomic status) and a certain *yun* (ups and downs of life). Together, *ming yun* makes up each person's fate or destiny. Ming is the life overview and does not change; yun, however, fluctuates from childhood through old age. One of the 12 zodiac animal symbols (earthly branches) is also assigned to each of the 12 life palaces, and "flavors" both the decade and that specific area of life. When these 12 palaces are examined together with major and minor stars, one can discover the fate (ming yun) and destiny (tian ming) of one's life.

The Zi Wei Dou Shu chart is plotted in a large rectangle (symbolizing a rice field), and is divided into 12 houses or boxes (plots of land). These are called the 12 life palaces, or *quons*. The destiny, or ming, palace is the most important of these 12, and is main focal point of a Zi Wei Dou Shu birth chart. It embodies the sum and substance of a person and discloses his or her destiny. The self, destiny, character, and one's likely fate are all found here. It divulges whether one's general outlook, inborn capabilities, level of achievement, and basic character will be influenced by the imperial (royal) energies, the martial (fighting) energies, or the psycho-social (humanitarian) energies. It shows one's physical characteristics, as well.

The Life Palaces

The parents palace reveals your parents, family background, elders, teachers, authorities, bosses, and clients. The energies located in this palace describe the social situation of your parents, their luck, how well they get along, their longevity, and their relationships with their children, if any. This palace also indicates the prospect of inheritance.

The karma palace reveals your moral, spiritual, and emotional aspects. It tells you how happy you will be, your outlook on life, your biases, and your hang-ups. Next to the destiny palace, this is the most influential of the life palaces. It can improve a bad destiny or deteriorate a good one. The Karma palace also reveals your spiritual enjoyment, your peace of mind, and how well you enjoy life. It is a looking glass into the soul, the emotions, and the intellect.

The property palace reveals the wealth, property, inheritance(s), investments, and standard of living you will have. It also governs your living environment and home life, whether good or bad.

The career or vocational palace reveals the type of career that is most suitable for you. It also determines the amount of success you can expect in your chosen career. Your work environment is also displayed here. When this palace is studied in connection with the destiny palace, it can also indicate how you should develop your career, and whether you are suited to work for others or be in charge of your own business.

The friends or peers palace reveals the kind of peers and colleagues you will have and whether they will be helpful to you or not. It also represents the relationship you have with your friends. Staff, close friends, colleagues, and people who work with you or for you are found here. This palace is also an important complement to the destiny palace. Here, you can spot whether your friends and colleagues are loyal or if they will betray you. The stars found placed here will describe your friends or hired help.

The travel or others palace reveals what kind of traveling you will do and whether you will need to relocate to achieve success. Journeys, voyages, changes, and international matters are manifest in this life palace. This house explains your dealings with others and with foreign countries. It also shows your level of sociability and describes your outward appearance.

The health or physical body palace reveals your general health, the kinds of diseases you may encounter, and your longevity. This palace is also concerned with your mental health, as well as any injuries caused by accidents.

The wealth or prosperity palace reveals your finances, and can predict whether you will have steady income or encounter losses. It also tells whether income is from hard work or from other sources, such as inheritance or windfall. Wealth, luck with money, and lifetime fortune are all found in this life palace. This palace is also studied in conjunction with the career palace to determine how you should make your money, and to find your wealth luck (strong or weak) and earning capacity.

The children or minors palace reveals whether you will have children or not, and what your relationship with them will be. It also reveals subordinates, employees, and students. This palace is also concerned with your ideas, or brainchildren. Information concerning minors, children, offspring, nieces, nephews, and all of your descendants will be found in this life palace.

The spouse or marriage palace reveals the character of your spouse and your love relationships. This palace can also predict whether your marriage will end in divorce, and whether there will be affairs. Spouses, unions, and intimate relationships will be addressed in this palace. Your love affairs, married life, sexual behaviors, and the number of marriages you will most likely have can also be found there. The stars present in this palace will indicate what kind of person your spouse is and whether or not your marriage will be successful and happy.

The siblings palace reveals the relationship between you and your siblings, as well as their respective characters. Step-siblings, business partners, and colleagues are revealed here, as well. This palace divulges the relationship with your siblings, your business partners, your schoolmates, and whether your relationships with these people will be helpful or not.

We will discuss these 12 palaces and the meanings of the individual stars occupying these palaces in greater depth in the next chapters.

Zi Wei Do Shu analysis shows the positions of both beneficial and detrimental stars in each palace to predict an individual's most likely future and fate. The 12 animal signs have fixed positions in the chart, while the location of the various palaces will differ based upon the birth information. For example, the Tiger may correspond to the siblings palace or the wealth palace, depending whether the person is male or female, and yin or yang. A life palace is affected and influenced by the palaces adjacent to it, opposite it, and in one of the harmonious trines below it. The opposite palace is a mirror image of the palace being analyzed. These two palaces will have the strongest influence on each other.

Interpretation begins with looking at where the major influential stars are placed. "Trines" (palaces that form a triangle) are strongly connected and highly relevant to each other in the interpretation. The harmonious connected palace trines are:

◈ Destiny/wealth/career palaces

◈ Children/elders/friends palaces

◈ Relationship/karmic luck/travel palaces

◈ Siblings/property/health palaces

The palaces directly opposite each other are interdependent and influence each other, as well. These include:

◈ The destiny and travel palaces

◈ The siblings and friends palaces

◈ The relationship and career palaces

◈ The children and property palaces

◈ The wealth and karmic luck palaces

◈ The health and elders palaces

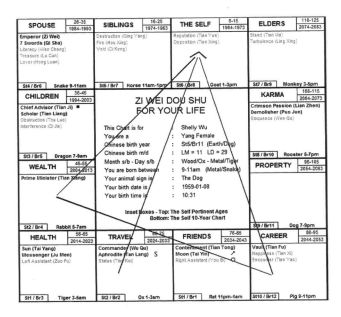

When looking at your chart, notice which decade (life palace) you are currently transitioning through. Each life palace brings a new beginning—the opportunity to change your way of life and to see things in a different light. A change in decades can also bring upheavals, but the middle of each decade is considered the pinnacle or high point of the period. The palace corresponding to your chronological age and the energies contained there are also very important to examine, along with the self/destiny palace itself.

In addition, one of the 12 animal earthly branches is assigned to each of your life palaces. Each animal provides a distinct character, or "flavor," to its particular palace. For example, if you find the Goat in your offspring palace, this indicates creative, gentle, and artistic children who will tend to be lazy and difficult to motivate. If the life palace is:

◈ In the sign of the Rat, it indicates concealment, charm, and frugality, and the yang Water element.

◈ In the sign of the Ox, it indicates endurance, stability, family, firmness, and country, and the yin Earth element.

◈ In the sign of the Tiger, it indicates nobility, courage, and action, and the yang Wood element.

◈ In the sign of the Rabbit, it indicates the arts, refinement, detachment, and the yin Wood element.

◈ In the sign of the Dragon, it indicates unpredictability, drama, and vitality, and the yang Earth element.

◈ In the sign of the Snake, it indicates wisdom, gradual development, physical beauty, and the yin Fire element.

◈ In the sign of the Horse, it indicates decisiveness, freedom, and speech, and the yang Fire element.

◈ In the sign of the Goat, it indicates artistic talent, propriety, benefactors, wealth, and the yin Earth element.

◈ In the sign of the Monkey, it indicates youthfulness, humor, and irrepressibility, and the yang Metal element.

◈ In the sign of the Rooster, it indicates application, resourcefulness, and candid speech, and the yin Metal element.

◈ In the sign of the Dog, it indicates anxiety, watchfulness, and loyalty, and the yang Earth element.

◈ In the sign of the Pig, it indicates resignation, chivalry, and physical comforts, and the yin Water element.

We will discuss these animal signs and the special features they contribute in Chapter 13. Next, let's examine the various stars and their meanings.

Chapter 11
The Stars

The traditional Zi Wei Dou Shu chart is calculated using the Chinese lunar calendar and the four pillars, which shows the placement of the King/Emperor star. This star, called *Zi Wei*, is the most powerful ming energy and the pivotal point around which the entire chart is built. In Taoist spiritual cultivation, the Zi Wei star has great significance and is considered the pathway to the highest spiritual realms. Take special note of where this star energy is located in your chart.

Before beginning, it will be helpful to familiarize yourself with the placement of the main star energies in your life chart. Depending on your birth data, stars will be placed in one of 12 life palaces in your birth chart. The star(s) placed in your destiny palace is referred to as your Ming Gong Zhu Xin ("main life star") and specifies your personal characteristics and general luck in life. Following is an overview of the main star energies and a general description of each one.

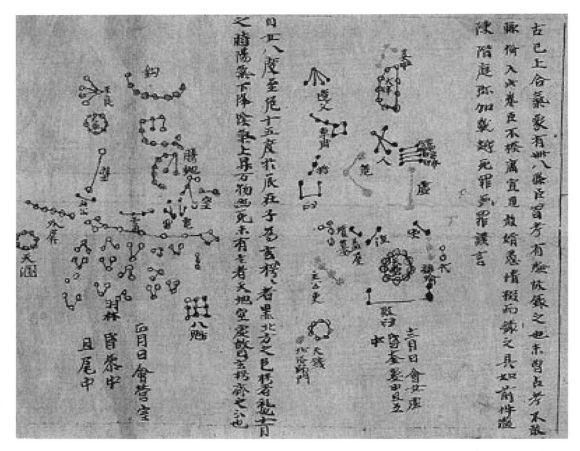

An ancient Chinese star chart.

The four major imperial (ruling) energies are the "leaders":

1. Zi Wei, the emperor/purple pole king star.
2. Tian Fu, the vault (palace treasury) star.
3. Wu Qu, the commander (armor, dance, music, finance) star.
4. Tian Xiang, the prime minister (involvement, mirroring) star.

The four major martial (aggressive) energies are the "fighters":

1. Sha Qi, the seven swords (general, power) star.
2. Po Jun, the demolisher (pioneer, ruinous) star.
3. Lian Zhen, the crimson passion (virtue/vice, virgin/villain) star.
4. Tan Lang, the Aphrodite (flirting, opportunity) star.

The six major psycho-social/literary (humanitarian) energies are the "supporters" and the "adapters." The supporters:

1. T'ai Yang, the sun (male yang energy, reputation, the crowd).

2. Ju Men, the messenger (giant gate, gloomy) star.

3. Tian Ji, the chief advisor (intelligence, motor, heavenly machine) star.

The adapters:

1. T'ai Yin, the moon (female yin energy, emotion, intuition).

2. Tian Tong, the contentment (lucky waif, unity) star.

3. Tian Lang the scholar (honest, blessings) star.

The four lucky "royal jewels":

1. Zuo Fu, the left assistant (aid, deputy I) star.

2. You Bi, the right assistant (support, deputy II) star.

3. Tian Kui, the status (laureate, stardust, angel I) star.

4. Tian Yue, the reputation (medal, delight, angel II) star.

The two major indicators of intelligence and talent:

1. Wen Qu, the eloquence (dissertation, arts minister) star.

2. Wen Chang, the literacy (discourse, literary minister) star.

The four life milestones, or "signposts":

1. Hong Luan, the lover (wedding, romance) star.

2. Tian Yao, the encounter (romance, socializing) star.

3. Tien Xi, the happiness (joy, birth) star.

4. Tian Xing, the opposition (punishment, sternness) star.

The main energy of travel, change, and movement is Tian Ma, the steed (pegasus, winged horse) star. The main energy of money is Lu Cun, the treasure (completion and abundance) star.

The six dark stars (Sha Yao) are the harmful or difficult energies:

1. Huo Xing, the fire (turmoil) star.

2. Ling Xing, the turbulence (siren, thunder) star.

3. Qing Yang, the destruction (trouble, lance) star.

4. Tuo Luo, the obstruction (worry, armor) star.

5. Di Kong, the void (nullity, misfortune, abrupt interference) star.

6. Di Jie, the interference (calamity, fate, constant interference) star.

Following is an explanation of the major star energies we will use in Zi Wei Dou Shu. The significance of the 14 major stars will be explained further in subsequent chapters.

The Rulers: The Four Leading Imperial Energies

Zi Wei is the leading energy of Chinese astrology, and the focal point of the Zi Wei Dou Shu astrological system. Where it falls in your chart will be the most powerful, favored palace and decade of your life, so take special note of where it is placed. Zi Wei is authoritative, pioneering, conquering, farsighted, and hot tempered. The emperor star brings luck, wealth, authority, prestige, protection and rescue to the life palace in which it is placed. It displays all the qualities of a strong, wise, courageous monarch and a natural pioneering leader who looks at the big picture. This energy is ambitious, demanding and royal. When placed in the destiny palace, its imperial status is ambitious. With favorable stars accompanying it, it produces virtue, leadership, and strong character. When it is found alone or accompanied by bad stars, it can become an irrational, hotheaded, extreme energy. It is very lucky to find the Zi Wei star placed in your career palace, as you may achieve greatness in your line of work.

Tian Fu symbolizes guarding the treasury of the King and represents great wealth. It is often found in the destiny of great leaders and entrepreneurs. This major prosperity energy quietly builds fortunes. When found in a woman's chart, Tian Fu reveals a sophisticated and powerful woman who may also feel isolated at times. Prosperity, possessions, preservation, caution, and integrity are the cornerstones of this energy. Found in the destiny palace, it produces a careful and detail-oriented person whose parents and elders played an important role in forming his or her character and personality. Where this star is placed is where you will amass substantial possessions and assets. It suggests inheritance and benefactors. If poorly aspected, however, it can represent the white collar criminal or embezzler.

Wu Qu is a powerful leadership energy of the imperial or royal group. It represents authority, and is responsible for entrepreneurial skills. This star indicates good luck with wealth, but also solitude, firmness, stubbornness, independence, and impatience. This star represents a strong and decisive leader who figuratively leads his or her army into battle. It symbolizes wealth, leadership, entrepreneurial skills, handicrafts, and metals. Wu Qu is an independent and impatient energy, sometimes bringing activity prematurely in the life palace where it falls. It reveals a strong personality when found in the destiny palace.

Tian Xiang is the emperor's minister, or general. It is a more passive energy than the other three imperial stars, and prefers to stay in the background rather than be in the spotlight. It is a loyal and hardworking energy of support and assistance. Bearing the seal of the emperor, Tian Xiang endorses verdicts that are passed down; therefore, its outstanding features are responsibility and accountability. This star also indicates the presence of a "right-hand man." With Tian Xiang, things tend to occur in twos. It represents repetition, helpfulness, responsibility, influence, and embroilment. Whether it is influencing for good or becoming embroiled in the bad, when placed in the destiny palace, it reveals an individual who gets involved.

The Fighters: The Four Major Martial Energies

Sha Qi is the leading energy in the martial group of stars. Its key features are aggression, force, severity, strategy, independence, and aloofness. It is an ambitious, reckless, hasty energy, with organizing and ordering abilities. When found in the destiny palace, this conquering star presages disquiet and chaos. It reveals clashes, power struggles, and turmoil in the family of origin. It also expresses an iron will, eager and conquering, and a cool-headed strategist, the power behind the scenes that must be reckoned with. Sha Qi commands respect in any life palace; however, it brings obstinacy, chaos, and rashness. This most powerful of the martial energies reveals much turbulence, adventure, excitement, and even danger wherever it is placed. Its specific location indicates an area of our lives where we tend to see things in black and white and where we will not compromise.

Po Jun is an ambitious, intense, and authoritative force. A mover by nature, this star embraces new things and discards the old and the obsolete. Po Jun is a strong and aggressive star that shatters and builds back up; it breaks down the old and makes way for the new. If it is found in someone's destiny palace, it can make that person pretty tough to get along with. Guided properly, however, he or she can learn to create good things from bad situations. This star is all about "out with the old and in with the new." It is also hope and fiery passion. This star energy is constantly in the thick of battle; it charges forward, uproots, tears down, and rebuilds. The life palace where this star is placed experiences upheavals and a lot of reorganization, so if you find this star in your chart, hold on tight and fasten your seat belt!

Lian Zhen is either pure virtue or pure vice, wickedness or innocence. This potent star reveals love affairs, aggression, and power. It indicates either respectability, honesty and virtue; or debauchery, dissipation, and licentiousness. This star has no grey areas or temperate middle zones. Lian Zhen is also one of the "peach blossoms"—those stars associated with romance, flirting, and love affairs. If positively positioned, it can bring success in dealing others; if poorly positioned; it can bring problems with infidelity, gambling, or alcoholism. Lian Zhen, the crimson passion star, represents blood relatives, emotions, the arts, politics, privacy, and femininity having to do with yin, female energy. You can expect plenty of romantic drama wherever this "passion" star is placed in a chart.

Tan Lang can either motivate you to get much done or make you very greedy and impatient. Like Lian Zhen, it is an energy of extremes. It is the main energy of sexuality and danger. Love and problems linked with love occur wherever it is placed. Its essence is indulgence, sensuality, and magnetism. Wherever it appears in your chart, you will experience relationship turbulence in that palace. This star can indicate exhaustive rounds of meetings and celebrations. It has also been connected with fights, power struggles, and triumphs or painful failures in matters of the heart. Those with this star in their destiny palace are full of sensual magnetism, artistic talent, and eloquence. These souls love the arts, languages, good wine, romance, and all the pleasures of life. They may have an interest in metaphysics, religion, and spirituality, as well, but can become frustrated with their desires and impetuous nature.

The Supporters and Adapters: The Six Major Psycho-Social/Literary (Humanitarian) Energies

T'ai Yang, the sun, brings a very public and "in the limelight" energy. It indicates success and popularity in whatever life palace it is found in, and bestows intellectual, literary, and public performance abilities. In the destiny palace, it indicates success with a crowd, being in the public eye, awareness, and prominence. It is associated with pure male yang energy, masculinity, openness, status, and elegance. The sun stands for all that is fiery, cleansing, and positive. Elegant, expansive and expressive, it can reveal an area of life in which we are boastful and blunt.

Ju Men represents a great door; as such, it is the energy of transition and change. It also represents the mouth, and reveals a convincing orator and speaker. Similar to Mercury in Western astrology, it is the astral signature of a consummate communicator. It also symbolizes litigation, privacy, caution, and suspicion. Positively expressed, Ju Men provides a good reputation and outstanding rhetorical or speaking abilities. Negatively expressed, it can indicate a problem with "foot-in-mouth disease." Flanked by negative stars or the obstruction catalyst, it also reveals gossip, slander, or a bad reputation. It is not an auspicious energy to find in the spousal palace, where it can indicate controversy and arguments with a partner.

Tian Ji represents strategic planning and innovative ideas. A pioneering spirit, mechanical ability, and physical agility are brought to the life palace in which this star is placed. Its presence indicates movement and speed, and can reveal that money is active, dynamic, and moving. However, the inconsistency of this energy can cause instability. When found in the destiny palace, this star indicates someone who learns quickly and is a great negotiator. In the relationship palace, it can represent instability in a marriage.

T'ai Yin, the moon, represents the mother, the wife, and the earth, as well as "feminine" traits: imagination, psychic skills, sensitivity, and intuition. It imparts spiritual gifts and a strong sense of the sacred. It also represents the soft nest of comfort and abundance. If the moon falls in your destiny palace, it bestows psychic and extrasensory abilities. Reproduction, tranquility, and hidden wealth are also gifts of the moon. It reveals a strong connection with women and accumulates wealth quietly and discreetly.

Tian Tong is the relaxed lover of life. It represents emotions, enjoyment, entertainment, and sensitivity. This star is gentle, fun-loving, and concerned with humanitarian pursuits. It is contented by nature, retiring, and happy to let others shine. It is a gracious energy that leans toward spiritual subjects. This star reveals a person who will spend much time in idealistic contemplation and daydreaming. It is a leisurely, joyous, and peaceful star; those with it in their destiny palace are frequently polite, humble, and at ease. They see no point in antagonizing others unnecessarily. If Tian Tong is found in the career palace, any pursuit that involves enjoyment, recreation, leisure, or entertainment is highly favored. This star of contentment also brings a love of luxury and the good things in life. It can indicate where you will have an easy time of things and where you might be a little lazy. It also indicates what aspect of life you will tend to over-romanticize.

Tian Liang represents protection, longevity, lateness, solitude, aging, and litigation. This beautiful energy also symbolizes the elderly, medication, insurance, accounting, numbers. It also has the practical connotation of housing and the environment. This is a lucky star that upholds principles and embraces orderliness. Its presence in the destiny palace ensures that major disasters and setbacks are averted, or at least diminished. Tian Liang represents passage through challenging times before reaping the harvest. Found in the destiny palace, it reveals an individual who has the ability to turn bad things into good, misfortune into good fortune. It is often found in the destiny palace of religious leaders. Those with Tian Liang in their destiny palace help others enthusiastically, in the way an older sibling takes care of the younger ones. This star is the astral signature of a priest, judge, or high-ranking official. Problem-solving and longevity are the key words with this star.

The Four Lucky Royal Jewels

Zuo Fu brings yang Earth assistance and enhances wealth and prominence. It stands for honor, kindness, and acceptance. It is a helper in whatever life palace it is found. It always strives for the best, motivating the individual to reach for the stars. Ever the optimist, this star can see its way safely through any crisis. It possesses great karmic wealth and brings relief and protection from the difficult stars or the obstruction catalyst.

You Bi brings glowing, yin Water energy, which symbolizes a constant flow of assistance, particularly in matters of the heart. It is most fortunate to find it in your relationship palace. It supplies honor, kindness, and assistance in whatever life palace it is found in.

Tian Kui brings yang Fire energy and assistance from benefactors, elders, mentors, superiors, and generally supportive people. It makes recognition possible. The entire life is enhanced by this star. If you find it in your chart, expect the appearance of helpful individuals. Where Tian Kui shines, luck seeks you out in the form of a timely helping hand. You may not be able to recognize these helpful people in the moment, but you will definitely recognize this star's influence in retrospect.

Tian Yue brings yin Fire energy and opportunities stemming from rules, regulations, policies, and authorities. It brings favorable contacts with the opposite sex and helpful people who guide, protect, and points you in the right direction. The life palace where it is placed, suggests from where this assistance will come.

The Major Indicators of Intelligence and Talent

Wen Qu brings yin Water energy, natural talent, and intelligence. It indicates a more informal or nontraditional education, especially in metaphysics or spiritual subjects. Verbal skills are indicated, as well as fame from utilizing this gift. Wen Qu often appears in the destiny palace of those with artistic abilities and highly developed senses. This artistic star also applies to self-expression, music, and the performing arts.

Wen Chang brings yang Metal energy, sophisticated social graces, the gift of persuasion, and a more formal or traditional education in time-honored subjects. Exceptional talent in writing is indicated, as well as the potential to become famous by using this talent. This profound teaching and speaking energy brings lively, intelligent, lucid, and clear discourse. This star also concerns literary matters, public education, and the arts.

The Signposts: The Four Life Milestones

Hong Luan indicates marriage, romantic associations, love, and possible pregnancy. It is a milestone energy of love and romance. When this star aligns every 12 years with the original birth position, romantic turning points (betrothal, engagement, or beginning of new relationship) occur. This enchanted star forms an auspicious pair with the happiness/joy (birth) star.

Tian Yao indicates enjoyment of the arts and a knack for entertaining, networking, and merriment. It is also an energy of romance—clandestine affairs, chance encounters, and frivolous romantic pursuits are found along its path. With Tian Yao, an accidental encounter with a stranger can send the heart aflutter and become the turning point in a once ordinary existence. The life palace this romantic energy is placed in will indicate the decade when this encounter will occur, and will delineate the specifics surrounding that encounter.

Tien Xi indicates celebrations, great happiness, and favorable activities. Like Hong Luan, it can presage major events such as marriage, the birth of children, or an important karmic relationship.

Tian Xing brings difficult situations and "heavenly punishment." Found in the destiny palace, it reveals an influential, fair-minded person with good leadership skills who can also feel alone and isolated at times. This milestone star can indicate a great loss, a death, or catalytic event that brings with it a new perspective on life. It reveals new horizons that open from adversity.

The Main Energy of Travel, Change, and Movement

Tian Ma brings pure yang Fire, mobility, activity, and action wherever it is found. This "steed" is a powerful stallion that flies across the sky with both grace and fortitude. In the destiny palace, it reveals an extremely busy individual—the busier, the better, in fact. Wherever it is found in the birth chart will divulge where change, travel, working abroad, or definite forward movement will occur. Tian Ma shines on high achievers.

The Main Energy of Money

Lu Cun (literally, "keeping wealth") generates wealth in the life palace in which it is found. This star contributes cautious and conservative yin Earth energy that brings financial and spiritual wealth and the ability to avert danger. A definite enhancer to any life palace, this star brings the good to new heights and thwarts the detrimental powers of dark stars. It is an indication of added protection and prosperity. This is also a healing star—the decade in which it is active will see a new beginning in which past hurts or losses are finally put to rest.

The Six Sha Yao: The Dark Stars

These stars hamper the major stars and negate the positive effects of assisting energies. In certain situations, they can help mitigate the negative impact of some of the more difficult stars (such as Sha Qi) in a life palace. The palace or palaces in which these stars are located will indicate when you will be prone to misfortune or untimely death caused by accidents or unexpected tragedies. From a more positive perspective, they exist as a balancing factor and as a reminder of possible misfortune.

Huo Xing generates unfavorable events that tend to happen quickly. Its presence casts a dark cloud over the palace in which it is placed. When found in the destiny palace, it reveals an intense, controlling, and abrasive personality, especially when it is accompanied by other negative stars. In the destiny palace, it can indicate a difficult childhood, an early departure from the parents, or other events that occur suddenly. More positively, the yang Fire energy of this star brings troubles into the open.

Ling Xing also brings troubles and unfavorable events that occur quickly; however, these troubles tend to be hidden. Sneaky and underhanded efforts may accompany this nasty little star. Found in the destiny palace, it reveals a chaotic childhood and many challenges throughout life. Like Huo Xing, it also indicates an intense, abrasive, and controlling personality.

Qing Yang brings yang Metal energy in the form of problems that arise suddenly, sabotage, and failure. These issues are in the open and can be predicted, but not avoided. This star indicates weapons, fighting, and injury, and can bring life-threatening accidents or attacks.

Tuo Luo brings yin Metal energy, and represents unexpected problems that are hidden. Its unexpected and undetected nature causes anxiety that can only be felt by the individual. Obstacles, blockages, and delays may cause additional difficulties. Tuo Luo doesn't bring life-threatening danger, but it can tarnish a good reputation with gossip or mockery, so caution is required wherever this star falls in a chart. Be on the lookout for subversive gossip or slander from within your own ranks.

Di Kong brings wastefulness and the careless squandering of resources. This yin Fire energy produces an unstable income and encourages unwise expenditures. This is obviously an unlucky star to find in the wealth palace. This dark star brings with it at least one major setback in the palace in which it is placed.

Di Jie is the most powerful of the dark stars. It brings turbulence, loss, crisis, and destruction in the palace in which it is found. This star wrecks havoc on the emotions and will reveal where constant interference will occur. The location of this energy can also give you the reason for your present existence.

Chapter 12
The Catalysts

In addition to the major stars, there are four powerful transforming stars, or catalysts. These life-changing stars are significant keys to interpreting your birth chart. The four transforming catalysts enhance, change, and convert the various stars in different ways. Three of the catalysts are helpful, and one is harmful.

The Helpful Catalysts

◈ Power: Hua Quan (literally, "transforms authority") brings direction, authority, power, influence, and supremacy. This catalyst transforms the star it is attached to into leadership, a high level of management, clout, ambition, determination, and initiative. It transforms into authority and is associated with the Fire element.

◈ Fame: Hua Ke (literally, "transforms success") brings success, reputation, recognition, self-satisfaction, and fame. It transforms into a good name and is associated with the Wood element. Personal distinction shines wherever this catalyst is placed.

◈ Prosperity: Hua Lu (literally, "transforms fortune") enhances the flow of fortune and good luck. It transforms into riches and is associated with the Metal element. It enhances the flow of fortune, riches, and luck. It also turns unfavorable matters favorable.

◈ Obstruction: Hua Ji (literally, "transforms to trouble"), also called the tribulation or cloud catalyst, is a very inauspicious star that negatively transforms other stars, situations, and life palaces. It usually indicates obstacles and dangers and is associated with the Water element.

The effects of Hua Quan on other stars

Zi Wei: Power makes the quick-tempered emperor positively hot-headed. This is a stubborn, unbending energy, especially early on in life. When the power catalyst is attached to this potent star, it produces a megalomaniacal greed for power. Great temperance will be required in order to achieve success.

Po Jun: The talent to create something from nothing as well as the drive to break through barriers into new territory will be enhanced. The power catalyst attached to Po Jun creates a powerful desire to mastermind projects and launch new ventures.

Wu Qu: The power catalyst augments the effects of the commander, which suggests that you will take charge and have a firm hold on the reins of the life palace in which it is placed. When these two stars combine, it reveals self-empowerment, quick reactions, and intense responses.

Tan Lang: The ability to mingle and entertain is enhanced. Socializing, indulgence, sensuality, physical attraction, and metaphysics are the key words when these two are attached. Power comes from attention from the opposite sex, meeting influential people, and social networking.

Tian Ji: The positive characteristics of movement are enhanced. Mobility, strategy, and agility are all improved in the life palace in which this combination is found. With Hua Quan, new ideas come quickly, but an excess of choices creates indecision.

Tian Tong: This star's ability to build fortunes from nothing is enhanced by the power catalyst. Hua Quan also insures that the contentment star will have an aptitude for handling people, and will be able to enjoy leisure activities of all kinds.

T'ai Yin: The moon's wealth energy and money management abilities are boosted by the power catalyst. Power comes, in part, from female supporters and associations with women. Calm, composed, and a good strategist, you plot for victory in a subtle way.

T'ai Yang: The sun's outgoing energy, status, and reputation are all boosted by the power catalyst. The sun with the power catalyst attached brings the public, crowds, and male supporters to your aid. Bored with tedious details, you excel at managing the larger picture.

Ju Men: These two stars together yield an articulate master communicator, public speaker, or spokesperson. Found in one of the relationship palaces, however, this combination reveals censure and disputes.

Tian Liang: Power added to the scholar enhances protection, solitude, litigation, and injury. This combination yields the inspector: loyal, lonely, and litigious, the inspector examines matters closely and reports its findings to the emperor. If these stars combine in your chart, being less rigid will serve you better. Focus on academic achievement, knowledge, and good judgment.

The effects of Hua Ke on other stars

Zi Wei: The emperor star with the success catalyst attached invites fame, recognition, and celebrity through groundbreaking organization and leadership. If accompanied by dark stars in the same life palace, this combination can indicate gaining popularity through misguided or unwise channels.

Wu Qu: The success catalyst brings in wealth, along with both personal and professional success. Known for contributing to a fiery temperament, this combination produces a fiery temperament and a blunt, direct personality. Exercise tact in your communication with others.

Tian Ji: The success catalyst highlights the chief advisor's fondness for strategy and action. Depending on the life palace in which it is placed, this combination achieves fame and success via novel or groundbreaking ideas. This combination reveals an intelligent, physically active fast learner.

T'ai Yang: Success comes with this combination via the media, the entertainment industry, or the public. However, this may be an isolated type of success. You would be advised to look closer at real benefits rather than at the mere pursuit of reputation. Despite being popular with many, you will always chafe against rivalry and experience a certain amount of competition.

Tian Liang: This is a very auspicious combination of energies and assures success in higher learning, knowledge, and literary pursuits. Focus more on academic pursuits rather than material wealth or possessions. Academic success will bring you the fame, good reputation, and material blessings you desire.

Tian Fu: The success catalyst adds power to the palace vault's many resources. This combination can create a financial wizard, especially when it is found in the wealth palace. It is indicative of success with money and an aptitude for financial topics.

Wen Qu: The success catalyst influences how a person promotes his or her name, reputation, and image. This combination reveals success due to eloquence, and in realms such as metaphysics, astrology, and spirituality.

Wen Chang: This combination reveals a talent for writing and all visual forms of art. You have a more formal education, skill set, and scope of knowledge. The success catalyst brings good luck in examinations. There is a potential for fame with this special combination of star energy and transforming catalyst.

T'ai Yin: With this combination, wealth, success, reputation, and fame come from associations with females or feminine supporters. You will be well-known within a close circle of friends, and you may use your intuition and psychic skills to become prominent.

The effects of Hua Lu on other stars

Po Jun: With the wealth catalyst attached to the demolisher star, don't be afraid to discard anything that doesn't work, as success will result from innovation and restructuring.

Wu Qu: With this combination, you have your own particular brand of skills and talent. You are an expert when it comes to putting plans into operation, and will be greatly rewarded financially for this. Take the reins of any project and see good results. Prosperity comes to the palace where it is found.

Lian Zhen: This star is all about the emotions; with the fortune catalyst it brings happiness (emotional wealth). Blood relations or family members bring assets or introduce auspicious situations.

Tan Lang: This combination assures wealth if you become involved in socializing and other pleasurable activities. Look for the hidden financial opportunities in networking, partying, and social liaisons. Physical exercise, dance, and body-building can also bring financial rewards.

Tian Ji: This combination of stars ensures unimpeded progress and quality of work in your career, but not necessarily great wealth. You are a good strategist and will gain financial security through lateral moves, rather than by climbing the corporate ladder.

Tian Tong: This combination brings great pleasure in life due to wealth, but not necessarily from a large fortune or inheritance. Wealth comes from activities connected with enjoyment, entertainment, leisure, or recreation. The wealth catalyst also uses OPM (other people's money) to quietly build a fortune from nil.

T'ai Yin: The fortune catalyst multiplies the moon's wealth energies tenfold. Fortune is accrued via associations, businesses, trades, or partnerships with women.

T'ai Yang: The sun symbolizes the crowd, the media, public matters, and males; from these sources, wealth flows. When the fortune catalyst combines with sun, the level of wealth will depend on the reputation, status, and relative level of fame of the individual. The more popular and famous the person is, the more money he or she will enjoy.

Ju Men: With this combination, fortunes can be made via speaking skills. Professions that entail public speaking, debate, or conversational skills, such as the law, sales, teaching, or training others, are favored financially.

Tian Liang: This combination indicates heirlooms, estates, or a family business. Many obstacles must be overcome to achieve wealth, and even then, problems may still follow. Financial corruption looms with this combination, so it is critical to keep all financial transactions aboveboard and beyond reproach.

The effects of Hua Ji on other stars

Wu Qu: In this placement, the commander's quick thinking lacks thoroughness. The obstruction catalyst has the commander's hands tied, so this combination is inauspicious for the execution of plans. There will also be dangers related to sharp metal objects.

Lian Zhen: This combination indicates diseases of the blood and heart and gynecological disorders. Serious physical injuries with blood loss, as well as problems and disputes with blood relatives, are also indicated. The life palace in which this difficult combination rests will likely reveal a broken heart.

Tan Lang: This star has to do with sensuality, socializing, and vices; obstructed, it can become self-indulgence, trouble with love affairs, compulsions, and addictions. Trouble and scandal can come from socializing and hobbies. When this combination is found in the health palace, sexually transmitted diseases can be a result.

Wen Qu: With this combination, there will be a price to pay for errors in speech. Slander, arguments, and endless complaints are the maladies that come with an obstructed Wen Qu. Failure is brought on by arrogance or trying to impress others with your knowledge.

Wen Chang: Errors in the written word cause calamity. Libel, problems with legal documents, and difficulties regarding certifications, diplomas, or licensing occur when the obstruction catalyst is attached to Wen Chang. Double-check all documents and contracts.

Tian Ji: This difficult combination results in impediments to movement and obstructions to the thought process. Long-term plans fail to materialize, and there may be losses and delays in travel plans, deliveries, and/or communications. Bad choices and failure are brought about by too many changes.

Tian Tong: The emotions take a devastating blow with the obstruction catalyst attached. Life may feel like an emotional rollercoaster. Mental stress can block the enjoyment of leisure activities and entertainment. Also, watch out for disasters at play, during free time, or while vacationing.

T'ai Yin: This combination reveals emotional problems, self-imposed stress, and inner turmoil. It is a very bad omen for wealth investments. The moon is dealt a blow by the obstruction catalyst, investment are devastated. Problems with women, as well as economic loss brought about by a female, are also indicated.

T'ai Yang: An obstructed sun indicates disapproval from crowds, the majority, and/or the public. In eclipse, ailments of the head, eyes, and heart will come to light. When an obstructed sun is placed in any of the "people" palaces, be cautious of males and of attracting disputes easily.

Ju Men: Ju Men represents the mouth; combined with Hua Ji, it can cause you to speak tactlessly and/or bring problems having to do with speech. Arguments, slander, lawsuits, and suspicions are all exacerbated with this combination, and losses may remain undiscovered.

Chapter 13

The Self or Destiny Palace

The focal point of a Zi Wei Dou Shu chart is the self or destiny palace, or *ming gong*. It reveals our pre-heaven nature (*xian tian*)—our personal specifications as determined by our manufacturer. This includes our temperament, talents, character, and potential. We look to the destiny palace to uncover our natural abilities and to see what life will bring our way.

Depending on the date and time of your birth, one or more of 14 major stars will end up in your self/destiny palace. The star energies placed there are your "main life stars," or *ming gong zhu xin*. Using the CD that accompanies this book, calculate your Zi Wei Dou Shu chart to determine which major star or stars reside in your destiny palace.

Write your destiny stars here: _____
_____.

Write down which of the 12 animal branch signs occupies your destiny palace: _____.

The first step of Zi Wei chart interpretation is figuring out which soul group you are a part of. This is determined by what stars are placed in your destiny palace. The soul groups include the imperial (royal) group, the martial (aggressive) group, and the psycho-social/literary (humanitarian) group. Yours is an imperial or royal destiny if Zi Wei, Wu Qu, Tian Fu, or Tian Xiang resides in your destiny palace. These energies are found in the self/destiny palaces of the "rulers"—those souls favored by birth to lead, to guide, and to be key figures in this life. Yours is a martial destiny if Tan Lang, Po Jun, Lian Zhen, or Sha Qi dwells in your destiny palace. These energies are the fiercest of Chinese astrology and are found in the self/destiny palaces of the "fighters"—those souls characterized by ambitious, aggressive, and authoritative action. Yours is a psycho-social/literary destiny if Tai Yang, Ju Men, Tian Tong, Tian Ji, Tian Liang, or Tai Yin is placed in your destiny palace. These energies are found in the self palaces of the "teachers"—those governed by intellectual, diplomatic, or humanitarian interests and pursuits.

What does it mean if one of the following major royal (ruling) energies is found in the destiny palace?

Zi Wei: It can be lonely at the top. Ask anyone with Zi Wei in his or her destiny palace. Rulers and leaders by divine right, those with the emperor star placed in this critical life palace are the movers and shakers in this world. This star represents luck, wealth, authority, prestige, protection, and rescue. Those with this most powerful of stars in their destiny palace are fated to be amongst the "royal class"—those souls favored by birth to lead and to guide. This leading energy of the Chinese astrological cosmos indicates a sophisticated, thoughtful, responsible person who may experience isolation and loneliness at times. In general, however, this is a strong individual with an objective, farsighted view of life, able to see problems and challenges from all angles. There is an excellent chance for fame and fortune. This is the classic archetype of the wise king or queen who is destined to be in a position of authority and respect. This king of stars rules the destiny palaces of judges, magistrates, CEOs, and heads of state. The Zi Wei star reveals a soul who is authoritative, pioneering, conquering, and farsighted. Those with this royal destiny are leaders in every sense of the word. They wield influence and evoke respect.

Tian Fu: This star in the destiny is the astral signature of a kind, conservative soul who has chosen to lead a peaceful life. With Tian Fu (literally, "heavenly luck") in the destiny palace, finances play an important role, for better or for worse. Typically, however, it is for the better. This star reveals a conservative and grounded person who enjoys success in examinations and who will have every opportunity to obtain great wealth. This is mainly due to a careful, cautious, and frugal nature. Parents and elders play an important role in forming this person's character and personality, which will ultimately bring success later on in life.

Wu Qu: Ah, the power behind the throne! This major star is the leadership energy of the royal group, responsible for entrepreneurial skills, good luck, and wealth, but also solitude, firmness, and stubbornness. Someone with this star in his or her destiny palace will be the "right hand man" of the powerful and the influential. It also indicates a strong, resilient, independent, yet impatient person who may tend to act too quickly. Wu Qu represents a decisive leader who figuratively leads his or her army into battle. People with Wu Qu in their destiny palace are usually slightly built, but with a resounding, resonant voice. This individual will be an implementer, involved with the details of putting ideas to work.

Tian Xiang: This star provides support and backing to others, as well as personal responsibility and influence. Also known as "the mirror," Tian Xiang indicates duplication or twinning: a twin birth, two sets of parents, two professions, two marriages, and so on. With this energy of duplication, you must be careful not to repeat past mistakes; break out of this circle and you will move forward. You are likely cautious and methodical, and recognized by the care and detail you apply to your dress, home, and office. Responsible and interested in details others may have missed, those with Tian Xiang in their destiny palace are upright and fit into everyone's ideal of the big brother or sister. This helpful soul goes out of his or her way to help others. Whether it is influencing for good or getting embroiled in the bad, this is a person who loves to get involved.

What does it mean if one of the following major martial (aggressive, fighting) energies is found in the destiny palace?

Sha Qi: Power, prestige, and presence are the calling cards of this major martial star. These are the bad boys and girls extraordinaire, and danger is their middle name. Risk, turmoil, and, above all, supremacy is their lifeblood. Sha Qi (literally, "bad energy") is the leading star of the ambitious, reckless, and hasty martial group. It brings suspicion and obstinacy, as well as an iron will, an aggressive character, and fearsome efficiency. With Sha Qi, there will always be a certain amount of going against the grain and chafing under restraint.

Po Jun: Brave, arrogant, and dashing, those with Po Jun presiding over their destiny palace reinvent themselves daily and change their colors more often than a chameleon. Today's project is not necessarily tomorrow's passion, as this star represents "out with the old and in with the new." Hopefulness, aggressiveness, a pioneering spirit, and an impulsive temperament characterize those with Po Jun ruling their destiny palace. They are always willing to dissolve ties to make way for bigger and better things. They also love to take risks. They can't tolerate a stagnant environment, but change for the sake of change may overtax their resources. For the person with Po Jun in his or her destiny palace, it will always pay to create a realistic plan and review it thoroughly before taking on the next battle.

Lian Zhen: A little moderation may be sorely needed in the lives of those with Lian Zhen placed in their destiny palace. An "either-or" star, it reveals aggression, debauchery, and licentiousness, or respectability, honesty, and virtue. There is no temperate middle zone with this star presiding over the destiny palace. It represents blood relations, emotional issues, the arts, politics, and privacy. As one of the peach blossom stars, it is also associated with romance, flirting, and affairs. Expressed positively, it can bring success and popularity. If poorly positioned, obstructed, or expressed negatively, however, Lian Zhen may produce a shady individual who has problems with infidelity, gambling, or alcoholism. Excesses may cause confinement.

Tan Lang: This star is a major martial energy of extremes. In the destiny palace, it is a magnet to the opposite sex. It offers that certain special something to the personality, sexual pizzazz perhaps. Tan Lang has no trouble attracting playmates; in fact, those with this major martial destiny fairly ooze sensuality. Because this is a martial star, however, it is also the energy of danger, of love affairs, of intense sensuality, and of problems linked with love. This energy also represents indulgence, sensuousness, the physique, and divination. This star in the destiny palace reveals an individual who is curious, who loves metaphysics and spirituality, and who will have an appreciation for the arts, languages, good wine, romance, and all the sensual pleasures of life.

What does it mean if one of the following major civil/literary (humanitarian, diplomatic) energies is found in the destiny palace?

T'ai Yang: If you are outgoing, popular, and always on the go, Tai Yang may be shining prominently in your destiny palace. The sun reveals a passionate, romantic, radiant soul who is more of a visionary. Male or female, those with Tai Yang placed in their destiny palace have a powerful masculine presence that is chivalrous, noble, generous, altruistic, just, and blunt. They were born to be in the public eye in some way. Women are especially competent and ambitious. Tai Yang is an especially good energy for those in the legal profession, broadcasting, and any kind of publicity. Although people with this destiny are able to gain prominence with ease, it will be to their advantage to look for real and tangible benefits rather than merely running after fame and reputation.

Tai Yin: The moon represents the mother, the woman, night, the earth, female yin energy, imagination, sensitivity, intuition, reproduction, tranquility, and wealth. It imparts spiritual gifts and reveals a strong connection to women, as well as to men with the moon in their destiny palace. Calm and composed, with intuition bordering on the psychic, those with Tai Yin in their destiny palace are subtle, deep, and discerning. Intelligent, well-known, and blessed with a first-rate social life, Moon natives enjoy the arts and spiritual subjects immensely. However, due to their extreme sensitivity, they can be overly emotional and too easily influenced. These traits are enhanced if the person was born at night.

Tian Tong: This political and civil-minded star bestows intellectual, literary, administrative, and diplomatic abilities and qualities. This humanitarian, gracious, gentle, and peaceful energy brings unity to others. The primary faults here are unpredictability and a lack of perseverance. This is a contented, relaxed lover of life who is happy to let others shine. Goals and ambitions are accomplished through persuasion, reason, and teamwork. Tian Tong represents protection, longevity, and solitude.

Tian Liang: This star is a power-hitter in the civil/literary group of stars. Those souls with Tian Liang in their destiny palace enthusiastically help others, just as an older sibling cares for the younger ones. This star represents protection, longevity, lateness, solitude, control, and litigation. It represents slow, organic growth, older individuals, and long-standing employees and associates who are in it for the long haul. Tian Liang is serious, responsible, disciplined, and a little sad. When found in the destiny palace, it often indicates difficult beginnings, Herculean efforts, and then success. This person has the ability to turn bad into good; the good things tend to come later, after difficulties. With this star in the destiny palace, there is also a tendency to take on too much. This person will have few real friends, but they will be helpful and faithful, and often older. Many with this destiny become priests, judges, or high-ranking officials, or engage in some type of public service.

Tian Ji: Tian Ji represents unity and friendship, the heavenly force that drives the cosmos. This star of intelligence also represents strategy, a pioneering spirit, mechanics, and agility. Placed in the destiny palace, it reveals much movement—changes of residence, traveling, and new locales are likely in store. Those with Tian Ji in their destiny palace are often the power behind the throne. When we pick a flower, we must not forget the humble bee that has prepared it; likewise, when we applaud a great singer, we must also remember the sound engineer and stage manager who made it all possible. Similarly, Tian Ji reveals a soul who keeps everything and everyone on track.

Ju Men: The "giant gate" star indicates that there will be many passages and changes in this life. This energy has a touch of mystery and the unusual. It represents the mouth, and as such reveals a convincing orator or spokesperson. The spoken word and verbal communication will play an influential role for better (eloquence, articulation) or for worse (misunderstandings, verbal gaffes, and gossip). Those with this star in their destiny palace are consummate communicators; as such, they are ideally suited for careers in teaching, sales, politics, entertainment, and the law. When Jun Men rules the destiny palace, prosperity does not come without competition and a great deal of discussion. Careers that rely on eloquence gain wealth; however, be cautious and guard against arguments and/or contentiousness.

One of the 12 animal signs of the zodiac, or earthly branches, also occupies each life palace, including the destiny palace. This animal sign may differ from the sign of your birth year. Find the animal sign that is placed in your destiny palace. Then, look at the three directional groups, each of which contains four signs of the zodiac.

Group 1 consists of the "four corners," or "posts": the Monkey, Snake, Tiger, and Pig. These four branches reside in one of the four corners of a Zi Wei chart. They have to do with movement, so someone with his or her ming gong (destiny) in a post corner will be perpetually on the move. Each of these signs may also invite problems unnecessarily, so the person's life path will likely be more chaotic in general.

When the Monkey is found in the destiny palace, the person will be:

◈ Changeable and contradictory—confident one minute, unsure the next.

◈ Clever, witty, and skillful.

◈ Poised and graceful—will excel at the performing arts.

◈ Inconsistent—will experience great gains, but also great losses; better to marry late in life.

When the Snake is found in the destiny palace, the person will be:

◈ Calm on the outside, but grasping and tumultuous on the inside.

◈ Perfectionistic—can miss the main point by focusing on the details.

◈ Savvy in business and prudent with money, but can invite problems in these areas unnecessarily.

◈ Ambitious, busy, and hardworking, but often lonely.

When the Tiger is found in the destiny palace, the person will be:

◈ Generous, big-hearted, popular, and admired. Enjoys as wide circle of friends.

◈ Wealthy; making money comes easy.

◈ Active and always on the move; prefers life in the fast lane.

◈ Tough and resolute; able to endure hardships.

◈ Does not like to be told no.

When the Pig is found in the destiny palace, the person will be:

◈ Sensitive and compassionate, and easily moved to tears by beauty and nature.

◈ Intelligent, generous, serious, busy, hardworking, kind, and gentle-hearted.

◈ Prone to invite problems.

Group 2 consists of the "four directions": the Rat, Rabbit, Horse, and Rooster. Each of these four branches resides in a palace associated with the four cardinal directions—North, South, East, and West. When these peach blossom branches (sometimes called the "four failures") are found in someone's destiny palace, partying, romancing, drinking, gambling, and overspending are usually the result. The arts or entertainment are where this person's charisma will help him/her succeed.

When the Rat is found in the destiny palace, the person will be:

◈ Distinctive, strong-willed, poised, smart, and practical, with uncommon judgment.

◈ Emotional, sensual, and easily seduced.

◈ Fair and even-handed, and devoted and loyal to friends; treats others equally regardless of socioeconomic status.

When the Rabbit is found in the Destiny palace, the person will be:

◈ Physically weak in younger years, yet stronger in adulthood.

◈ Sensitive, observant, and clever, and able to see what others cannot.

◈ Sociable and romantic; easily involved in affairs of the heart.

◈ Sometimes suspicious and cautious due to prior difficulties.

◈ Prone to arguing over trivial matters.

◈ Prone to feeling isolated; has few friends.

When the Horse is found in the destiny palace, the person will be:

◈ Witty, friendly, talkative, with a sunny personality, but sometimes prone to arrogance.

◈ Financially successful if brought up well.

◈ Lecherous and exploitive if brought up poorly; will flatter others in order to please.

When the Rooster is found in the destiny palace, the person will be:

◈ Dependable, hardworking, and observant.

◈ A lover of romance; can easily fall prey to affairs of the heart.

◈ Strong and independent; not open to the suggestions of others.

◈ Arrogant a times, which alienates others or causes failure.

◈ An avid traveler, particularly to historical sites.

Group 3 consists of four earths: the Dragon, Ox, Dog, and Goat. Each of these four branches is associated with the earth element. They are also called the "four graves," as earth is heavy and not easily moved or changed. Those with one of these branches placed in their destiny palace are easily stuck and have difficulty with change. They must work harder than others; success comes only when they can break out of their ruts.

When the Dragon is found in the destiny palace, the person will be:

◈ Intelligent, clever, and helpful.

◈ Courteous, well-mannered, and tranquil in appearance.

◈ Balanced, impartial, relaxed, unhurried, and sometimes a bit indecisive or too casual.

◈ Can invite sorrows or disaster with few to turn to.

◈ Loathe to move out into the world; personal development and success come after moving away from home or birthplace.

When the Ox is found in the destiny palace, the person will be:

◈ Private, independent, and solitary; not easy to get to know.

◈ Willing to take on responsibilities without considering personal interest; has a strong desire for praise.

◈ Trusted and respected, but quick to anger when crossed.

◈ Loathe to move out into the world; personal development and success come after moving away from home or birthplace.

When the Dog is found in the destiny palace, the person will be:

◈ Steady and tranquil externally, but prone to depression.

◈ Needy; requires much support and encouragement from loved ones.

◈ Smart, hardworking, and efficient, and not afraid to fight for justice.

◈ A bit unmotivated; often needs prompting and external motivation to succeed.

◈ Loathe to move out into the world; personal development and success come after moving away from home or birthplace.

When the Goat is found in the destiny palace, the person will be:

◈ Shy and sensitive, and seemingly easily irritated; actually quite strong inside, however.

◈ Idealistic, but must push hard to achieve concrete goals.

◈ Narrow-minded; does not readily accept outside opinions or ideas.

◈ Isolated and lonely at times.

Now, let's move on to the other 11 palaces.

Chapter 14
The Elders, Parents, and Authority Palace

This palace tells of the relationship with one's parents, mentors, teachers, and superiors. It also indicates the prospect of inheritance. As always, the stars found in this particular palace will tell a lot about how your relationships with these people will play out.

Zi Wei: This star reveals well-to-do, financially secure parents. However, they will also be opinionated, strong-willed, and unyielding, which can make you feel overpowered, overwhelmed, or overshadowed.

Tian Fu: This star reveals dedicated parents who leave behind an inheritance or legacy for you. They will have money and property, and will treat all of their children well. This star reveals a very auspicious and affectionate relationship.

Wu Qu: There will be unfavorable relationships with parents and elders due to a lack of attention or separation. Your parents will be strong-willed, unyielding, tough, and/or severe.

Tian Xiang: Your parents are prudent, stable, and open to their children's ideas. They provide a loving and supportive environment. This star also indicates a possible duplication of parents (two sets of parents or godparents).

Sha Qi: This star presages angry, hot-tempered parents with strong personalities and iron wills. This makes for a chaotic living situation. Sha Qi indicates clashes, power struggles, and a controlling, disciplinarian environment.

Po Jun: This star reveals unusual parents who may be different from the norm. The parents are self-starters, entrepreneurs, or business owners who are progressive in their thinking, but your relationship with them is rocky. Po Jun tears down in order to rebuild, which makes this an inauspicious placement. It may reveal squandering or wasting family wealth or inheritance.

Lian Zhen: Masked by outwardly cordial natures, parents or those above you will be difficult to read. Parents are emotional, changeable, and unpredictable in their behavior. This star also indicates a difficult relationship with all blood relatives due to poor communication.

Tan Lang: This indicates a good relationship even though your parents tend to be selfish. Very complex family dynamics, with a possible Oedipal or Electra complex with the opposite sex parent, are also indicated. The relationship with your parents is not an easy one, especially with your mother.

T'ai Yang: The sun in the elders palace indicates parents with outgoing, energetic, and radiant personalities. It reveals that your father and any other male figures will have a profound effect on you. However, much controversy surrounds your parents, elders, and/or senior employees.

Ju Men: This star placed in the Elders palace reveals arguments with your parents or authority figures. Verbal activity is prominent in the family of origin as are unnecessary squabbles. Parents quarrel endlessly between themselves.

Tian Ji: Instability is brought to the elders palace by the presence of this star. Much movement and activity is centered on your parents. Their life together is unstable, and too much change brings distractions and a restless mind.

T'ai Yin: As a feminine energy, the moon places an emphasis on the mother when it is found in the elders palace. Difficult or adverse stars in the same palace can indicate a rocky or lukewarm relationship with the mother or female family members, particularly during the formative years.

Tian Tong: This relaxed, peaceful lover of life represents emotions, enjoyment, and sensitivity. In the elders palace, it reveals clients, parents, and authority figures who are warm, loving, and emotional. However, their assistance to you is limited.

Tian Liang: Tian Liang represents the elderly, medication, insurance, accounting, numbers, and the armed forces. Its presence in the elders palace suggests a supportive environment with a significant age difference between you and your parents. You were likely born late into their relationship.

Chapter 15
The Karmic Luck Palace

This palace reveals your thoughts and behavior. It also describes the temperament you were born with, how happy you will be, and how long you will live. This "happiness" palace, as it is sometimes called, indicates your spiritual enjoyment and peace of mind, as well as your emotions and demeanor. Read on to find out how the major stars will affect your karmic luck palace.

Zi Wei: You may frequently feel lonely, isolated, and/or misunderstood by others. Opinionated, forthright, fair, and open-minded, you are an individual of high integrity. You have a strong will and natural leadership abilities.

Tian Fu: You search for stability, but experience constant turbulence and changes. You have a steady and forgiving mind, but too many changes and upheavals can undermine this stability. You have an open mind, a cheerful disposition, and a positive outlook on life.

Wu Qu: The commander in your karma palace reveals that you will enjoy abundant material possessions and make a very good living. Wu Qu represents wealth, leadership, trading, crafts, and entrepreneurial skills; your success comes by means of these channels.

Tian Xiang: This placement reveals that you are an upright, sympathetic, idealistic individual who tends to miss opportunities. You have a duel nature, and disturbing thoughts repeat themselves. Embroilment in conflict may be a common theme in your life.

Sha Qi: You will enjoy hustle and bustle in all aspects of your life. An indication of inner turmoil and disquieting thoughts. You

159

are active both mentally and physically, with deep poetic thoughts; however, this placement also brings isolation and a very challenging path in life.

Po Jun: This symbolic "army breaker" star reveals a busy, active individual who has revolutionary and inventive ideas to offer. You are gallant, impulsive, brave, a bit arrogant, and dashing, as well as a quick and decisive thinker.

Lian Zhen: Representing opportunity, indulgence, and sensuality, Lian Zhen in the karmic luck palace represents decadent pursuits. Gambling, drinking, and carousing can lead to trouble. Your preference for excitement creates a lack of focus and undisciplined thoughts.

Tan Lang: This star indicates a materialistic, hedonistic, leisure-oriented individual who can also be philosophical and artistic. Flirting, creative thinking, and idealism preoccupy your mind. Decadent pursuits and self-indulgence can lead to trouble.

T'ai Yang: You bring a feverish intensity to all that you do, particularly to your love affairs and romances. Benevolence, openness, and status-seeking are the key ingredients of your mental makeup. You excel in macro-management, leaving the details to others. This placement makes for a better planner than an implementer.

Ju Men: This placement brings suspicion and unsettling thoughts. You are a serious personality, and tend to become depressed and anxious about too many small matters. Your inherently distrustful character can lead to obsessive thoughts. For you, too many details creates confusion, so keep things simple.

Tian Ji: You are constantly thinking and pondering; sometimes racing thoughts occupy your mind. You crave new knowledge and love to uncover primordial mysteries. You have a tendency to dabble in many fields, so your arsenal of facts is eclectic.

T'ai Yin: You will have a talent and passion for metaphysics and the full breadth of spiritual subjects. As a devoted student of the arts, religion, and spirituality, both psychic and material wealth can be yours. You will spend much time in quiet contemplation.

Tian Tong: With this star in your karmic luck palace, you have the ability to build something from nothing. Your placid exterior hides deeply felt emotions. This placement produces a jovial, happy personality—you are a gentle soul who is happy to let others shine. Kindhearted and easy-going, you are a contented and good-natured person.

Tian Liang: You are likely a spiritual, cerebral, classy, and highly opinionated individual. Life is enjoyable in a large part because of your love for and enjoyment of the arts. You also enjoy antiques and learning about history. You tend to process things slowly and deliberately, and you possess an extraordinary memory.

Chapter 16
The Property Palace

This palace governs how many assets (property, investment, inheritances) you are likely to have. It also describes your living environment, whether good or bad. Read on to find out how the major stars affect this palace.

Zi Wei: With this placement you will prefer to live on high ground, literally—at higher altitudes, in mountainous areas, or on one of the top floors of an apartment building. You have the ability to become very rich and may inherit an estate or property.

Tian Fu: You may own quite a few properties and have numerous types of residences during your life. Tian Fu reveals that this will be very profitable for you. This star indicates large properties, an inheritance, and the accumulation of tangible resources.

Wu Qu: You most likely live in a residence of quality and will own several significant properties in your lifetime. You have the capacity to accumulate significant assets with this placement, but it is quality, not quantity, that distinguishes this star from some of the other financial energies.

Tian Xiang: This star offers prosperity due to inheritance. It also suggest a doubling of some sort: two different family homes, a duplex, a two-storied home, or a residence that has two separate living areas. This star is very dependent on surrounding stars.

Sha Qi: This is a very unstable influence to find in your property palace. With other more favorable stars present or with the fortune catalyst attached, however, you could be very successful buying and selling real estate. The home is self-contained and free-standing, not an apartment.

Po Jun: You will be happiest in a state-of-the-art, modern home filled with gadgets and the latest electronic devices. You may own property later in life; however, you may tear it down and renovate it beyond recognition.

Lian Zhen: Your assets are either up or down; you will experience wealth followed by bankruptcy, possibly multiple times. There will be frequent moves and much work involved in maintaining your properties. You may live with blood relatives, especially female ones, at some point in your adult life due to a downswing in luck.

Tan Lang: You could reside near a sports arena, a fairground, or an entertainment venue. In business, you could be very successful through socializing, entertaining, sports, or physical therapy. Mixing business with pleasure will be most lucrative for you; you have the ability to generate considerable wealth through your social network.

T'ai Yang: With the sun in your property palace, you will prefer sunny or temperate climates, and your home itself will be bright and sunny. Frequent moves and multiple living environments are often seen with this placement. Constant changes or shifting of circumstances prevent your retaining property and assets.

Ju Men: You reside on low ground, in a shady area, and/or on one of the lower floors of an apartment building. Your home may be near a courthouse, restaurant, or pub. There will be a preference for exciting, noisy, or busy environments. Be cautious of lawsuits or verbal disputes on or regarding your property or home.

Tian Ji: Frequent moves are in store for you if Tian Ji is placed in your property palace. Traveling and new locations are the norm with this star/palace combination. Much movement surrounds your home; you may live close to a busy intersection, train station, or airport.

T'ai Yin: The moon in your property palace reveals your preference for peaceful, quiet living arrangements and a tranquil lifestyle. You probably dislike metropolitan areas, preferring instead to live in the country or a quiet, hidden area.

Tian Tong: Property comes to you rather easily; you may receive an inheritance in the form of a large sum of money, trust account, or property. You will be most prosperous and productive in a peaceful environment. You may have experienced upheavals in your home early on in life.

Tian Liang: This star is a blessing to find in this palace, as it is an indication that you will inherit property. You are also likely to remain in one house for a considerable length of time. The family home may be old and/or near a retirement home, hospital, or older establishment.

Chapter 17
The Career and Vocation Palace

This palace indicates how you should develop your career, and whether you are better suited to work for other people or go into business for yourself. It indicates what kind of career you should pursue and what sort of achievement you can expect. Read on to find out how the major stars affect this important life palace.

Zi Wei: You work with powerful, successful, and influential people. You hold down a job that requires self-sufficiency and independent thinking. Whether you work for a small business or in a large company, you will have a say in the day-to-day decision-making. This can also be an indication of entrepreneurial endeavors; you may launch and manage your own business or even establish a global firm or multinational enterprise.

Tian Fu: A steady career path awaits you. You would be a boss, CEO, manager, or director in any financial line of work. Although work is steady, it can also lack a certain creative spark and become dull. Success for you will lie in secure and safe business operations.

Wu Qu: You have special skills and/or areas of expertise. This star is found in the career palaces of engineers, mechanics, technical personnel, and those involved in military service. You will be employed in an independent, self-directed position and will have a say in the running of the business.

Tian Xiang: Due to your stable career, wealth is well within your grasp; however, you may lack ambition. Interest is key to your work motivation. You may have two different vocations or sources of income.

Sha Qi: This star indicates a dramatic turn of events related to your work or career. It is a bad omen for high-risk businesses or any form of financial speculation. People management is your forte, so a supervisory role or a career in human resources would suit you best. You seek positions of power and independence.

Po Jun: Your career will be in a constant state of flux. It will be torn down and then rebuilt many times. Many changes will find you out in the forefront of innovations. Expect to wear many hats as circumstances change and your talent for blazing new trails is tapped.

Lian Zhen: This is the sign/palace placement for a politician. You may find yourself called to be an officer, military, court judge, or elected official. Females will be extremely successful in professions that require regular contact with men. You will achieve better success in a structured environment, in a stable, salaried position.

Tan Lang: Career success comes by way of using your extraordinary communication skills and charisma. Multitalented, charming, and adventurous, you could be quite successful in a career in the entertainment business. In general, people-oriented professions or jobs working with the public suit you.

T'ai Yang: A career in the public eye is revealed by Tai Yang in the career palace. This placement indicates a profession in publicity, engineering (electricity), communications, politics, or foreign affairs. This will likely be a high-profile profession in the limelight.

Ju Men: You have the ability to start your own business from scratch. You will be drawn to careers in which you use your verbal skills, such as public relations, marketing, sales, the law, radio, or teaching— or any profession that relies heavily on speech is indicated.

Tian Ji: You will be required to travel for your work or change residences often due to job relocation requirements. A 9-to-5 job would be disastrous for you; an avant-garde profession is a must. One might find you as an activist, a futurist, an artist, or even a religious leader (of a new sect, of course). Planning and new ideas are your forte.

T'ai Yin: The moon is 100-percent yin, so your career will likely involve females or women's issues. As it is also a wealth energy, you may be called to a career in finance, a night job, working underground, or a late evening shift.

Tian Tong: You prefer easy, undemanding jobs in a casual or loose work environment. Careers that are connected with recreation and enjoyment of any type will suit you well. Perseverance is the key to your vocational success. You may well hold down a job in the entertainment industry, the arts, or travel. You would make a first-rate resort owner, manager, or travel agent.

Tian Liang: You will thrive in a supervisory, planning, or problem-solving capacity. A traditional career in medicine, teaching, or accounting is also favored. Management will be your best career path, as will judicial professions of all types.

Chapter 18
The Friends and Staff Palace

This palace shows whether your friends and subordinates are loyal or if they will betray you. It can describe your friends or hired help. It also shows their relationship with you, and if they will help or hurt you. Your business partners, good or bad, can be determined with the stars placed in this palace. Read on to find out how each major star will affect you when found in this palace.

Zi Wei: You will have powerful, influential friends in high places. You assist them and, in turn, they are in a position to grant you many favors. This placement also indicates strong and competent employees or partners.

Tian Fu: This star is a sign of upright and honorable friends, some of whom may be influential society types, powerful CEOs, or successful entrepreneurs. This placement reveals long-standing friends who are reliable and whom you can count on to act in your best interest. What they lack in flexibility they make up for in loyalty.

Wu Qu: This placement reveals strong, confident friends, but you may experience obstacles, communication difficulties, and/or challenges with them due to forceful behavior. Wu Qu is an auspicious star to find in this location if you run your own business, as it indicates vigorous employees who get things done. Be tactful with your friends to avoid driving them away.

Tian Xiang: This is a favorable placement indicating supportive and involved friends. Your comrades are true peers of a similar age and with a similar background. As matters happen in twos with this star, friends and staff perform dual roles. Be cautious of friends becoming two-faced or of a rivalry between two different groups.

Sha Qi: Friends and staff are strong and independent, but may possess dreadful tempers. These hard-headed individuals have powerful personalities and have hard lessons to learn in this life. You must be careful about associating with a wild group or bad individual and thus becoming a part of these hard lessons.

Po Jun: This star indicates independent and rebellious friends, staff members, and underlings. If you are a business owner with employees, beware of them undermining you or your company. Friends are wasteful of your resources, and many times they are troubled personally. You may have a difficult time making and keeping friends because you tend to associate with problematic people.

Lian Zhen: You will have many friends and effortlessly attract associates of the opposite sex. Your friendships will tend to be exciting or risky in some way. You will consider many of your blood relatives to be your friends. Being too focused on passion could get you into trouble.

Tan Lang: You will have many acquaintances of varied interests and from many different backgrounds, but few true friends. You will enjoy a lot of socializing and partying. Friends of the opposite sex may have a secret agenda that has nothing to do with platonic friendship.

T'ai Yang: High profile friendships are indicated here. You must guard against private information becoming public via friends, employees, or staff. Because you will be in the public eye, you may also be the target of blame or become a scapegoat for others. There is a certain superficiality amongst your friends.

Ju Men: Many arguments are in store for you. Friends bicker amongst themselves and with you. Gossip, idle talk, and backbiting are also revealed with this placement. Slander, lawsuits, and arguments are burdensome; "friends" may try to bring you down and harm your reputation.

Tian Ji: There will be many changes in your friendships, some occurring very rapidly. You will have numerous friends from many different backgrounds, but these associations will tend to be short-lived. Traveling, socializing, and meeting new people appeals to you, as does any change in routine.

T'ai Yin: Women and female friends will be of great importance in your life and in business. It represents quiet, gentle employees who work for you in the background. The majority of your friends and staff will be women. With favorable stars placed in the same life palace, these friends help you; under the influence of bad stars or the obstruction catalyst, they do not.

Tian Tong: You will enjoy a myriad of friends, most of whom will be involved in a relaxed or leisurely lifestyle. Joyful social occasions plus interactions with interesting people from all walks of life equal very pleasurable moments. However, if you are a business owner, Tian Tong can indicate lazy or unmotivated employees.

Tian Liang: Your friends are helpful to you, but will tend to be older. With this placement, you will tend to be a loner and will have few friends. However, the friends you do have will stand the test of time and be in it for the long haul.

Chapter 19
The Travel and Sociability Palace

This palace represents the public, travel, and foreign relations. It reveals your level of sociability, describes your relationships, and indicates your fate while traveling, either for work or for pleasure. This palace also will show if relocating to another country would be auspicious for you. Read on to find out how each of the major stars affects this life palace.

Zi Wei: Traveling is favorable for you and could put you in touch with some very influential people. This placement indicates that you will receive assistance while traveling, and experience an upturn in luck after moving or relocating to a foreign country. You will gain many friends and earn respect from others while on your voyages.

Tian Fu: Assistance is forthcoming when traveling or on the move. This assistance may be financial, as Tian Fu represents the palace treasury. You will feel equally comfortable at home or abroad. You may choose to invest your finances in overseas projects or open an offshore bank account.

Wu Qu: You must move away from your birthplace, sometimes even your homeland, to earn any substantial wealth. Although Wu Qu in this palace brings success through travel, it also indicates greater effort required and hectic activities after moving to a foreign country.

Tian Xiang: Others enjoy traveling with you due to your personable and pleasant companionship. Tian Xiang makes for an agreeable travel palace; you will have good luck overseas or in your dealings with foreign countries. As things tend to happen in twos with this star, you will not be one to stay long in one location.

Sha Qi: This star indicates difficult changes and unlucky events that occur during travel. You have greater success closer to your place of birth or hometown, rather than away in a foreign land. Trade or business exchanges with other countries or oversees companies could end in disappointment or disaster. This an active and controversial energy that reveals many difficult moves or changes in location.

Po Jun: There is no rest for the weary with Po Jun in your travel palace. You can expect to encounter much action with little result, and you will have to depend on a specialized skill or knowledge. Despite this, you will love to travel and may even decide to sell all of your possessions and relocate to a foreign land.

Lian Zhen: This could indicate an accident or injury after a move to a foreign land. Emotional attachments or issues involving blood relatives may surface. This combination of star energy and travel palace may reveal illegal immigration or a problem with a foreign visa.

Tan Lang: Your love of romance, excitement, and adventure leads you to new and interesting locales. This also reveals a love affair or marriage with someone from a foreign country or culture or who comes from a much different background. Great pleasure is experienced overseas and others will assist you during travel.

T'ai Yang: The sun in your travel palace indicates success when traveling and more success in your career when you are away from home. Fame, recognition, and status come to you after transferring to a foreign land. Your name will be etched on the hearts of many and your benevolence will be rewarded.

Ju Men: This placement suggests that others speak poorly of you overseas. You could experience slander, gossip, and possibly litigation after moving to another country. Gossip also surrounds you when traveling. This causes you to keep your activities hush-hush.

Tian Ji: This star in your travel palace indicates constant activity and movement. You will likely move to a foreign county and be kept both physically and mentally active. You will have better luck making a living if you move far from your birthplace. Your restless nature will have no trouble with this kind of existence.

T'ai Yin: With the moon in your travel palace, women will assist you on your travels and you will love to stay out late or travel at night. If you move to a foreign land, tranquility will follow you. You will receive much assistance when traveling, allowing you to achieve your goals and enjoy an abundant harvest. You will gain respect and a helpful benefactor overseas.

Tian Tong: This placement is an indication of a turn for the worse after relocating to a foreign country. Watch for accidents or mishaps during vacations or leisure time. With dark stars accompanying Tian Tong in this palace, beware of vehicle accidents or injuries while on vacation. Despite this, you make friends easily while on your travels.

Tian Liang: Older or elderly people assist you when traveling. You gain respect overseas or away from home. You will overcome a certain amount of turmoil if you move far from home or to a foreign place. This move will likely be permanent.

Chapter 20

The Health Palace

This palace describes your body and your health in general, both mental and physical. Hidden illnesses that you may be prone to are also found here; this includes physical handicaps and internal disorders. When interpreting the health palace, stars represent body parts, and the dark stars, such as Huo Xing and Ling Xing, represent illness.

The health palace is usually examined in conjunction with the destiny palace. A favorable destiny palace can supersede even the most dismal health palace; conversely, if all stars in the health palace are favorable and the destiny palace is obstructed or filled with dark energies, true health will be elusive. Both palaces must be used to pinpoint weaknesses and evaluate your overall health. For example, if either the destiny or the health palace contains Sha Qi, Qing Yang, Tuo Luo, Huo Xing, Di Jie, or Di Kong, they are weak and poorly placed. In this case, you may suffer continuous health misfortunes and illness. Following is how the various star energies will affect your health palace.

Zi Wei: The Zi Wei star represents the head, the brain, and the area between the eyebrows. With other favorable energies, it reveals very good health throughout your life. Obstructed or with dark stars also present, you may suffer headaches, dizziness, a weak nervous system, and/or insomnia. Zi Wei may cause problems in your digestive system, spleen, or stomach; you may experience indigestion, acid reflux, or other problems with digestion.

Tian Fu: There are usually only minor illnesses with Tian Fu, such as poor digestion or swollen legs. This star can also indicate stomach or digestive problems, possible rib injuries, or lung weakness, but all in all, you will benefit from good health. There may be some circulatory problems, such as edema, when you are older. Found together with the Zi Wei star, it means that you are seldom ill and will enjoy excellent health.

Wu Qu: Your lungs and respiratory system will be weak if any of the dark stars are present in the health or destiny palace. Lungs, nose, face, and teeth can all be at risk with this star. Because this star is connected with the Metal element, it can reveal injuries from sharp metals or surgeries. Found together with Tian Xiang, a hidden disabling illness may surface.

Tian Xiang: You may experience urinary system dysfunction, bladder disease, edema, diabetes, and/or skin maladies and allergies (ringworm, psoriasis). With dark stars in tow, contagious diseases or hereditary illnesses may surface.

Sha Qi: You will likely experience many illnesses during your childhood. Diseases of the respiratory system and/or breathing difficulties may also plague you. Your colon, large and small intestines, and rectal area are all susceptible to problems, as well. Hemorrhoids, impotence, and incontinence are found with Sha Qi in the health palace.

Po Jun: Po Jun brings misfortune and frequent illnesses during childhood. Diseases and dysfunctions of the reproductive system (miscarriage, irregular or painful menstruation) and a host of genitourinary problems are frequently seen. Disorders of the abdomen, kidneys, and bladder can also afflict you. Po Jun reveals poor health in general and chronic or hidden illnesses that show up later in life.

Lian Zhen: You will be plagued with many health problems such as insomnia, poor blood circulation, or heart disease later on in life. However, the main issues with this star are psychological and emotional problems and diseases of the nervous system. Diseases of the blood, bodily fluids, mouth, teeth, tongue, and lips are also frequently seen.

Tan Lang: Representing love and problems with love, Tan Lang brings with it the potential for genitourinary disorders and sexually transmitted diseases. Diseases of the gall bladder, liver, and spleen are also seen.

T'ai Yang: Tai Yang in the health palace reveals problems with the head, eyes, heart, or circulatory system. Surrounded by favorable energies, there are usually very few illnesses or physical mishaps; obstructed or accompanied by dark stars, however, the sun becomes eye pain, injury, or disease; bleeding in the brain; and diseases of blood qi (high blood pressure, heart disease).

Ju Men: There could be problems in and around the mouth area. Diseases of the throat, digestive system, stomach, esophagus, and duodenum are also possible. Frequent illnesses in childhood, including respiratory problems and ear, nose, and throat infections, are also indicated.

Tian Ji: Tian Ji can reveal problems with the liver, gall bladder, or nervous system. Alcoholism, emotional breakdowns, and ailments of the limbs or extremities are frequently seen. If the obstruction catalyst is attached or if it is surrounded by dark stars, Tian Ji reveals a wound that results in a scar, most likely on the forehead. There is also the potential for hyperactivity, ADD, and learning disabilities due to injury and/or emotional volatility.

T'ai Ying: T'ai Ying placed in your health palace puts you at risk for diabetes, edema, urinary tract disease, kidney depletion, and yin disorders in women (miscarriage and infertility). Diseases and dysfunctions of the head and eyes, such as myopia and retinal degeneration (especially the right eye), are also seen with this placement. Hidden or mysterious diseases of the genitourinary system and the breasts and psychological disturbances are particularly troublesome when T'ai Yin is obstructed or met with the dark stars.

Tian Tong: You will enjoy basically good health with the exception of some significant emotional or mental concerns. Obesity and weight-related issues, along with a tendency toward physical inactivity or lethargy, is frequently seen when Tian Tong is found in the health palace. The kidneys, bladder, or urinary system may also be vulnerable if this star is obstructed or accompanied by other difficult stars.

Tian Liang: The spleen, liver, gallbladder, and digestive system may cause trouble. This star frequently also brings small but chronic health problems, but impressive longevity, as well. Combined with dark stars, it can indicate a brain tumor or other cranial disease, a weak nervous system, arteriosclerosis/heart disease, and problems with mobility (arthritis).

Chapter 21
The Wealth and Prosperity Palace

This palace is concerned with your level of income, and whether you have to work very hard for it or often have "windfall" fortunes. It describes your financial situation in general. This palace also indicates how you should make your money, your wealth luck (whether it is strong or weak), and your earning capacity. This chapter will tell you how each of the major stars affects this life palace.

Zi Wei: You possess power in financial matters and can generate wealth in a variety of ways. Easy money is likely, but it may be unstable—abundant one minute and gone the next. Generally, you will be well-to-do and will be drawn to careers in finance and money management.

Tian Fu: You have a tremendous capacity to generate wealth for yourself and for others. You could easily find yourself responsible for overseeing large sums of money. You will have significant wealth when this star combines with other favorable financial energies (such as Wu Qu). However, if this star is obstructed or paired with dark stars, it can reveal legal problems surrounding money.

Wu Qu: The potential for great wealth is present with this star/palace combination, as well. Wu Qu represents wealth, leadership, entrepreneurial skills, handicrafts, and metals, so it is through these channels that financial prosperity will flow. It augers momentous wealth when paired with other favorable financial energies (such as Tian Fu) or the wealth catalyst.

Tian Xiang: Depending on surrounding stars, auspicious financial events come in sets of two. However, the same goes for financial setbacks. Karma will determine whether this is a positive or negative influence.

Sha Qi: This powerful energy bestows the ability to take risks. Found placed in your wealth palace, it encourages taking risks with money, financial speculation, stock trading, and gambling. Substantial wealth is possible with Sha Qi, but only if you avoid risky investments. This most powerful of the aggressive martial stars indicates disputes and conflicts brought about by earnings.

Po Jun: This star (also known as the "destroyer") in your wealth palace suggests that money comes and goes and that you may have difficulty saving. Investment in new projects or businesses will be successful; however, money is not stable and you will need to learn to manage it carefully and frugally. On a more positive note, you are an exceedingly resourceful individual when it comes to creative ways to make a fortune.

Lian Zhen: You deal with financial matters with blood relatives, and these dealings are kept confidential. Trust accounts and inheritances occur frequently with this placement, as well. Wealth is generated through struggle, competition, and controversy.

Tan Lang: You love money, but also love gambling, excitement, and risk. Money from the opposite sex comes to you easily. There is the possibility of quick money or unexpected financial windfalls. People of the opposite sex affect your money either positively or negatively, depending on the other stars present in this palace. With negative energies, money is lost through gambling or bankruptcy.

T'ai Yang: With the sun in your wealth palace, there is no problem getting money to flow in; the problem is keeping it. With this extravagant energy, you like to spend rather than save. The more you make, the more you want to spend, and this may be motivated by a desire for status and an affluent appearance. You could incur debt due to others.

Ju Men: Wealth is generated by way of your voice or communication skills. If this star is surrounded by other positive energies, it gives the gift of oration or public speaking. If it is obstructed or joined by negative stars, it suggests that wealth is blocked by slander, misspeaking, gossip, or financial litigation.

Tian Ji: Due to Tian Ji's unstable and inconsistent nature, this is not an auspicious star to find in your wealth palace. Money comes and goes, but its flow is sufficient for your needs. You will earn your wealth working by yourself or in solo efforts. You learn quickly and are an excellent negotiator.

T'ai Yin: The moon in your wealth palace indicates the potential for a limitless fortune. Calm, composed, and clever, you have a natural talent for tucking away a nest egg and accumulating savings for future security. Compounded funds that may be hidden will be your primary source of fortune. You accumulate wealth quietly and without fanfare.

Tian Tong: With this star in your wealth palace, you will be content with whatever level of financial prosperity you attain. Always happy to let others shine, you will not gain financially at the expense of others. It is because of this kind and altruistic attitude that fortune will shine upon you. You have the ability to start your own business from scratch and will be financially comfortable in old age.

Tian Liang: This problem-solving energy attracts tribulations and then proceeds to solve them. Unfortunately, bad times must be experienced before a change for the better. Tian Liang placed in your wealth palace indicates that you may be in a constant process of solving financial troubles. Greater effort is required in order to straighten out money issues. Disputes and unrest are brought about by earnings, inheritance, trust funds, or winnings.

Chapter 22
The Children Palace

The children palace reveals the relationship with your children, your subordinates, and your students. It also represents the quality of your ideas (brainchildren), projects, and creative efforts. In this chapter, you will learn how each of the major star energies affects this important life palace.

Zi Wei: Finding the Zi Wei star in this palace suggests that you will have few children and that it will be more favorable for you to have them later in life. This star reveals active and intelligent offspring—more females than males, although boys may come along later on. Your children are strong and confident, but difficult to control because of their strong wills.

Tian Fu: This star in your children palace indicates that you will have many children. You will forge a good relationship with them and will have a strong influence on their lives. You enjoy a filial and stable bond with your offspring as well as with your employees, if you are a manager or business owner.

Wu Qu: You will have few offspring, and more than likely they will be with your second spouse. Wu Qu in this palace indicates strong, confident children (and senior employees, if in business). Your children will be very strong-willed, with minds of their own, and may be a challenge to educate.

Tian Xiang: It will be better for you to have a daughter as a firstborn. This "mirroring" star of duplication means that things will come in twos, revealing the possibility of twins or a premature birth. This star suggests that you will have obedient, truthful, and sensible children in whose lives you will be exceptionally involved.

Sha Qi: You will have few children, but they will have extremely strong characters and be difficult to control. Sha Qi is a risky energy to find in your children palace, as it can be a sign of miscarriages, birth defects, or genetic disorders. Sha Qi suggests that you will have aloof children who will hide what is going on inside of them. They will have many hard lessons to learn.

Po Jun: Po Jun placed in the children palace indicates active, rebellious children. The firstborn will be the most difficult to raise and may be in poor health as a child. He or she may be scarred, born prematurely, or endure some kind of unfortunate setback or blow. When placed in this palace, this "demolisher" star unfortunately reveals a difficult or blocked road to pregnancy (infertility, miscarriage, abortion). The children's relationships with each other may also be damaged.

Lian Zhen: Your offspring will have logical minds and enjoy taking things apart to find out how they work. They must be very cautious with fire and electricity. Children and employees will tend to be secretive, so it will be imperative to keep an open dialog with them. All in all, you will have a positive relationship with your offspring.

Tan Lang: Finding the "pleasure" star in this palace can reveal a child born out of wedlock. You will have two or three curious and capricious children who are charming and sociable. They must be cautious, however, as this tendency can turn into a fondness for partying, drinking, and gambling.

T'ai Yang: This bright and shining influence is a powerful energy to find in your children palace. It reveals very active, helpful children and employees who will find themselves in the public eye and will enjoy a certain amount of recognition and fame. The sun indicates difficult pregnancies with possible miscarriage(s) or therapeutic abortions.

Ju Men: You will have talkative children with advanced verbal skills who are nevertheless difficult to communicate with. These are sassy, impish offspring who like to talk back and challenge your authority. There will be many disagreements between you. When other auspicious stars are present, your children will be linguistically gifted. However, if this star carries the obstruction catalyst or is joined by any of the dark stars, the opposite will be true. Speech impediments or structural abnormalities of the mouth (harelip, cleft palate) may occur.

Tian Ji: This is not a pleasant star to find in this palace. Your children are forward-thinking and smart, but may face dangers of various kinds. This star brings great risk to the children from machines and automobiles. Your offspring (and your best ideas) will come later in life, and there will be many challenges with them.

T'ai Yin: This feminine yin energy reveals female offspring and very favorable relationships with your children and employees. Your daughters will be quiet and introverted, and will enjoy financial security.

Tian Tong: A very favorable relationship is in store for you and your children. At times, the lines separating you and them may be blurry, and you could have more of a friendship with them rather than an adversarial, parent-child relationship. Although your relationship with them will be good, their health may be fragile.

Tian Liang: This star reveals gentle and supportive children who are intelligent and studious and who will care for you in your old age. They will love the fine arts and may come along later in your marriage. Their maturity will surpass their age. Firstborns are frequently daughters with this placement.

Chapter 23
The Relationship Palace

This palace covers all significant romantic attachments, not just marriage. It indicates whether you will enjoy a happy marriage/union/relationship or an adversarial one. It also explains why some people marry many times and why some stay single for life. It describes your married life, indicates what kind of person your spouse is, and reveals whether or not your partnership is thriving. If there are no stars found in this palace, look to its opposite palace of career for guidance.

Zi Wei: Your spouse or partner is the domineering boss in your relationship. Although he or she can be responsible and a good partner, he/she may not meet your emotional needs. Despite this, it will be very difficult, if not impossible, for you two to part ways. There may be multiple marriages to the same individual.

Tian Fu: Your spouse is good with the family finances. If the Zi Wei star is also present, it is an indication of a second marriage. Your later marriage will be happier than the first, and you will share many interests in common with your spouse. This star also suggests that your spouse will be conservative, traditional, and guarded.

Wu Qu: Your spouse or partner will be slight or short of stature and shy, yet have a resonant, deep voice. He/she may be difficult to communicate with; the relationship will suffer from bickering, arguments, and internal strife. This is an inauspicious placement as it generally points to a domineering spouse. It will be better for you to marry later on in life.

Tian Xiang: As matters come in twos with this star, it is a clear indication of more than one marriage or significant relationship.

There is a good possibility that you will marry an old acquaintance, your high school sweetheart, or someone from your home town.

Sha Qi: This star is no friend to the unions palace. It reveals that your spouse has a very strong personality and that you will marry him or her suddenly. This star also reveals that you put up a happy front for others that hides an inner discontent or unhappiness with your relationship. It describes your spouse as an independent, silent type who is hard to read. There will be many hard lessons to be learned in this palace.

Po Jun: Because this star is all about "out with the old and in with the new," it is disastrous to find in your relationship palace. You and your spouse will have very little in common, and divorce is almost certain. There will be at least two marriages, one of which may be unusual in some way (marrying a cousin or a brother-/sister-in law, a marriage for citizenship, an arranged marriage, and so on). You will have rocky relationships in general, especially early on in life.

Lian Zhen: Arguing, affairs, and a possible divorce are likely in the stars for you. Your spouse or partner may be friendly one minute and pick a fight with you the next. Lian Zhen is an indication of a spouse who has emotional problems, bipolar disorder, or other psychological disturbances. Abundant passion that cannot be contained causes relationship problems. A strong blood factor is at play with this star; in the unions palace, it can reveal operations, injuries, and/or accidents involving the spouse or significant other.

Tan Lang: This energy of extremes is the main star of sexuality, danger, love, and problems connected with love. Wherever it is placed will reveal fights, power struggles, and romantic triumphs or painful failures in matters of the heart. Placed here, it represents indulgence, sensuality, and the form of the body (physique). Full of sensual magnetism, your partner loves romance, but this causes turbulence in your relationship.

T'ai Yang: Passion can turn cold quickly with Tai Yang in your relationship palace. With this very public and "in the limelight" energy, your spouse will be in the public eye in some way. He or she will have success and popularity and possesses an energetic and radiant personality. Unless it is obstructed or surrounded by dark stars, your spouse/partner will be benevolent, open, and elegant.

Ju Men: This is an argumentative placement. It reveals that your spouse will be talkative, but will have very little of substance to say. Communication difficulties cause marital strife, and you will constantly be drawn into arguments by your spouse. Ju Men (also called the "gloomy" star) may lead to jealousy, slander, and dishonesty. It can also represent litigation, privacy, and suspicion if surrounded by dark stars.

Tian Ji: Tian Ji reveals a partner who has an active mind and quick intelligence. He or she loves to learn new things, but may lack perseverance. Eclectically talented in many trades, he/she is highly intelligent, but unstable. Much traveling with be required of your spouse or partner, and this may be a catalyst that ends the relationship. This a very unstable energy to find in the unions palace.

T'ai Yin: With the moon in your unions palace, your spouse or partner will be tranquil, graceful, and wealthy, and distinguished by literary, spiritual, reflective, feminine "yin" qualities. Placed here it reveals a supportive spouse who is financially fortunate or wealthy in his or her own right. There may be a significant age difference between you and your partner.

Tian Tong: This is a beautiful energy to have in your unions palace. It describes your spouse or partner as a contented soul who goes through life as a happy-go-lucky adolescent. Self-effacing and always ready to start anew, he or she is happy to let you shine. This is a gracious, learned, gentle soul who leans toward the fine arts and spiritual subjects, and will spend much time in quiet meditation and self-cultivation. He or she is emotional, sensitive, and able to build something from nothing.

Tian Liang: This radiant star achieves results with persuasion rather than force. Your spouse may be much older than you, and brings heirlooms, an estate, or a family business to your union. He/she is not one to toil or struggle, and will display a certain degree of sophistication as he/she pursues the good, easy life. This star indicates longevity, but also loneliness. Your spouse or partner will be principled and orderly, and will be employed in a career that has to do with the elderly, medication, insurance, accounting, mathematics, or the military.

Chapter 24
The Siblings and Peers Palace

This palace concerns your relationships with your siblings and peers. This is where you can look to find information on business partners, colleagues, and fellow students, as well. The strengths and weaknesses of your rivals are also located in this palace. Following is how each major star will affect this particular life palace.

Zi Wei: This star reveals strong and dependable siblings, powerful rivals, and prominent or high-ranking colleagues. Your siblings are helpful, but you may not get along with them because they tend to be bossy or want to be treated like kings. You will have two or three siblings, and they will tend to overshadow you or be more successful.

Tian Fu: This star reveals multiple siblings who are of some assistance, but not much support. These siblings may be favored by the parents. Business associates and rivals will see failures, and the favored siblings could end up disappointing the parents. All in all, you will experience a harmonious relationship with your siblings and working partners.

Wu Qu: This star reveals few but strong and opinionated siblings who have commanding personalities. You will experience disharmony and disagreements with them. Business associates will be direct and straightforward, difficult to deal with at times, but able to produce swift and effective results.

Tian Xiang: This star placed in your siblings palace indicates many siblings and is generally quite favorable unless the obstruction catalyst is attached or it is accompanied by dark stars. You will have many siblings, and amongst them there will be similar personalities or even twins. The "mirror" star placed here reveals reunions with associates from your past who become your business partners.

Sha Qi: This martial, fighting star indicates disharmony with, petty jealousies among, and conflicts with a small number of siblings. They will be unable to communicate with you, and you may feel very distant from them. This star in your siblings palace reveals some challenging times and hard life lessons for them.

Po Jun: The oldest sibling will carry the heaviest burden with this aggressive martial star. There will be illnesses and possibly a wide age gap between siblings. This is a family of hot-tempered rebels, and you will find yourself assuming a lot of responsibility early in life. This placement does not bode well for relationships between you and your fellow students, working partners, or rivals. Battles may become bitter and relationships destroyed.

Lian Zhen: This changeable star indicates siblings who are sometimes helpful and sometimes not. Business partners will have tricks up their sleeves and could undermine you. Lian Zhen represents blood and death, so you could lose a sibling at an early age. Sometimes this is through divorce or adoption, however.

Tan Lang: You should have harmonious relationships, but be wary of siblings or work associates who feel that they have an unquestionable right to your possessions or property. You will get along better with your siblings if you live separately; otherwise you could have difficult relationships. This is also an indication of half-siblings, step-siblings, or a blended family.

T'ai Yang: This masculine energy points to brothers or male relatives who are significant in your life. Siblings or business associates will achieve success and be in the public eye in some way. When the obstruction catalyst is attached to the sun, it veils its energy; this should caution you regarding unscrupulous employees, male business associates, and/or men in general.

Ju Men: You must be wary of siblings, peers, or work colleagues engaging in slander, disagreements, and gossip. Unfavorable relationships with siblings are often found with this placement. Ju Men brings problems and misunderstandings due to miscommunication or verbal abuse.

Tian Ji: Your siblings will be on the move and will tend to come and go in and out of the family circle. You may fall victim to some behind-the-scenes scheming on their part, underhanded trickery on the part of your business associates, or fast-talking con men who are here today and gone tomorrow. You will have few siblings, and you will have more sisters than brothers. They are all intelligent, but there may be arguments between them. Tian Ji is also a sign of a blended family or siblings from different parentage.

T'ai Yin: This feminine energy indicates that you will have sisters. When reflected from the opposite palace of friends, however, it indicates a female friend who will be as close as a sister. This star is an indication of gentle siblings who are financially well-off and advantageous for you to associate with.

Tian Tong: This star reveals talented, peaceful, and fun-loving siblings with whom you may be close friends. They are relaxed lovers of life and happy to let you shine. Siblings and business partners are emotional, sensitive, and able to build exciting projects from almost nothing. They may make a living in a career that has something to do with leisure, entertainment, or recreation.

Tian Liang: This star in your siblings palace indicates that you will take care of your younger siblings as a parent would and that you will have favorable relationships with them. You may have many siblings, and there could be significant age differences between you. This star also reveals that one of them may leave you an inheritance. In business, Tian Liang indicates older partners who pass down a legacy, a practice, or a business.

Chapter 25

Interpreting Your Zi Wei Dou Shu Chart

In Chapter 13, we learned that the focal point of a Zi Wei Dou Shu chart is the destiny palace, or *ming gong*. You also learned about the 14 major stars (the *ming gong zhu xin*, or "main life stars") and how they affect your life path. You also found out which soul group (royal, martial, or psycho-social/literary) you are a part of.

Write your destiny stars again: _____

_____.

And write down which of the 12 animal signs occupies your destiny palace: _____.

Again, the emperor, vault, commander, and prime minister stars are the most beneficial ones of Chinese astrology. Where they are placed will be the most powerful and protected areas of your life chart. The seven swords, Aphrodite, crimson passion, and the demolisher stars are the most aggressive and complicated ones of Chinese astrology. Where they are placed there will be fighting, difficulties, and power struggles.

Next, notice where the four transforming catalysts are found in your chart and write down which star(s) they are attached to:

Power: _____ Fame: _____

Fortune: _____ Obstruction: _____

After examining your self/destiny palace, look to your karmic luck palace to establish a complete character profile. The basic equation is self/destiny palace + karmic luck palace = personality. Each palace in your chart also represents a specific decade. The age at which the decade transit occurs is in the top right-hand box of each life palace. Start in your self/destiny palace and move through your chart, decade by decade, to see the various influences. Notice which palaces are in trine (separated by three palaces) with the others, thereby combining their energies. For example, to analyze wealth, look to the self and career palaces.

Forecasting

In addition to the Chinese natal chart, which is fixed for life, there is a mobile (moving) part of your chart—a 10-year cycle (in blue on the accompanying CD) and an annual or yearly cycle (in red on the CD). Each of these energies moves to a new position in one's chart each year. The decade (in blue) and yearly (in red) cycles are merely smaller cycles contained within the larger life cycles. These "transits" come back regularly to the positions they originally occupied at birth. They reactivate the potentialities of the life palace they pass through. They also raise obstacles or urge us to iron out difficulties. By observing which life palace is transiting over your self palace each year, as well as where the four catalysts come to rest, you will shine light on that year's forecasts.

When I was trying to decide what birth chart to use as an interpretive example for this book, I toyed with several ideas before finally settling upon the unlucky soul I would put on the hot seat. After lending my analysis to thousands of charts over the years, I found it only fair to put the scrutiny on me—the good, the bad, and the ugly.

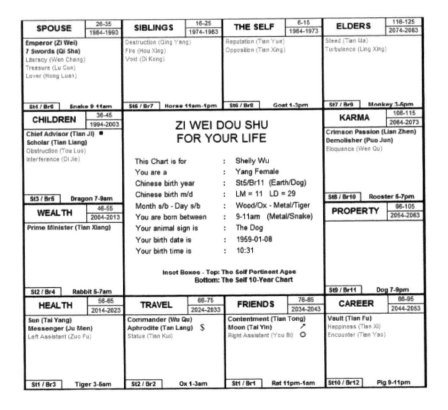

Name: Shelly Wu

Born: January 8, 1959, 10:31 a.m.

Earthly branch: Dog (Xu)

Heavenly stem: Earth

Birth hour: Snake

Manifest as: Dog on the Mountaintop

Stem: yang female

Lucky elements: Earth and Metal

Unlucky element: Fire

Destiny: mixed

Soul group(s): imperial and martial

Destiny palace stars: Wu Qu and Tan Lang

Having no major stars in the self palace is indicative of a late bloomer who doesn't come into his or her own until midlife. This person may also feel emptiness and frustration. This is true in my case. When none of the 14 major stars are present, then, we must borrow stars from the palace directly opposite the self/destiny palace; these become the resident energies of both palaces. This will be the case with any empty life palace or one that contains only minor energies. So we must look to my travel palace to find the major destiny energies.

Present in this palace are two major stars, Wu Qu and Tan Lang. Wu Qu is a major energy in the imperial or ruling group and reveals a soul blessed by birth to lead, to protect, and to be a key figure in this life in some way. Wu Qu is sometimes called the "military minister" due to the speed and quick thinking it contributes. It represents a decisive leader who figuratively leads his or her army into battle. It is a quick, intense, and temperamental energy—the astral signature of an individual who feels the need to lead in some type of public service. This person is likely involved in the nuts and bolts of planning and putting ideas to work. The commander star is also responsible for entrepreneurial skills, and reveals a destiny of one who is the "right hand man" to the powerful and influential. Its presence indicates a strong and resilient personality as well as a competitive spirit; women in particular are generally very comfortable with and competitive in the company of males. It indicates good luck, but also solitude, firmness, and even stubbornness. Indeed, this is all very true for me. I am stubborn and tenacious, and I prefer to give orders rather than take them. This star energy also allows me to get a large amount of work done in a small amount of time when necessary. I am also an independent and impatient person who tends to act too quickly.

Aphrodite (Tan Lang) is a major "peach blossom" energy and the most powerful star of pleasure and romance. Those with Tan Lang in their destiny palace are eloquent, love to entertain lavishly, and possess exceptional people skills. This star's energy is all about making strong connections with others. This is an indulgent energy of sensuality, physical love, socializing, and enjoyment; it has the ability to captivate the opposite sex. Unfortunately, it is also the main culprit responsible for my unrelenting love life dramas. Romance and sensuality cause trouble with Tan Lang in the self/destiny palace, and I am resigned to the fact that love and all its attendant problems will be the tumultuous common denominator of my existence.

On a different note, metaphysics, religion, spirituality, and free thinking also characterize those with Tan Lang in their destiny palace, as does a strongly empathic nature. People with this placement often pursue astrology, divination, or other spiritual arts. This has certainly been true in my case. Lian Zhen in my karma palace combined with the Aphrodite star in my self palace, reveals an artistic personality. Moreover, the combination of Tian Yue in my self/destiny palace and Tian Kui opposite it symbolizes the pen. This literary, writing energy, combined with the next batch of stars present, begins to build a more complete picture.

Tian Fu in my career palace, Tian Xiang in my wealth palace, Wu Qu and Tan Lang in the travel palace, and Wen Qu in my karma palace all reveal a housewife turned entrepreneur. According to the chart, this happened between the ages of 46 and 55. Indeed, I didn't start my writing career until this time.

To take a glimpse at the bad news, notice the obstruction catalyst (solid square block) attached to the fast-moving energy of Tian Ji in my children palace. Tian Ji has to do with machines, automobiles, fast movement, and impediments to strategy or movement. The additional presence of the two dark stars, Tuo Luo and Di Jie, in the children palace added strength to an already risky situation. Unfortunately, reality bore this out as true, as well. The fateful day happened on a hot August afternoon in 1988. My only son was hit and almost killed by a reckless driver who was obliviously speeding down our quiet residential neighborhood street. Fortunately, after enduring a painful recovery with the help of his doctors, he has grown into a fine young man. After all, he was born into a year of the resilient, enduring Ox! More mundanely, my health palace contains Tai Yang, the sun, which reveals a weakness in my eyesight. I am, in fact, so myopic and nearsighted that my optical prescription requires what I call "the creature that ate Tokyo" glasses. I am completely dependent on these glasses or contact lenses.

In Zi Wei astrology, just as in life, we have to take the good with the bad. This system can give you insight into what is likely to happen if you take a certain course of action. It can be a useful tool to advise you on the best course of action to take in order to achieve the ends you desire. Once you learn the essence of each of the various stars and life palaces, you will begin to put together a comprehensive astral profile of your fate and destiny and how you fit into the universe.

Part III
The Eastern Astrological Subspecialities

Chapter 26
The I-Ching

The I-Ching, or Book of Changes, is an ancient Chinese process of divination that dates back to about 3,000 BCE. However, it may have been in use even thousands of years earlier by Siberian shamans, who used cracked tortoise shells as their method of divining the future. The I- Ching represents one of the first efforts of humanity to understand its place within the universe. Later, when it became a book, it provided a common source of wisdom for both Confucianism and Taoist philosophies. To many Westerners, the I-Ching seems mysterious and obscure, not to mention incredibly complex. Yet it's treasured by millions in the East as a valued oracle and tool for divination.

How can something that's thousands of years old be effective in a modern society? Those consulting the I-Ching may use it for advice in everyday decisions and for spiritual guidance. It can also be used in path-working, rituals, and opening astral doorways. The I-Ching is actually a simple binary system of zeros and ones, similar to the language of modern computers. In this system, broken and solid lines are grouped into hexagrams. Each hexagram is gener-ated line by line, and contains a unique arrangement of six lines. There are a total of 64 hexagrams.

In divination, each line has a special meaning based on its placement in the hexagram, which is read from the bottom up. The patterns, or oracles, reveal the answer or answers to the question or problem at hand. Coins, sticks, cards, stones, or the traditional yarrow stalks can be used, but always in threes. These items are tossed into the air, and the numerological total will determine the type of line in the hexagram, which is built from the base upward. A question is best phrased in a "yes or no" form, although it need not be spoken nor written. This process is repeated until

An oracle used during the Shang Dynasty (c.1300 BC) for divination. Such oracles were often made of tortoise shell.

the six lines are built. Today, there are extensive interpretations that can be brought to bear on this method: Confucian, Taoist, feminist Goddess, and the list goes on. Because of free will, the I-Ching only hints at the future and does not actually delineate it. Real magic works from the inside out, and self-knowledge is an absolute necessity to avoid falling into the snares of self-delusion. Here are the 64 hexagrams of the I-Ching in order:

1. The Creative
2. The Receptive
3. Difficulty at the Beginning
4. Youthful Folly
5. Waiting (Nourishment)
6. Conflict
7. The Army
8. Holding Together (Union)
9. The Taming Power of the Small
10. Treading (Conduct)
11. Peace
12. Standstill (Stagnation)
13. Fellowship with Men
14. Possession in Great Measure
15. Modesty
16. Enthusiasm
17. Following
18. Work on What Has Been Spoiled (Decay)
19. Approach
20. Contemplation (View)
21. Biting Through

22. Grace
23. Splitting Apart
24. Return (The Turning Point)
25. Innocence (The Unexpected)
26. The Taming Power of the Great
27. The Corners of the Mouth (Providing Nourishment)
28. Preponderance of the Great
29. The Abysmal (Water)
30. The Clinging (Fire)
31. Influence (Wooing)
32. Duration
33. Retreat
34. The Power of the Great
35. Progress
36. Darkening of the Light
37. The Family (The Clan)
38. Opposition
39. Obstruction
40. Deliverance
41. Decrease
42. Increase

43. Breakthrough (Resoluteness)
44. Coming to Meet
45. Gathering Together (Massing)
46. Pushing Upward
47. Oppression (Exhaustion)
48. The Well
49. Revolution (Molting)
50. The Caldron
51. The Arousing (Shock, Thunder)
52. Keeping Still (Mountain)
53. Development (Gradual Progress)
54. The Marrying Maiden
55. Abundance (Fullness)
56. The Wanderer
57. The Gentle/The Penetrating (Wind)
58. The Joyous (Lake)
59. Dispersion (Dissolution)
60. Limitation
61. Inner Truth
62. Preponderance of the Small
63. After Completion
64. Before Completion

The traditional manner of consulting the I-Ching was to toss up a bundle of yarrow sticks or coins with holes in the center over and over again in a very long and ritualistic process. The modern equivalent would be the three coin method, in which three coins are thrown six times. When the coins land, the combination of odd or even sides (head or tails) yields a particular result, called a "line." The line can either be an unbroken horizontal line, or a horizontal line with a break in the center. In I-Ching, each throw generates one line in the hexagram, starting from the bottom and working upward.

Each side of the coin is given a numerical value: "heads" counts as two, and "tails" counts as three. The total is then added to give a score. So three coins that land as "heads" would give a score of six; three coins landing as "tails" would give a score of nine; and one coin landing as "heads" and the other two coins landing as "tails" yields a score of eight; and so on. Any even score yields a broken line, while an odd score yields a solid line. And finally, any score of 6 or 9 yields what is called a "changing" or "moving" line, which will invert the final result. For example:

◈ 3 heads = 6 = a broken line (--- ---) which changes to a firm line (------).

◈ 3 tails = 9 = a firm line (------) which changes to a broken line (--- ---).

◈ 2 heads and 1 tail = 7 = a firm line (------) that does not change.

◈ 2 tails and 1 head = 8 = a broken line (--- ---) that does not change.

Depending on the answer you receive, you can try different approaches to the same question. You may frame it slightly differently, clarify it, or alter it entirely.

The I-Ching is a wonderful means of making decisions and thinking out the finer points of any situation. If you would like to explore this subspecialty of Chinese astrology further, there are a myriad of resources available to you in bookstores and on the Internet.

Chapter 27
Feng Shui

Feng shui (literally, "wind and water") was first practiced in China 3,000 years ago and became an official state science. In ancient China, wind and water were the strongest known natural forces. If you were to imagine an invisible stream of energy moving over your head like the wind, that would be *feng. Shui* is represented by the water in the earth, such as an underground stream. Feng shui is the historic discipline of manipulating the invisible and subtle energies of the cosmos (qi) to create harmony between people and their environment. The essence of feng shui is that an individual or business can, by proper orientation of a house or office according to these ancient principles, attract favorable cosmic influences. One way to do this is by using the colors of the five creative elements: green (Wood), red (Fire), yellow (Earth), white (Metal), and black (Water). According to feng shui theory, you would incorporate these colors in the appropriate area in the form of furniture, rugs, bedspreads, decorative items, and so on. Today, feng shui practitioners ply their trade throughout the world, but in no place are they more revered than in Hong Kong, where it is rare that a building is planned without the advice of a feng shui master.

The theory of the five elements is the foundation of feng shui. How you should use them is determined by your Chinese astrological birth chart. A feng shui practitioner can tell you:

1. Your best sleeping directions.
2. Your best work (sitting at a desk) directions.
3. Your best area for creativity, studying, and practicing a discipline.

4. Your "good entrance direction," which brings luck and supportive people into your life.

5. Your "bad entrance direction," which can drain you or make it difficult to save money.

6. How to attract love possibilities using a romance remedy.

Feng shui is not magic, however; rather, it allows us to live in harmony with our environment.

Cosmic energy (qi), also called earth luck, is different from heaven luck (which is the destiny that is readable in the various astrological charts) and man luck (what we make of our life). Qi is the same energy that the yogis call prana, that the ancient alchemists tried to capture, that acupuncture regulates, and that Eastern martial arts (karate, tai-chi-chuan, qigong) use. It's also the same cosmic energy that is used in holistic medicine—reiki, for example. Some also compare it to the Holy Spirit that falls upon Christians in tongues of flame during the Pentecost. There is both good qi (sheng qi) and bad qi (sha qi).

Feng shui diagnoses the status of a home and proposes possible solutions, or "cures," to improve the situation. A feng shui practitioner will stand in front of your home and determine its orientation or direction with a special compass called a *lo pan*. The practitioner will then look at the important areas of your floor plan (bedrooms, entrances, offices) to determine what annual energy exits there. You will be advised of your home's most prosperous areas and how to enhance them. You will also be told of any important areas that may be prone to accidents, arguments, lawsuits, loneliness, setbacks, or delays, and how to reduce these negative influences. Careful observation of the surroundings of the home is also involved. Hills, mountains, creeks, pools, other buildings, and dominant winds are noted. This information is combined with the birth data of the inhabitants and the date the home was built to determine a master plan. Your natal Zi Wei Dou Shu chart can also be used to supplement the feng shui cures. Each of the 12 life palaces are associated with a cardinal direction, which may or may not be favorable for you. For example, if the palace that contains the sign of the Rat (corresponding to the North) is mainly occupied by favorable energies, then the Northern direction is favorable for you. However, even if your astrological chart is auspicious, there will always be periods of vulnerability when misfortune can step in if the environment allows it. According to the old Chinese masters, living in a malefic house can usher in catastrophes such as injuries, fires, floods, accidents, robberies, adulteries, divorces, illnesses, and bankruptcies.

Creating a Feng Shui Garden

A garden is a place you can go to relax, to unwind, and to connect with the earth. Using the principles of feng shui, you can create an unique, private retreat where you can go to escape the fast-paced world, to dream, and to reflect. Feng shui gardens are about putting everything in their proper place. Of course, spring is the perfect season to plan and create a feng shui garden, but the winter months can be a great time to do the planning and designing.

When planning your garden, there are some principles you should keep in mind. Beneficial energy flow is created with wavy or curvy shapes and lines, whereas negative energy is generated by sharp, straight, or angular lines (called "poison arrows"). Create a balance of yin (dark, soft, passive) and yang (light, hard, active) plants, objects, and water. And keep in mind the producing/generating and controlling/destructive relationships between the five elements of Wood, Fire, Earth, Metal, and Water. Stand in the center of your outdoor space and use a compass to determine the eight directions. Then, refer to the following guide to place the colors, symbols, numbers, and elements in their appropriate areas.

North

◈ Represents creativity, personal growth, new ideas, inspiration, prospects, career, music, art.

◈ Use the Water element.

◈ Good area for metal decorations, wind chimes, tool sheds, fountains, ponds, and hot tubs.

◈ Incorporate wavy or curved lines.

◈ Avoid stone, clay pots, earthenware, rock gardens.

Northeast

◈ Represents knowledge, wisdom, meditation/reading, inner journeys, spiritual and intellectual growth, nature.

◈ Use the Earth element.

◈ Good area for stone benches, rock gardens, metal tools, stones, boulders, statuary, brick, flagstone, and anything made from the earth.

◈ Incorporate low and flat surfaces.

◈ Avoid plants and trees

East

◈ Represents new life and growth, rebirth, rejuvenation, harmony, health, family life, nutrition, healing.

◈ Use the Wood element.

◈ Good area for fruit trees, herbs, medicinal plants, steam rooms, saunas, tai chi and other exercises, plants.

◈ Incorporate tall columns and cylindrical shapes.

◈ Avoid metal garden furniture, tools, white flowers, metal decorations, and ironwork.

Southeast

◈ Represents wealth, abundance, material possessions, communication.

◈ Use the Wood element.

◈ Good area for cultivation and display of specimen plants and flower gardens.

◈ Incorporate cylindrical shapes, posts, and columns.

◈ Avoid metal garden furniture and accessories, garden tools, and white flowers.

South

◈ Represents opportunity, dreams, aspirations, awards, fame, recognition, achievement, happiness, longevity, festivity.

◈ Use the Fire element.

◈ Good place for barbecues, fire pits, torches.

◈ Incorporate pointed, serrated, and/or triangular shapes.

◈ Avoid ponds, waterfalls, fountains, and sprinklers/misters.

Southwest

◈ Represents marriage, romance, motherhood, love, relationships, partners.

◈ Use the Earth element.

◈ Good place for seating/dining for two, team sports.

◈ Incorporate low, flat surfaces.

◈ Avoid wooden furniture, gazebos, fences, gates, birdhouses, the color green.

West

◈ Represents children, creativity, harvest, socializing, and entertaining.

◈ Use the Metal element.

◈ Good place for outdoor entertaining, a bar, playground, convalescing, healing, sun-bathing, and tanning.

◈ Incorporate circles, domes, and arches.

◈ Avoid barbecues, firepits, the color red.

Northwest

◈ Represents trade, interests outside of home, international travel, fatherhood, mentors and benefactors, helpful people, supporters.

◈ Use the Metal element.

◈ Good place for statues of deities, angels, cherubs, animals, wind chimes, music.

◈ Incorporate circles, domes, and arches.

◈ Avoid barbecues, firepits, grills, the color red or red flowers.

Chapter 28
Chinese Palmistry

Palmistry came to China around 3,000 BC. Palmistry is the art of character reading and foretelling the future through the study of the palm. There are several branches of this particular art. Chiromancy is the study of the lines on the palm. These lines are formed during fetal development and are the best indicators of personality traits and characters. This was palmistry in ancient times. Later the various marks and mounts on the palm were also examined. Chirognomy is the study of the general shape and texture of the hand, fingers, and fingernails. Dermatoglyphics is the study of the ridges of the fingertips (fingerprints). Nowadays this is used as a personal identification tool and in criminal/forensic sciences.

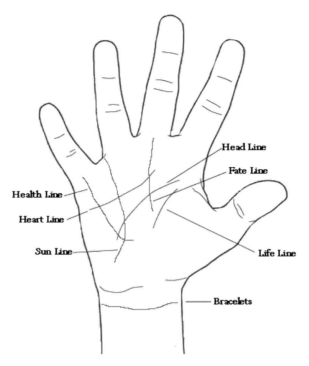

Head Line

Fate Line

Health Line

Heart Line

Sun Line

Life Line

Bracelets

The palm lines

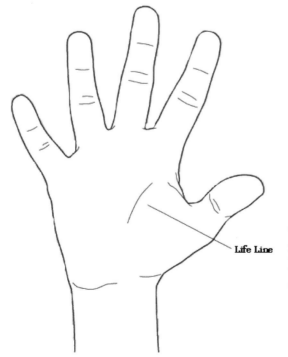

Life Line

This line symbolizes how vigorous you are as well as your enthusiasm for living. If it is long and defined, you have great potential and a sense of adventure.

The life line

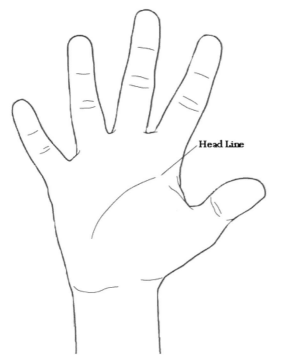

Head Line

This is an indicator of how you use your intelligence. A strong line indicates that you think before acting. Some breaks represent lack of focus. The slope of the line is associated with creativity.

The head line

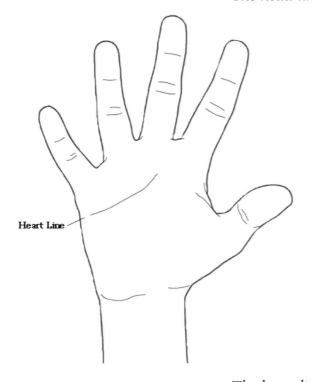

Heart Line

The heart line represents your emotions and health. When this line is straight, the emotions are ruled by the mind, and sentimentality is mixed with good instincts.

The heart line

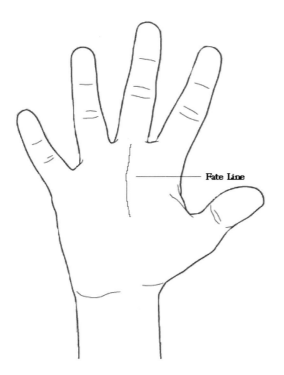

A strong line indicates balance and strength. Breaks in the line could mean that major changes will affect your life.

The fate line

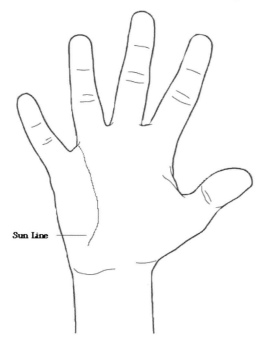

The sun line on your palm relates to luck, success and fortune. A long vertical sun line indicates a lucky life with many blessings. A blurred line suggests a lack of focus. A hard worker's line curves toward the thumb.

The sun line

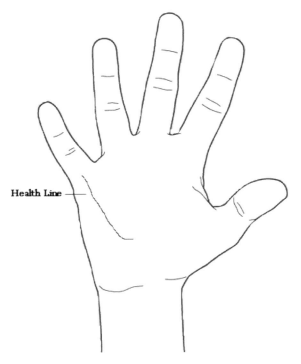

Health Line

The health line (also known as the Mercury line) shows vitality and important life changes. It can also indicate an intuitive nature. No discernable health line means a lifetime of good health. A health line crossing the life line suggests ill health and inherited diseases. A wavy line suggests digestive problems, and a blurred line shows a lack of stamina.

The health line

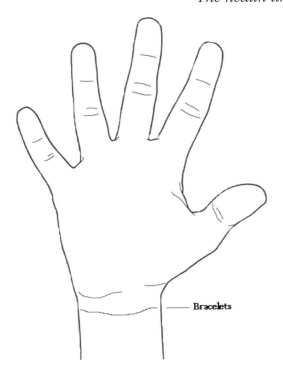

Bracelets

The stronger and more defined the bracelets are, the better your general health is likely to be.

The bracelets

The Life Line

The life line does not indicate how long you will live; rather, it reveals the quality of your life. It is an index of how much vitality, strength, and energy you will have. A life line running close to the thumb indicates a person of low vitality. It is sometimes found on the hands of people who suffer chronic fatigue syndrome. A life line that makes a wide curve shows a person with a great deal of vitality and get up and go. If the head line is stronger than the life line, this shows a person who is more mentally than physically active. A chained life line indicates delicate health. Little lines rising indicate an active personality. Outward swinging lines indicate a love of travel. Most of the small lines on the life line refer to particular events at certain times in your life.

If your life line:

◈ Runs close to your thumb, you have low vitality and are often tired.

◈ Has a wide curve, you have high vitality and lots of energy.

◈ Is bigger or wider than your head line, you are more active physically than mentally.

◈ Is chained, you have weak health.

◈ Has small rising lines, you have an active personality.

◈ Has outward-swinging lines, you love to travel.

The Head Line

The head line represents the way you think, not necessarily how smart you are. It concerns the mental processes, as well as willpower and mental fortitude. The head line is the prominent line below the heart line. An average head line ends somewhere under the ring finger. A short head line indicates a person whose thinking is simple and straight to the point. A long head line indicates a person who thinks things through very carefully. A straight head line indicates clear, concentrated thinking. A curved head line belongs to a person who likes to play with new ideas. Sloping head lines belong to creative people. Horizontal head lines belong to people who look at the practical side of life. Chained head lines belong to highly strung people. A fork in the headline shows the ability to see more than one point of view. A floating head line is indicative of someone with a carefree attitude. A head line that starts under the index finger indicates a brilliant mind.

If your head line:

◈ Ends around your ring finger, your head line is average.

◈ Is short, you think simply and directly.

◈ Is long, you're a thorough and careful thinker.

◈ Is straight, you think clearly and are able to concentrate.

◈ Is curved, you are ready to play with new and different ideas.

◈ Is sloped, you're a creative thinker.

◈ Is horizontal, you think in practical terms.

◈ Makes a chain-like pattern, you are strung-out.

◈ Has a fork in it, you are open-minded and capable of seeing many points of view.

◈ Floats (is disconnected), you have a carefree attitude.

◈ Starts under the index finger, you are brilliant!

The Heart Line

The heart line reflects the emotional side of your personality and relates to all matters of the heart. The heart line is not just a way of telling what will happen, but also a way of finding out *why* things happen. Imagine two heart lines extending from the edge of the hand below the little finger to between the first and second fingers. The first line is a deep curve while the second heart line is straighter. The curved line is active in romantic matters, while the straight line is passive. The curved heart line is aggressive in love, whereas the straight one is receptive. The curved heart line is demonstrative, while the straight line thinks about it. Interestingly, the curved line is much more common on male hands, and the straight line is more common on female hands. A heart line that becomes a steep curve below the index and middle fingers indicates someone who has a strong sexual desire. If the heart line ends up under the index finger, it indicates someone who is choosy about his or her partner.

If your heart line:

◈ Curves steeply under the index and middle finger, there's strong sexual desire.

◈ Ends under the index finger, you're picky with your lovers.

◈ Ends under the middle finger (this is rare), you may feel lonely or deprived of love.

◈ Is straight and short, you have no need for romance, but a strong sex drive.

◈ Has two or more lines branching off, this shows the number of sides to your emotional nature.

◈ Points downward with a branch and touches the life line, you're easily hurt in love.

◈ Is the same as your partner, you will have a successful union or marriage.

The Fate Line

The fate line (also called the destiny line) indicates the influence the world will have on you. Strong fate lines belong to people who settle into a pattern of life early. Weak fate lines tend to belong to people who are unsettled and tend to change jobs a lot. Fate lines starting at the very bottom of the palm indicate people who settle into their life path early. When the fate line ends at the head line, it indicates a person who seems to lose his or her way somewhere between 30 and 40 years of age. Most fate lines end at the heart line. However, if the fate line runs all the way up almost to the middle finger, this person will tend to be active right up into old age. A fate line that is tied to the heart line indicates a restricted childhood. Two fate lines are found on people who pursue two careers at the same time. The absence of a fate line indicates a person who lacks stability. It is also found on the hands of alcoholics and drug addicts.

Palm readers also look at other lines and marks on the palm—for example, the ring of Solomon around the forefinger, the girdle of Venus above the heart line, the bracelet lines on the wrist, relationship lines under the little finger the fate line from the wrist to the middle finger, the sun line from the wrist to the ring finger, and so on. Again, all the lines are read to produce a complete reading.

Other Means of Interpretation

For a palm reader, the length of the fingers indicates information about the individual's character. Here's a synopsis:

◈   Long fingers: analytical, academic, likes attention to detail.

◈   Short fingers: practical, intuitive, and instinctive.

◈   Proportionate hands: balanced personality.

Texture is important on both the back and front of the hand. Softness means sensitivity and refinement, while a rough hand shows a coarse nature. Of course, calluses mean the person works hard using his or her hands. Flexibility of the hands and fingers directly represents how flexible and easygoing the person is. The length of nails is also important. Longer nails that taper at the tip mean creativity, while square nails mean orderliness. Color indicates how blood circulates through the client's body. A pinkish hand means he or she is healthy, while yellow means too much bile is being produced. Blue means there is a circulation problem. The "mounts" at the bases of the fingers are also significant:

◈   The Mount of Jupiter (base of the index finger) shows ambition, leadership, religion, and love for nature.

◈   The Mount of Saturn (base of the second finger) denotes seriousness, wisdom, balance, and sadness.

◈   The Mount of Apollo (base of the ring finger) represents brilliance, artistry, happiness, and success.

◈   The Mount of Mercury (base of the fourth finger) shows industriousness and shrewdness.

◈   The Mount of Venus (base of the thumb) means love, sympathy, music, and passion.

◈   The Mount of the Moon (edge of the hand) shows imagination, coldness, and selfishness.

◈   The Plain of Mars (the rest of the hand) denotes courage, bravery, and aggression.

Chapter 29
The Emperor's Destiny Chart

Find the season of your birth, and match it up with your birth time to see the yellow emperor's lifetime prediction for you.

Spring—February 4 to May 4:

11 p.m. – 1a.m. Rat (Zi)	Crown
1 a.m. – 3 a.m. Ox (Chou)	Chest
3 a.m. – 5 a.m. Tiger (Yin)	Feet
5 a.m. – 7 a.m. Rabbit (Mao)	Shoulders
7 a.m. – 9 a.m. Dragon (Chen)	Knees
9 a.m. – 11 a.m. Snake (Si)	Hands
11 a.m. – 1 p.m. Horse (Wu)	Abdomen
1 p.m. – 3 p.m. Goat (Wei)	Hands
3 p.m. – 5 p.m. Monkey (Shen)	Feet
5 p.m. – 7 p.m. Rooster (You)	Shoulders
7 p.m. – 9 p.m. Dog (Xu)	Knees
9 p.m. – 11 p.m. Pig (Hai)	Chest

Summer—May 5 to August 6:

11 p.m. – 1 a.m. Rat (Zi)	Abdomen
1 a.m. – 3 a.m. Ox (Chou)	Hands
3 a.m. – 5 a.m. Tiger (Yin)	Feet
5 a.m. – 7 a.m. Rabbit (Mao)	Shoulders
7 a.m. – 9 a.m. Dragon (Chen)	Knees
9 a.m. – 11 a.m. Snake (Si)	Hands
11 a.m. – 1 p.m. Horse (Wu)	Crown
1 p.m. – 3 p.m. Goat (Wei)	Chest
3 p.m. – 5 p.m. Monkey (Shen)	Feet
5 p.m. – 7 p.m. Rooster (You)	Shoulders
7 p.m. – 9 p.m. Dog (Xu)	Knees
9 p.m. – 11 p.m. Pig (Hai)	Chest

Fall—August 7 to November 6:

11 p.m. – 1 a.m. Rat (Zi)	Shoulders
1 a.m. – 3 a.m. Ox (Chou)	Hands
3 a.m. – 5 a.m. Tiger (Yin)	Knees
5 a.m. – 7 a.m. Rabbit (Mao)	Chest
7 a.m. – 9 a.m. Dragon (Chen)	Feet
9 a.m. – 11 a.m. Snake (Si)	Hands
11 a.m. – 1 p.m. Horse (Wu)	Shoulders
1 p.m. – 3 p.m. Goat (Wei)	Chest
3 p.m. – 5 p.m. Monkey (Shen)	Abdomen
5 p.m. – 7 p.m. Rooster (You)	Knees
7 p.m. – 9 p.m. Dog (Xu)	Feet
9 p.m. – 11 p.m. Pig (Hai)	Crown

Winter—November 7 to February 3:

Time	Animal	Body Part
11 p.m. – 1 a.m.	Rat (Zi)	Abdomen
1 a.m. – 3 a.m.	Ox (Chou)	Knees
3 a.m. – 5 a.m.	Tiger (Yin)	Chest
5 a.m. – 7 a.m.	Rabbit (Mao)	Shoulders
7 a.m. – 9 a.m.	Dragon (Chen)	Feet
9 a.m. – 11 a.m.	Snake (Si)	Crown
11 a.m. – 1 p.m.	Horse (Wu)	Hands
1 p.m. – 3 p.m.	Goat (Wei)	Knees
3 p.m. – 5 p.m.	Monkey (Shen)	Chest
5 p.m. – 7 p.m.	Rooster (You)	Shoulders
7 p.m. – 9 p.m.	Dog (Xu)	Feet
9 p.m. – 11 p.m.	Pig (Hai)	Hands

If you were born under the Emperor's Crown:

This is the luckiest of birth placements and the astral signature of literal or figurative royalty. You will be blessed in this life and will lead and advise others. Riches, honor, and fame are all within your grasp. You will not want for worldly possessions or be without resources. Benefactors will always be available to help you.

If you were born under the Emperor's Hands:

You will have a lucky life, aided by those in a position to grant you favor. You will not have to worry about food, clothing, or shelter. Your childhood and early years are smooth and you accumulate many possessions. This is the astral signature of wealth and prosperity.

If you were born under the Emperor's Shoulders:

You will have a mixed life, as this is the sign of a late bloomer. Early life is difficult and perhaps even bitter, but success comes during midlife and old age is sweet. Children and grand-children are plentiful, and you will be blessed by helpful people. A lucky sign overall.

If you were born under the Emperor's Chest:

Clothes, food and the necessities of life come to you effortlessly. Those born on the Emperor's chest are talented in the arts: writing, music, dance. Middle life is happy and prosperous, old age is serene. Honor, prosperity and long life are the gifts of this astral signature.

If you were born under the Emperor's Abdomen:

You were treasured by your parents, but the family reputation may have been tarnished. Although you are cultured and bright, you must shine on your own and rely on your own accomplishments. Old age brings a comfortable retirement and wealth.

If you were born under the Emperor's Knees:

This difficult placement means that your efforts tend to be fruitless, frustrating, or without reward. This is the astral signature of the wanderer who travels on life's roads. You will have a lifetime of hard work and labor, especially during your middle-age years. Although youth and middle age are arduous, old age is smooth and you will not want for food, shelter, or honor.

If you were born under the Emperor's Feet:

This position represents a lifetime of travel, difficult beginnings and endings, and many changes. Difficult interpersonal relationships are found in this position, and there may be more than one marriage. Partnerships after middle age are the most harmonious, and retirement is pleasant.

If you were born under the Emperor's Knees or Feet, there is no need to worry as this does not mean that you are destined to a life of poverty or squalor.

Chapter 30

9 Star Ki

9 Star Ki (*ki* is the Japanese equivalent of the Chinese qi) is one of the most ancient forms of divination. This astrological system is based upon the principles of Chinese and Japanese astrology and philosophy, the trigrams from the Yi-Jing (I-Ching), and the principles of yin and yang. 9 Star Ki astrology is centered on your principal 9 Star Ki number, which has its basis in the feng shui magic square, or *lo-shu*. This ancient tool has been in use for more than 5,000 years. An important underlying assumption in 9 Star Ki astrology is that the universe is full of energy that flows around and through everyone. This energy works in nine stages, and each cycle or stage has its own unique quality. The cycles repeat themselves in the same order every 9 days, every 9 months, every 9 years, and every 81 years (9 multiplied by 9). We acquire the ki energy of whatever cycle we are born into. By using the 9 Star Ki astrological system, we can determine our position in the lo-shu matrix at birth and throughout life, and derive valuable insights regarding our personal qualities, relationships, and destiny.

To calculate your first (annual) 9 Star Ki number, add all four numbers of the year you were born, reduce the number to one digit, and deduct the result from 11. Here are some examples:

1973	1997
$1 + 9 + 7 + 3 = 20$	$1 + 9 + 9 + 7 = 26$
$2 + 0 = 2$	$2 + 6 = 8$
$11 - 2 =$ number 9	$11 - 8 =$ number 3

If the outcome is 5, men adopt the number 2 and women adopt the number 8. Number 5 belongs to the center and does not have a trigram. 9 Star Years begin on February 4 of each year, so if you were born prior to February 4, use the ki number that is assigned to the previous year. For example, someone born on January 8, 1953 would use the birth year of 1952, and someone born on February 1, 1972 would use the previous year of 1971 for his or her calculations.

Annual Ki Table								
9	8	7	6	5	4	3	2	1
Fire	Soil	Metal	Metal	Soil	Tree	Tree	Soil	Water
1901	1902	1903	1904	1905	1906	1907	1908	1909
1910	1911	1912	1913	1914	1915	1916	1917	1918
1919	1920	1921	1922	1923	1924	1925	1926	1927
1928	1929	1930	1931	1932	1933	1934	1935	1936
1937	1938	1939	1940	1941	1942	1943	1944	1945
1946	1947	1948	1949	1950	1951	1952	1953	1954
1955	1956	1957	1958	1959	1960	1961	1962	1963
1964	1965	1966	1967	1968	1969	1970	1971	1972
1973	1974	1975	1976	1977	1978	1979	1980	1981
1982	1983	1984	1985	1986	1987	1988	1989	1990
1991	1992	1993	1994	1995	1996	1997	1998	1999
2000	2001	2002	2003	2004	2005	2006	2007	2008
2009	2010	2011	2012	2013	2014	2015	2016	2017

According to 9 Star Ki, and just as in traditional Chinese lunar astrology, we embody the characteristics of the year in which we were born. There are nine distinct personality types.

1 Water

To fully appreciate the qualities of the 1 Water star, we must look at the qualities of water as it is found in nature. On the one hand, you have the lively, brisk mountain streams and waterfalls; on the other, you have deep, slow, calm ponds, lakes, and oceans. 1 Water people tend to fall into one or the other of these categories. The spirited, youthful nature of a fresh mountain stream brings out a spirit of adventure. Water does not have its own shape and needs something to contain it; without this containment, there is chaos and destruction. Likewise, 1 Water people can be chaotic and undisciplined. However, the opposite can also hold true: From time to time, the 1 Water can seem *too* disciplined and rigid. The sensitive, philosophical, and intuitive side of this sign can be seen in the many artists, writers, and composers who were born under it. This brooding, reflective quality is similar to the energy of deep water. The trigram *k'an*, which represents the middle son, brings out a diplomatic quality in some 1 Water stars. If you are a 1 Water, you would make a good arbitrator or lawyer, and a good listener in general within your family and community. Although you may seem quiet on the surface, you hear all sides of the argument and will often come up with a win-win situation. People born as 1 Waters are the deepest thinkers within the 9 Star Ki astrology system, and are perhaps the most intense and spiritual, as well. They generally find listening easy, and written communication comes naturally to them.

1 Water people are also very insightful. As the most "yang" of the numbers, they are generally very comfortable engaged in worldly pursuits, but they are strongly attracted to the yin, spiritual aspects of life, too. This combination gives 1 Water people very strong intuition. Evolved 1 Waters seek out people, religions, books—anything, really—that will provide structure in their life. This inherent drive for structure is not the result of weakness; on the contrary, this personality is strong and flexible and, like water, can "flow" in virtually any direction. Therefore the search is for definition, not pampering or restraint. 1 Waters are also very interested in observing others and in romantic relationships. Although they keep their thoughts and feelings well-hidden, they have a deep respect for communication.

2 Soil

There is a maternal quality that 2 Soil individuals possess when they are in service to others. They are not natural-born leaders, but work quietly in the background to get the job done. It is good to have a 2 Soil around when there is work to be done; for steadiness and reliability, this sign is unbeatable. They are consistent, steadfast, and very supportive. However, they should not be mistaken for blind followers. They have strong ideals and are extremely public-minded. The quality of soil represented here could be described as earthy loam or compost, which encapsulates its nurturing, helpful nature. The earthy, maternal nature of a 2 Soil is expressed not only within the family but also within the larger family of humanity, as well. There have been many examples throughout history of 2 Soil leaders whose main goal was to serve others—for example, Abraham Lincoln, John F. Kennedy, and Tenzin Gyatso (the Dalai Lama), to name a few. 2 Soils are also gentle and have a strong, patient quality. They are generally sociable, hardworking, and public-spirited, and make excellent teachers or organizers. Busying themselves by helping others gives them great satisfaction. They need to be within a group; without the support of an organization, they can lose direction and spirit. They tend to be over-fastidious and fussy in their working methods, which can cause them to get bogged down in detail and irritate others. On the plus side, they derive great strength from using their natural talent for diplomacy. They feel more at home on the land or in the woods. Gardening or walking in the country are good forms of recreation for them. Because 2 Soils play such a supportive role, they sometimes find it difficult to say no to the requests and demands of others, even when they would rather be alone or away from the action. It is advisable that they make quiet time for rejuvenation. They find it difficult to hide from the activities of the world for too long, though, due to their thirst for social interaction. They are not the "get rich quick" type; rather, they can find great prosperity through sustained, steady effort.

3 Tree

3 Trees are born with the full force of springtime within their souls. Like the season, they are endowed with plenty of vitality and energy and are capable of strong, powerful action. They are very positive and optimistic, going about their tasks vigorously and expecting others to keep up. In their pursuit of growth or new pastures, they tend to lead the way and leave the details to others. People who dislike change and interruption may dislike the vigorous and optimistic nature of the 3 Tree. They are open and honest, and can be candidly frank to the point that they alienate friends and colleagues. Only after they get their point of view across first will they listen to the thoughts and opinions of others. These strongly opinionated people can have grandiose ideas, but if they can work with others who can stabilize their visions, they can be extremely creative people. As the eldest son of the 9 Star family, 3 Trees are likely to be precocious. Many born under this sign have success early in their lives and move on as soon as they become bored. The full energy of spring that the sign represents also gives 3 Trees a strong, virile nature. Celebrities born under this sign are often regarded as heartthrobs or sex symbols. 3 Trees are humorous and outspoken, but frequently get themselves into trouble through their direct and honest sense of humor. Fortunately, their eloquence can just as easily get them out of awkward situations. Spontaneity, humor, and charm are amongst the strongest assets of a 3 Tree. They are also invaluable in providing fresh insights and new opinions. As their upward motion energy suggests, 3 Trees are very active. They like to explore and choose their own path. People born in the 3 Tree position like to win, but evolved 3 Trees also have the capacity to feel joy when others succeed. This being the case, enlightened 3 Trees are extremely pleased when everyone wins. For this reason, they can be very effective leaders. 3 Trees make good performers and often act spontaneously, sometimes without considering the ramifications of their actions. Therefore, they tend to learn through experience.

4 Tree

The 4 Tree's nature is governed by air. The trigram wind can denote anything from a slight breeze to a full-fledged hurricane. The 4 Tree is one of the most emotional of the nine signs. Although they appear gentle and easygoing at times, they can also be stubborn, impulsive, capricious, and moody. Although they have a similar nature to that of the 3 Tree, they are more practical, thoughtful, and reliable. They have great common sense and sensitivity to others, which can work for them and against them. When this sensitivity is combined with good listening skills, 4 Trees can be gifted counselors. However, their trusting and sometimes gullible nature makes them too easily influenced by more powerful individuals. Their sensitivity makes them deeply appreciative of the arts in all their forms. They are gifted with excellent verbal skills, and make charismatic orators, leaders, and political figures. The natural element of wind can cause them to change their mind—and their direction in life—frequently. On the other hand, the same wind works positively, allowing them to spread their influence to others, as well.

4 Trees take everyone at face value, which can cause difficulties in relationships. Therefore, it is advisable that they seek the advice of a friend or someone they trust before committing to

a long-term relationship. 4 Trees can provide very powerful and practical advice within their field of expertise. The archetype of the absent-minded professor fits well here. However, their responses to questions that are outside of their preferred field of knowledge may be less practical. If they are pushed into a field or vocation that is of little personal interest, they will be miserable; they chafe against oppressive situations. 4 Tree people have a great love for life, and focus upon those things that can provide the deepest personal meaning. Therefore, they tend to be romantics and idealists. Because of their capacity for analytical thought and devotion to their *métier*, their genius can be expressed in many different ways.

5 Soil

This sign is at the center of this system of astrology, so if you are a 5 Soil you will always find yourself at the center of what is going on. At work you will frequently be in the hub of discussions or arguments, and will probably feel left out if this is not the case. In family life, you will let your opinions and needs be known to those around you. You have a great capacity to control situations and are likely to take the lead. People often look to you for leadership and guidance. Although this can be fulfilling and exhilarating at times, friends can lean on you a bit too much and sometimes take advantage. If you are caught off guard or not feeling well, this could be draining for you. At these times, you need to protect yourself from being exploited. The 5 Soil position symbolizes the beginning and end of a cycle. Likewise, you could have a life of ups and downs, some of them extreme. However, you should not take this as a negative, as 5 Soil people have great resilience and bounce back easily after times of trouble. It is not unusual for 5 Soil individuals to make similar mistakes throughout their lives, but their resilient nature helps them deal with challenges far more easily than any of the other eight characters. You tend to take criticism or advice as a threat, which can make you either defensive or even more determined. You are bold and determined, sometimes aggressively so, and can bring about enormous change through the reinvention or destruction of old systems or patterns. Because you are at the center of this astrological system, others will naturally gravitate towards you, and you will enjoy the attention. As a result, you may find yourself in unusual circumstances—involved with someone much older or much younger or involved in a love triangle, for instance. There may be further complications in your relationships due to divorce, stepchildren, and so on. Health-wise, you have a great capacity to bounce back from stress-related illness and general health problems. For this reason you must remember to exercise and challenge yourself. The 5 Soil person is a good manager and controller of ventures, projects, and households. The 5 Soil can be found in all walks of life, from very humble surroundings to the highest circles of wealth and power. The evolved 5 Soil knows that he or she can have a profound influence upon the well-being of others and will use his or her energy toward that end.

6 Metal

The most obvious trait of this sign is natural leadership and authority. This can be in politics, the military, fashion, or the fine arts. Many 6 Metals have broken new ground and paved the way for future generations. With the full force of heaven present in their trigram, they can be extremely moral, direct, and noble. The consistent nature of the three lines can also make them rational, careful, and sometimes even rigid. They are active and sociable, but more reserved than the 7 Metals. They tend to be perfectionists and are quietly self-critical. The worst mistake that anyone can make with a 6 Metal friend is to criticize him or her. Most 6 Metals place a lot of emphasis on family values. If this is your sign, you are a natural leader in the family and the community, and will often give up your outside interests to return to the home if that is what the situation warrants. If you do not have a family of your own, you may well be at the center of the action in the workplace. You are a born leader in most situations. In relationships, you are the most loyal of all the nine signs. You are most comfortable in a relationship in which you can take the lead. Despite the fact that you are governed by the full force of yang energy, the opposite side of this nature can come through, as well, showing up as strong intuition, logical, rational thinking, and a wise approach to family and relationship problems. The 6 Metal Person is very good at providing solidarity and purpose to a group or an event. 6 Metals have a strong sense of ethics and propriety. Choosing a practical approach over idealism, they can be strict and strong-willed when applying their authority. Many mechanics, machinists, engineers, and jewelers are 6 Metals. Evolved 6 Metals are socially oriented and work for the greater good of the team or family. They share their opinions on life by setting a strong example through their behavior, rather than verbalizing their ideas. They practice what they preach. They are good financial managers and excel at producing finished products. Although most 6 Metals are mainstream thinkers, with little interest or belief in methods that are not tried and true, they can also have very strong powers of intuition. In some cases, this intuition can become so pronounced that some would call it psychic.

7 Metal

The time of year associated with the 7 Metal is late autumn, when farmers traditionally celebrate the harvest with relaxation and enjoyment. Number 7 Metals are great pleasure-seekers who, more than any other of the 9 signs, enjoy spending money on fashion, entertainment, and eating out. With their capacity to listen and be receptive to others, they make great hosts. If this is your sign, you are charismatic, optimistic, flamboyant, and graceful, and you probably dress and appear younger than you are. Like the 6 Metal, you have leadership qualities, but these are displayed in the advice you give others or the direction you suggest in the workplace. You have a capacity for fun and are endowed with a good sense of humor. With your free and independent nature you are not keen on long-term commitments at work or in relationships. As the symbolic "youngest daughter" in the 9 Star Ki system, you have the accumulated experience and wisdom of the rest of the family to help you. Your eloquence and sense of timing makes you an exceptionally good speaker; indeed, many 7 Metals are famous orators or politicians. 7 Metals often vacillate between their outgoing, fun-loving, and sociable side, and a deeper, reflective, more spiritual nature. The 7 Metal personality reflects the sensual feel of the early evening hours and the setting sun. 7 Metals are often interested in fashion, clothing, jewelry, and beauty. Although they appear to be emotional and superficial on the surface, on the inside they are solid. The evolved 7 Metal is very organized and will have a practical response to almost any situation. This trait provides balance to an otherwise excitable and overly emotional nature. They are verbally gifted and can easily sway the opinions of others. Due to their natural sensuality and general attractiveness, 7 Metals are easily noticed in and promoted quickly through the ranks of an organization. Although they can be extremely practical and patient, they flourish best when receiving the attention and support of others.

8 Soil

As the symbolic "youngest son," the 8 Soil benefits from the combined experience of the older brothers and sisters. They often have good financial sense and accumulate wealth during their youth, either through their own hard work or through an inheritance. If an 8 Soil's investment or business fails before middle age, he or she is quite likely to succeed again. If this is your sign, your success in achieving material wealth tends to be achieved more through your single-mindedness than through any subtlety, charm, or creative talent. The most "yang" of the three soil types, you tend to move slowly and persistently as you learn from your experiences. Although you have a strong, stable character with enormous reserves of energy, you need to retreat into your "cave" from time to time, which makes you seem reserved and cool to others. Of all the nine signs, you are perhaps the hardest to get close to; you generally conceal your feelings and only display them when provoked. When you are challenged, you can dart out of your sequestered shelter and deliver a powerful argument. You also have a strong sense of what is right and just; indeed, many 8 Soils are involved in human rights. With your strength and forethought, you can bring about change and revolution in people's lives. Your main asset is your composed, solid nature that can ride out most difficulties in life. Your experience and your hidden strength can be of enormous help to family, friends, and colleagues. The 8 Soil is up for anything that fits in with his or her plans, and usually, these plans include lending a helpful hand to anyone and everyone. 8 Soils are kindhearted, fair-minded, and family-oriented. When they feel that justice has not been served, they are quick to speak out and take remedial action. These individuals alternate between periods of reserved, deep thought and extroverted action. They are deep thinkers as well as boisterous revelers. The evolved 8 Soil will study important issues before taking action. They often have a very straightforward set of plans concerning their career and what they want to accomplish next, but they are not afraid to become involved with new ideas and directions. They are courageous travelers and make personable road companions. Although they tend to move often, 8 Soils love family. Even if their experiences keep them from settling down at an early age, the thought of family is always there. As they age, their love and respect for their elders deepens.

9 Fire

The 9 Fire person has all the qualities that the sun bestows—inspiration, enlightenment, charisma, and status. 9 Fires have an enormous capacity to see the obscure and steer a path through troubled waters. In politics, particularly in times of change and revolution, they can inspire a nation. Their natural active energy attracts them to stagnant situations that require major change. Of all the nine stars, this is the one that is most at home in the field of communication, especially when it concerns the emotions and personal experiences. These traits, along with their warm, passionate nature, can also make them successful in theater and film. 9 Fires can be proud, vain, sophisticated, and critical. If this is your sign, the sensitive nature that underlies your strong, successful surface image can erupt stormily, but you are also the quickest to forgive and forget. Like your brother the middle son (1 Water), you do not like to have your space invaded; as a result, you have plenty of contacts, but few real close friends. Your capacity to see clearly and understand the big picture does not help you deal with the minutiae of day-to-day living (such as repairing the washing machine or changing the oil in your car). However, appearances are important to you; in your clothes, your cars, and the contents of your home, you pay considerable attention to detail. You also dislike individuals who are sloppy or untidy or who display poor manners. The world would be a much duller place without the colorful, sophisticated, inspiring number 9 Fire. You lift the spirit and inspire those around your with your attitude and skills. 9 Fires are good at developing new ideas and initiating fresh activities, but in order to reach a successful conclusion, their path must be well-defined. Their temperament can change quickly, so it is sometimes difficult to know what their mood will be next. Outgoing and enthusiastic, these individuals are brilliant on the surface, but their plans and opinions are not always carefully thought out. The evolved 9 Fire will use his or her good fortune, charisma, and outgoing nature to develop a business or profession that will balance his/her somewhat chaotic existence with the more substantial, material aspects of life. When 9 Fires learn to channel their flamboyant nature, they can obtain the social approval and support they crave. Many 9 Fires are very successful in public relations and sales positions, but often have difficulty settling down in a long-term job or marriage.

Index

Adolescence, and life stage, 52

Adulthood, and life stage, 52

Aging, and life stage, 53

Arguing, pillars of, 111-112

Best sign compatibility, 104-105

Birth hour pillar, 88

Birth, and life stage, 51-52

Blossoms, peach, 99-100

Career palace, 128, 163-164

Catalysts,

    Hua Quan, 143,144

    stars, 143-147

Characters, eight, 13-19

Chen, 29-30

Children palace, 128

Chinese palmistry, 197-204

Chou, 23-24

Combinations,

    and trine signs, 102-103

    compatible, 101-103

    in-kind, 101-102

Compatibility,

and multiple signs, 105-106

and pillars, 99-106

best signs, 104-105

combinations, 101-103

Conflict, pillars of, 108-109

Cross, literary, 100

Crosses, the three, 99-101

Dark stars, 141

Day pillar, 13, 15, 55-86

Death, and life stage, 53-54

Decline, and life stage, 53

Destiny palace, 149-156

Dog, 40-42

and Earth, 41

and destiny palace, 155

and Fire, 41

and Metal, 41-42

and Water, 42

and Wood, 41

hour of, 96-97

Dormancy, and life stage, 54

Dragon, 29-30

and destiny palace, 155

and Earth, 30

and Fire, 29-30

and Metal, 30

and Water, 30

and Wood, 29

hour of, 92

Earth, 71-75

Earth,

as lucky element, 115-116

as unlucky element, 119

yang, 72-73

yin, 74-75

Earthly branches, twelve, 56-60

Eight characters, 13-19

Elements,

lucky, 114-117

unlucky, 118-120

Embryo, and life stage, 51

Emperor's Destiny Chart, 205-208

Feng shui, 193-196

Fire, 65-70

Fire,

as lucky element, 115

as unlucky element, 118-119

yang, 66-68

yin, 68-70

Four pillars, 13-19

Four steeds, 101

Friends palace, 128, 165-166

Goat, 34-36

and destiny palace, 155

and Earth, 35

and Fire, 35

and Metal, 36

and Water, 36

and Wood, 35

   hour of, 94

Hai (Pig), 42-44

Health palace, 128, 169-171

Heavenly stems, ten, 55-56, 58-60

Horse, 32-34

   and destiny palace, 154

   and Earth, 33-34

   and Fire, 33

   and Metal, 34

   and Water, 34

   and Wood, 33

   hour of, 93-94

Hour pillar, 13, 15, 87-98

Hua Ji, 143, 146-147

Hua Ke, 143, 144-145

Hua Lu, 143, 145-146

Hua Quan, 143, 144

I-Ching, 189-192

Incompatibility, and pillars, 107-112

In-kind combinations, 101-102

Karma palace, 128, 159-160

Life stages, 46-54

Literary cross, 100

Literary energies, and destiny palace, 151-153

Mao (Rabbit), 27-29

Map, star, 14

Martial energies, and destiny palace, 151

Metal, 76-81

Metal,

   as lucky element, 116-117

   as unlucky element, 119-120

   yang, 77-79

   yin, 79-81

Monkey, 36-38

Monkey,

   and Earth, 37

   and destiny palace, 153

   and Fire, 37

   and Metal, 37

   and Water, 37

   and Wood, 37

   hour of, 95

Month pillar, 13, 15, 45-54

Multiple signs, and compatibility, 105-106

9 Star Ki, 209-216

Opposition, pillars of, 109-111

Ox, 23-24

Ox,

   and destiny palace, 155

   and Earth, 24

   and Fire, 24

   and Metal, 24

   and Water, 24-25

   and Wood, 23-24

   hour of, 89-90

Parents palace, 127-128, 157-158

Peach blossoms, 99-100

Penalties, pillars of, 111-112

Pig, 42-44

Pig,

    and destiny palace, 154

    and Earth, 43

    and Fire, 43

    and Metal, 43-44

    and Water, 44

    and Wood, 42-43

    hour of, 97-98

Pillar,

    birth hour, 88

    day, 13, 15, 55-86

    hour, 13, 15, 87-98

    month, 13, 15, 45-54

    year, 13, 15, 21-44

Pillars,

    and incompatibility, 107-112

    compatibility between, 99-106

    four, 13-19

    of arguing, 111-112

    of conflict, 108-109

    of fighting, 111-112

    of opposition, 109-111

    of penalties, 111-112

Pregnancy, and life stage, 51

Prime, and life stage, 52-53

Property palace, 128, 161-162

Rabbit, 27-29

Rabbit,

    and destiny palace, 154

    and Earth, 28

    and Fire, 27-28

    and Metal , 28

    and Water, 28

    and Wood, 27

    hour of, 91-92

Rat, 21-23

Rat,

    and destiny palace, 154

    and Earth, 22

    and Fire, 22

    and Metal, 22-23

    and wood, 22

    hour of, 89

Relationship palace, 177-179

Rooster, 38-40

    and destiny palace, 154

    and Earth, 39

    and Fire, 39

    and Metal, 39-40

    and Water, 40

    and Wood, 39

    hour of, 95-96

Ruling energies, and destiny palace, 150-151

Self/destiny palace, 149-156

Sexagenary cycle, 18-19

Shen, 36-38

Si, 31-32

Siblings palace, 129, 181-182

60-year cycle, 18-19

Snake, 31-32

Snake,

    and destiny palace, 153

    and Earth, 32

    and Fire, 31

    and Metal, 32

    and Water, 32

    and Wood, 31

    hour of, 92-93

Spouse palace, 128-129

Star chart, 134

Star map, 14

Stars, 133-141

Stars,

    adapters, 135

    catalysts, 143-147

    dark, 141

    4 life milestones, 135, 140

    4 lucky royal jewels, 135, 139

    4 major imperial energies, 134, 136

    4 major martial energies, 134, 137

    main energy of money, 135, 140

    main energy of travel, 135, 140

    6 major psycho-social/literary energies, 135, 138

    2 major indicators of intelligence, 135, 139-140

Tiger, 25-27

Tiger,

    and destiny palace, 153

    and Earth, 26

    and Fire, 26

    and Metal, 26

    and Water, 26-27

    and Wood, 25

    hour of, 90-91

Travel palace, 128, 167-168

Trine signs, 102-103

Tze, 21-23

Unlucky elements, 118-120

Void, and life stage, 54

Water, 81-86

Water,

    as lucky element, 117

    as unlucky element, 120

    yang, 82-84

    yin, 84-86

Wealth palace, 128, 173-175

Wood, 60-65

Wood,

    as lucky element, 114

    as unlucky element, 118

    yang, 61-63

    yin, 63-65

Wu, 32-34

Xu, 40-42

Yang Earth, 72-73

Yang Fire, 66-68

Yang Metal, 77-79

Yang Water, 82-84

Yang Wood, 61-63

Year pillar, 13, 15, 21-44

Yin (Tiger), 25-27

Yin Earth, 74-75

Yin Fire, 68-70

Yin Metal, 79-81

Yin Water, 84-86

Yin Wood, 63-65

You (Rooster), 38-40

Zi We Dou Shu, 123-125, 129-131, 133

Zi Wei Dou Shu, interpreting, 183-186

About the Author

Shelly Wu is the author of *Chinese Astrology*, *Chinese Sexual Astrology*, and *The Karma Sutra*. Her columns and articles have been featured in the Associated Press, on ABC News and the BBC, as well as in *Psychic Interactive*, *Your Stars*, *InTouch*, and *LIFE* magazines. Wu teaches Chinese astrology at the Online College of Astrology, and can be heard on radio talk shows worldwide.